MAKE MONEY WITH

SOYBEAN OPTIONS

USING GRANDMILL'S OPTION TABLES

Published by Windsor Books
P.O. Box 280
Brightwaters, N.Y., 11718

Manufactured in the United States of America

ISBN 0-930233-35-2

TABLE OF CONTENTS

WHAT THIS BOOK IS ABOUT

This book is different from any other book you may have read on Soybean Options. When you have finished reading and studying this book, you will have a new perspective on options. Maybe for the first time you will feel that you now are in control of your option positions – no more of that feeling that once you have taken your trade, you must simply hope for the best and take whatever comes.

No more of that! You should feel a new confidence in the outcome of your option trading. You should feel that finally you are in control of the situation. And, best of all, you will know whether your option trade will be profitable under a variety of conditions **before you commit your money**.

How will this come about? Because you will be using the new Soybean Option Tables – an entirely new approach to option trading.

You will have a new understanding of options and how they function when you have finished this book. It will be like a person who has looked at a clock face many times, and then one day he removed the face to look behind it to see the synchronous movements of the wheels, cogs, and levers which have moved the hands of the clock. And so here we will look behind an option's facade to discover how the 3 option market forces work together to alter an option's value.

This is not a trading system. Instead it is a practical method of trading options based on the option tables. The tables are the heart and core of the book. All the rest of the book is built around the tables. The spread sheets, the graphs, and other information all support and augment the tables.

Another thing. This book is meant to be both informative and instructive. By "instructive" is meant, "to learn by doing". So, in a sense, it is like a text book. You will be asked to work out some problems and questions with the objective of becoming skillful in the use of the tables. Your expertise with the tables will be the most important skill which could turn you into a most profitable option trader. It is advisable that you do all the questions. Each question has a purpose and each answer is explained when necessary. The questions themselves are progressive – that is, they start off easy and progress to difficult ones.

One last point. If you are an experienced option trader, skip Part 1 and go directly to Part 2. Part 1 is for those people who are new or nearly new to option trading. The option basics are reviewed in Part 1.

OPTION TRADING BASICS

Part 1 is for those traders who are new to option trading. Experienced option traders should proceed directly to Part 2.

Compared to futures, how are options different?

Even though you may be new to option trading, it is likely that you are experienced in trading futures. Now you want to try your hand in options because you are seeking more security and safety than you had in futures trading. You have heard that options are safer – none of those unpleasant limit moves against you which you experienced in futures when things went wrong. You heard correctly. There are no limit up or limit down price moves in options. You are in a safer form of trading, and, in addition you will be using the new option tables, which should give you an edge.

The reason why I expected you to have traded in futures already, is that options are the next logical step after futures. Look at the heading above each table at the back of the book and you will see the words, "Option Values on Futures". That means that the future's price is the basis of the option's price. In other words, the future's price is the most important factor in option trading. All option prices are dependent upon the futures' prices. But it is safer to be in options than in futures as you will see later.

When you traded futures, you gave your broker an order to **buy** a contract when you expected prices to rise, and you gave him an order to **sell** a future's contract when you expected prices to fall. You use the same words in options: "buy or sell". The word "buy" has almost the same meaning in options as it has in futures, but the word "sell" has a different connotation. This difference will be explained later. But, first, let's become familiar with option terminology.

Two kinds of options

There are 2 distinct kinds of options: a **call** option and a **put** option. They are opposites, like up and down. Think of the call as belonging to the "up", and the put as belonging to the "down".

Each of these two kinds of options can be bought or sold. Therefore, the words "buy or sell" can be used with either a "call" or with a "put". This means that you have a choice of 4 orders to say to your broker when you wish to take an option trade. The 4 orders are: Buy a call, Sell a call, Buy a put, Sell a put. But in order to be in a position to give those orders to your broker, you must know the trend of the future's price.

Know the trend

You should never take an option or a future's position without some hint or reason why prices will move in the direction you desire. Otherwise, you are guessing and there is no place for guessing in either option or futures trading. What, then, should a new trader do, to find the price trend?

The most common aids to finding a price trend are: (1) a graph or chart of the underlying future's price. Most traders plot the high, low, close at the end of each trading day. (2) Using the crossover of 2 moving averages of different time length. (3) Subscribing to a newsletter which gives option or future's recommendations. (4) Read and find fundamental information which will help you to make a decision. While not all of the above will be useful to you, they are better than having nothing. Having no idea of the trend could be disastrous. Most traders do all 4 of the above.

Buying a call

You "buy a call" when you believe prices are rising or about to rise. But before you call your broker to give the order, you will have checked out the call by using the tables at the back of this book. The table will have told you if the call will be profitable, and by how much. You will taught to do this in Part 3.

Buying a put

You "buy a put" when you believe prices are falling or about to fall. Now, this is where you could get confused with futures because, when prices fell with futures, you **sold**. Now you are being told to **buy** when prices are falling. "How come?", you wonder, "What's happening?"

It sounds confusing — and it is. But, here is the explanation.

(1)   About futures, first: You sold a future's contract when the price of the underlying commodity was declining. Note again, it was the price of the commodity itself which was declining.

(2)   About options: you buy a put when the underlying **future's** price was declining. Note in (1) above it was the commodity price which was declining, e.g. the S&P 500 Index, Soybeans, Gold, etc. Whereas, here, we are talking of the future's price declining — two different things.

(3)   Remember, there are only two kinds of options to buy. Either you buy a call or you buy a put. You buy a call to profit from rising prices. You buy a put to profit from falling prices.

Margin requirements

When you traded futures you were required to deposit margin money into your account. But that is not the case with options. No margin is needed when you buy a call or buy a put. It is like buying an article at the market — you pay the price for it and it is yours — end of transaction.

Therefore, when you buy a call, for example, you pay the price, and the call is yours. No more money is required — not even if prices go against you. In future's, remember, you sometimes were asked by your broker to deposit more money into your account if prices went against you. But not when you buy a call or buy a put — you pay the price for it and it is yours.

In other words, the most money you can lose when you buy a call or a put is the premium (option price) which you paid for it. You will never be asked for more. By the way, in this book the words "option price" and "option premium" and "option value" have the same meaning. Sometimes one is used, sometimes another.

While it is comforting to know that you do not deposit margin when **buying** a call or a put, such is not the case when **selling** a call or a put. You must deposit margin money into your account when you **sell** a call or a put because it is risky — not as safe as buying a call or a put.

Selling a call

This is the opposite of buying a call because you pay out money when you buy it, but you take in money when you sell a call or a put. That's right, you have the money deposited into your account. Again, it is like a market. You own the market, and when you sell an article to a customer, you take his money and deposit it into your cash register. It's the same here. You sell a call to some trader, he pays its price, and the money he pays for the call is deposited into your account. Also, your broker will ask you to deposit margin into your account for reasons which are described next paragraph.

Now comes the big difference between buying and selling a call. You will remember that the most money that you could lose when buying a call was the price that you paid for it. Not so when **selling** a call. You could lose plenty! And that's why the broker makes sure that you have extra money into your account — just in case prices go against you. He is preparing for the worst.

If you are new to option trading, you will be asking, "How could I lose money when I have already had the option premium deposited into my account? I would have thought that I had made money right from the start!" You are right, of course. You are money ahead at the start. But the middle and the end have yet to come, and that's where the risk and danger are.

"What danger?", you may ask. Think about this, — the person who bought the call from you is also hoping to make a profit. He is hoping the price will rise, because that's why anyone buys a call — to make money from a price rise. Now here's the bad news. If the buyer of your call makes a profit, then that profit has to come from somewhere. And, unfortunately for you, it comes out of your pocket, or to be more precise, it comes out of your account. That's why your broker asks you to put up margin, in case this calamity happens — the calamity being that the buyer actually makes a profit from you. If it is a big profit, you could get an urgent call from your broker to deposit still more money into your account to cover a loss. So you can see now that **selling** an option is risky and the amount you could lose is unlimited. It's not like **buying** an option where the most you can lose is the price you paid for it.

At this point you are probably thinking, "I'll never put myself in that risky position. I'll never sell a call or a put." Well, don't be too hasty. There is big money in it if you do it right. In fact, many of the people who make the largest profits in options are traders who sell options on a large scale.

By "doing it right" is meant that there are ways to protect yourself against serious losses. You will learn some of them when you learn how to use the option tables later in this book. But three simple protection methods will be mentioned now.

4

First, you can get out of an option position anytime you wish. You don't have to stick with it until the expiration date. If you feel nervous, or if you have already made a profit, then get out of the position — just like you got out of a future's position when you traded futures. For example, if you had sold a March option call, and if prices were going against you and you were getting nervous about it, just pick up the phone and tell your broker to buy a March call. The "buy" will cancel the "sell" and you would now be out of the market.

Second, you can place a stop order with your broker — just as you have done when trading futures. All you have to do is to decide how much you are willing to lose from selling the option, and tell your broker to place a buy order at that price level. If prices went against you, you would be taken out of the market at that price.

Third, and the best way to protect yourself against loss from selling a call is to sell a call only when you are fairly certain that prices will fall for sure. That way, the other fellow can't make a profit because he needs rising prices. That way, you keep the money that you received when you sold the call. Simple, isn't it? Just don't sell a call unless you are pretty sure that prices will fall. How can you be sure that prices will fall? Well, you can never be 100% sure but you are keeping charts and moving averages, etc., so you should have some ideas of the price direction.

Selling a put

Much of what was written above also applies to selling a put. As mentioned before, selling can be risky. So take precautions. The best precaution is to sell a put only when you believe prices will rise (just the opposite direction when selling a call, as above).

Keep in mind that a put makes money only from falling prices. So if you will sell a put only when prices are going to rise, according to your charts and moving averages, then you are fairly safe.

Summary

You have learned about (1) buying a call (2) buying a put (3) selling a call (4) selling a put. They are the 4 basic moves. In addition to those four, you can use them in combination with a future's position, or you can use them in spreads. All of these more complex moves are shown to you later in the book.

As mentioned above, you have learned the 4 basic moves and you will learn more complex moves later. But there are several things about options which are not mentioned in this book because they are not needed to make money from options, when you use the tables. For example, there are such items as: the history of options, beta, delta, the Black-Scholes formula, etc. which you can learn later if you are interested, but it is doubtful if they will add to your profit power. Your best tool for trading options is the skillful use of the option tables. When you have completed this book, you will be more knowledgeable in trading options than most people.

PART 2

THE OPTION TABLES

As mentioned before, the option tables are the heart and core of this book. This is likely the first time you have seen such tables. From these tables you will learn much about options that you didn't know before. But the option table's purpose, first and foremost, is to enable you to *plan your option position and note its likely profitability under a variety of conditions — before you commit your money to the trade.*

That last sentence above is the key to the proper use of the tables — to be able to select winning trades and to reject losing trades, before you pay out a cent to your broker. You see, what is a good profitable prospect one day could be a loser under other conditions. The tables are designed in such a way that you will automatically use the table which is best suited for the conditions of time, price and volatility at the time you take the trade. There are more details on these conditions later. Bur for now, let's inspect a table closely and analyze its composition.

FUTURES – Table No: 55

13	12	11	10	9	8	7	6	5	4	3	2	1	0		
125.4	125.2	125.0	125.0	125.0	125.0	125.0	125.0	125.0	125.0	125.0	125.0	125.0	125.0	$1.25	IN THE MONEY
101.9	101.7	101.4	101.1	100.8	100.6	100.4	100.1	100.0	100.0	100.0	100.0	100.0	100.0	$1.00	
81.4	80.8	80.2	79.6	78.9	78.3	77.6	76.9	76.0	75.4	75.1	75.0	75.0	75.0	75¢	
64.6	63.7	62.7	61.6	60.5	59.4	58.1	56.8	55.0	53.4	51.5	50.4	50.0	50.0	50¢	
49.8	48.7	47.5	46.1	44.7	43.2	41.4	39.5	36.9	34.2	31.2	28.0	25.8	25.0	25¢	
38.4	37.2	35.8	34.3	32.7	31.0	29.1	26.8	23.8	20.6	16.8	12.4	7.5	0.0		AT THE MONEY
29.2	28.0	26.6	25.1	23.6	21.9	20.0	18.0	15.3	12.2	8.7	4.7	1.4	0	25¢	OUT OF THE MONEY
21.6	20.5	19.3	18.1	16.8	15.5	13.9	12.1	9.9	7.5	4.9	2.0	0.2	0	50¢	
17.3	16.3	15.1	13.8	12.5	11.2	9.6	8.0	5.9	4.0	2.0	0.5	0	0	75¢	
12.5	11.7	10.8	9.9	8.8	8.0	6.8	5.7	4.2	2.8	1.5	0.3	0	0	$1.00	
8.7	8.1	7.4	6.6	5.8	5.1	4.3	3.4	2.3	1.5	0.5	0	0	0	$1.25	

WEEKS TO EXPIRATION

- to nearest tenth.   WM GRANDMILL (1985) LTD.

Above is a portion of Option Table 55. The entire table is located in Part 4, near the back of the book. Note the following.

1. THREE MAIN DIVISIONS

The tables are separated into 3 main divisions (1) in the money (2) at the money (3) out of the money. Look at each above.

(a) In the money. The "in the money" area is in the top half of the table. It is the profit area for both a call and a put. Whenever you buy a call or a put, its value will wander about the table as prices rise and fall. But whenever the value of the call or put is in the "in the money" area, then you usually have a profit. For example, if you bought a call "at the money" when the future's price was $7.00, and later if the future's price rose to $7.50, then the option's value would be "in the money" by 50¢.

(b) At the money. The "at the money" line is composed of a single row of values in the center of the table — and yet it is the most important row of values in the entire table. It is so important that all the other numbers in the table are dependent upon it. The values of all the other numbers above and below the "at the money" line are derived from this single row of values.

Where did that "at the money" line come from? Why is it so important? A few pages back you were told that an option's value is based upon the underlying future's price. We are doing Soybean Options – therefore the values of the options in the tables are derived from the soybean futures' prices. The "at the money" line, therefore, directly reflects the future's price, the very base of all option values. That's why it is the most important line of values in the table.

An example may help. Suppose the March Soybean future's price was $6.50 and you bought a March option call at a strike price of $6.50. Then you would be buying exactly "at the money" – exactly at the future's price.

To repeat, the "at the money" price is the key price in these tables. Let's look at one specific price. Look at Table 55 again, a page or so back. Look at column 8 (the 8th week to expiration). You can see that the "at the money" option price is 31.0¢ ($1550, each cent represents $50). All the values which you see in column 8 are related to and derived from the "at the money" price of 31.0¢. If that 31.0¢ price was the change slightly, then all the option values in column 8 would change slightly. The "at the money" price is the key price in the table.

(c) Out of the money. The "out of the money" area is the lower half of the table. This is usually the loss area. Example: if you had bought a call "at the money" and if the future's price had *fallen* by 25¢, then your call's value would now be in the "out of the money" area, and your call would have lost money.

The same applies to a put. Remember, a put makes money when the price falls, and loses money when the price rises — just the opposite of a call. If you had bought a put "at the money" and if the future's price was to *rise* by 25¢ then your option's value would now be in the "out of the money" area — the losing area.

7

2. THE TIME TO EXPIRATION

We are still looking at the composition of an option table. Look back at Table 55 and you will see a black row with white numbers at the bottom of the table. The numbers in the black row indicate the number of weeks remaining to the expiration date. All option contracts have an expiration date. The expiration date is always a Friday in the preceeding month. For example, the July option expires in June on a Friday as determined by the following rule.

To find the expiration date for Soybean Options, count back in the preceeding month a total of 6 trading days. If the 6th day is a Friday, then that date will be the expiration date. But if the 6th day is not a Friday, then use the preceeding Friday. For example, if you counted back 6 trading days and the 6th day was a Thursday, then keep on going until you come to the preceeding Friday. By "counting back" is meant counting like this: June 30th, June 29th, June 28th, etc., trading days only. For example, the expiration date for the September 1988 Soybean Option was August 19th, a Friday. The expiration date for the May/88 Soybean Option was April 22nd, a Friday. By the way, Chicago corn and wheat options also expire on the same dates as the soybean options.

Time is your worst enemy when trading options. Time erodes option values at an alarming rate. As the weeks pass and the expiration date draws closer, you will see your option's value shrinking rapidly. Let's take a look at the damage done by the passing of time.

Look back again at Table 55. Follow this closely. Suppose you bought a call "at the money" at the 5th week to expiration. Look in the table and you will see that you would pay 23.8¢ for it. Let's suppose that the future's price remained steady for the next 5 weeks, for this example – no price change. Look at the table and you will see that one week later your call option is now worth only 20.6¢. Another week passes and the call is now worth only 16.8¢ then 12.4¢, and so on until it expires worthless at 0¢.

An option's value declines more rapidly as the expiration date draws closer. Farther away, though, the effects of time erosion are much less. Look back along the "at the money" line to the 17th week column and you will see that value loss by time is much less than near the expiry date.

You probably have heard already about the effects of time on option values. But likely this is the first time that you have seen the effects laid out before you in black and white. Every table is different in that each has its own speed of time erosion e.g. table 25 is different from table 15. Also, each kind of option is different in time erosion speed e.g. the soybean option rate is different from the S&P option rate of erosion.

Can you use time erosion to your advantage? Now that you have seen the devastating effects of time on an option's value, you may wonder, "Is there something I can do to minimize the damage caused by the passing of time, or even better, can I use it to my advantage?" The answer is Yes, in both cases. It makes a difference, though, whether you are buying or selling.

(a) Buying a call. You buy a call because you expect prices to rise. What you will need is lots of time to achieve your objectives and you want as little time erosion as possible. The solution, then, is to buy your call fairly far away in time, say, around the 20th week. There is less time erosion there and 20 weeks gives ample time for prices to rise.

(b) Selling a call. This is a different situation from buying a call, described above. In this case you sell a call to a person who expects prices to rise, otherwise he wouldn't have bought it. He hopes to make a profit, and the profit will come from your account. Therefore, you must try to protect yourself. Here's what to do. Sell the call close to the expiration date, say, 5 weeks away from the expiration date. The erosion by time is severe at that time. An option value's erosion by time is to your advantage and to the other fellow's disadvantage. The faster his call's value deteriorates, the better for you. To repeat, when selling a call or a put, use a short time span.

3. STILL EXAMINING AN OPTION TABLE

Another copy of Table 55 is printed below for convenience sake. Use it, it's handier. Look at the end of the table where you see the areas "in the money" and "out of the money" with the numbers 25¢, 50¢, 75¢, $1.00, $1.25. These numbers represent the amount by which the future's price rises or falls. Remember, it is the change in the future's price which changes an option's value. A price rise puts it in the money. Example, suppose you bought a call "at the money", and later the future's price rose 50¢. Then the new value of your call option will be found on the 50¢ row, in the money — at whatever week you were using.

Another example, and this one is a bit complicated, so follow it closely in Table 55. Suppose you buy a call at 25¢ "out of the money", at the 10th week to expiration, for 25.1¢. (Find it in the table). Two weeks later the future's price declined by 50¢. How much is your call worth now? Answer: 11.2¢ Did you get that answer? Here's how it was done. (1) You took the call in the 10th week and 2 weeks passed which places your call in the 8th week column. (2) The future's price fell by 50¢ so you move down two rows from the row where you originally took the call. This places you now in the 75¢ "out of the money" row. (3) If you look at the junction of the 8th week column and the -75 row (-75 means 75¢ "out of the money", and +75 row means 75¢ "in the money" in this book) you will see 11.2¢.

IT'S PRACTICE TIME

Below is Table 55 and some questions. Find the answers in Table 55. Some are easy and some are tricky. Don't skip any. The answers are printed at the end of the questions.

1. You buy a call "at the money", at the 8th week to exp. How much did it cost?
2. You buy a put at -25¢ (out of the money), at the 12th week. What is its cost?
3. You buy a call at -12.5¢. (12.5¢ out of the money – get used to these abbreviations) at the 6th week to expiration. How much did it cost? (you will have to interpolate for this answer for this answer and several more below)

9

BEAN FUTURES – Table No: 55

15	14	13	12	11	10	9	8	7	6	5	4	3	2	1	0		
126.1	125.7	125.4	125.2	125.0	125.0	125.0	125.0	125.0	125.0	125.0	125.0	125.0	125.0	125.0	125.0	$1.25	IN THE MONEY
102.6	102.2	101.9	101.7	101.4	101.1	100.8	100.6	100.4	100.1	100.0	100.0	100.0	100.0	100.0	100.0	$1.00	
82.5	82.0	81.4	80.8	80.2	79.6	78.9	78.3	77.6	76.9	76.0	75.4	75.1	75.0	75.0	75.0	75¢	
66.3	65.5	64.6	63.7	62.7	61.6	60.5	59.4	58.1	56.8	55.0	53.4	51.5	50.4	50.0	50.0	50¢	
51.8	50.8	49.8	48.7	47.5	46.1	44.7	43.2	41.4	39.5	36.9	34.2	31.2	28.0	25.8	25.0	25¢	
40.6	39.6	38.4	37.2	35.8	34.3	32.7	31.0	29.1	26.8	23.8	20.6	16.8	12.4	7.5	0.0		AT THE MONEY
31.3	30.3	29.2	28.0	26.6	25.1	23.6	21.9	20.0	18.0	15.3	12.2	8.7	4.7	1.4	0	25¢	OUT OF THE MONEY
23.6	22.6	21.6	20.5	19.3	18.1	16.8	15.5	13.9	12.1	9.9	7.5	4.9	2.0	0.2	0	50¢	
19.3	18.3	17.3	16.3	15.1	13.8	12.5	11.2	9.6	8.0	5.9	4.0	2.0	0.5	0	0	75¢	
14.0	13.3	12.5	11.7	10.8	9.9	8.8	8.0	6.8	5.7	4.2	2.8	1.5	0.3	0	0	$1.00	
9.8	9.3	8.7	8.1	7.4	6.6	5.8	5.1	4.3	3.4	2.3	1.5	0.5	0	0	0	$1.25	

WEEKS TO EXPIRATION

ARE IN CENTS – to nearest tenth.

WM GRANDMILL (1985) LTD.

4. You buy a call at the 5th week, at 10¢ out of the money. How much did it cost?
5. You sold a put at the 10th week to exp. at 40¢ out of the money. How much premium was placed into your account?
6. You buy a call at the 12th week, at the money. Five weeks later the future's price has risen by 75¢. How much is your call worth now?
7. You buy a put at the 10th week, at the money. Five weeks later the future's price has risen by 50¢. How much is the put worth now?
8. You buy a call at 12.5¢ out of the money at 12 weeks to exp. Three weeks later the future's price has risen by 25¢. You decide to liquidate your position and take the profit. How much profit did you make?

Answers: 1. 31.0¢ 2. 28.0¢ 3. 22.4¢ 4. 20.4¢ 5. 20.9¢ 6. 77.6¢ 7. 9.9¢ (a put loses money when prices rise) 8. 6.1¢ (You paid 32.6¢ for it and received back 38.7¢, which gives you a profit of 6.1¢ before commissions.)

THE THREE PRIME MOVERS OF OPTION PRICES

Changes in option prices are caused by 3 market forces.

1. The time remaining to the expiration date. We dealt with the weeks to expiration a few pages back. We noted that the erosion of an option's value by the passing of time, was greatest as it approached the expiration date.

2. A price change in the underlying future. This was shown in Table 55 where you saw how an option's value increased as it moved into the "in the money" area which was caused by an increase in the underlying future's price.

3. Volatility. The changes in an option's value caused by time and price, are obvious.

10

But the changes caused by volatility are subtle. Volatility can creep into option trading unnoticed, causing an increase or decrease in the option's value. What, then, is volatility? **What causes volatility?**

It is caused by human nature. Such human traits as euphoria and fear, as expressed by the trading public, cause a change in volatility. It can also be called bullishness and bearishness. When the future's market is dull and uninteresting, then volatility is low. But when excitement or nervousness is exhibited by a mass of traders, then volatility will increase and so will option prices.

What must you do, you may wonder. You are asking, "How can I handle volatility? What must I do to protect myself against this subtle force?"

The answer is, not to worry! Because these remarkable option tables had the volatility rate incorporated into them. You will see it clearly later. But for the moment, just know that when you start to use the option table selected for your trade, you will be automatically using the table which closely reflects the volatility rate of that day. As far as is known, this is the first book to confront volatility head-on, and to do something about it in such a practical manner. To sum up: all 3 of the forces which affect an option are in the tables — time, price, volatility.

HOW THE SOYBEAN OPTION TABLES WERE CONSTRUCTED

The tables were constructed from actual Soybean Option figures – the numbers as they actually occurred in daily option trading from Jan. 1985 to April 1988.

All option times up to 30 weeks from the expiration date were used. Also every option month was used and all strike prices, as well as all the variations of volatility.

Each option value in a table is an average of all the option values which occurred at that point. For example, look at Table 55. Look at the "at the money" price in column 9 and you see 32.7¢. This number, 32.7¢, was the average of all the numbers which occurred at that juncture. There may have been several numbers ranging from 32.2 to 33.2 cents, for example, at that particular place which averaged out at 32.7¢. All the values horizontally and vertically were derived from actual trading prices. In other words, empirical data was used. Therefore, when you are using a table to plan your option trade, you will know that you are using values which have occurred previously under similar conditions of time, price, and volatility.

You may ask, "Are the option values in the tables accurate?" The answer is Yes. But, if you asked, "Are the option values 100% accurate?" Then the answer is no, because an average cannot be 100% accurate. It is an average of a closely related group of numbers, and as such, it has a relative accuracy, according to the closeness of the number group. "Relative accuracy", let's use that phrase to denote the accuracy of an average value in this book. The tables, then are relatively accurate, as befits an average. It would be impossible for an average to be 100% accurate.

HOW TO FIND THE "AT THE MONEY" PRICE

As mentioned before, the "at the money" option price is the most important price in the option table because it is directly related to the underlying future's price upon which the option depends. One would think, therefore, that such an important price would be plainly printed for all to see. But it isn't so. Strangely, it is not quoted in the option page of a newspaper or on a quote screen. Therefore, it is up to each one of us to calculate it ourselves from the data available in the newspaper or elsewhere. That's what this chapter is about — to teach you how to find the "at the money" price from an option quote page.

Below is a sample quote worked out for you. It is a segment of a soybean option quote page as might be found in a newspaper. Only the pertinent parts of the quote page are used so that it will be easier to understand. At the left are the strike prices, then a column of option prices. At the right is the future's price.

strike price	calls Sept.	
700	30	the September future's price is $7.10
725	20	

Note that the Sept. future's price will fall between the two strike prices. This means that the "at the money" price is between the two option prices of 30 and 20.

Problem 1: to find the "at the money" price for the Sept. option.

Method: there are 3 differences which must be used.

Step 1. (a) the difference between the future's price and the lower strike price, which is: 725 - 710 = 15. Let's say that "a" is 15.
(b) the difference between the two strike prices: 725 - 700 = 25 (this number will always be 25). Let's say that "b" is 25.
(c) the difference between the two option prices: 30 - 20 = 10. Let's say that "c" is 10.

Step 2. Use the formula a/b x c
Substituting the numbers above, we get $\underline{15} \times 10 = 6$ or 6¢
25

Step 3. The answer, 6¢, is added to the lower option value, to get 20 + 6 = 26¢. ***Therefore the Sept. option "at the money" price is 26¢.***

You try one:

strike price	calls Sept.
700	32
725	27

The Sept. future's price is $7.20

Find the "at the money" price for the Sept. option.

Answer: Did you get 28¢? If not, follow this working:

Step 1. find the three differences.
(a) the lower strike price – the future's price = 725 - 720 = 5, a = 5

(b) the difference between the two strike prices is always 25. b = 25

(c) the difference between the two option prices, 32 - 27 = 5. c = 5

Step 2. use the formular a/b x c, to get $\frac{5}{25} \times 5 = 1$

Step 3. add the answer to the lower option value: 27 + 1 = 28¢, the "at the money" price.

You probably noticed that the lower strike price was used. But you can use the upper strike price if you wish – the only difference being that you must **subtract** the answer from the upper option value to get the "at the money" price.

Try Another:

strike price	Sept.
700	37
725	23

The Sept. future's price is $7.10

Find the "at the money" price for the Sept. option.

Answer: Did you get 31.4¢? If not, follow the working below.

Step 1. (a) 725 - 710 = 15 for "a"
(b) 725 - 700 = 25 for "b"
(c) 37 - 23 = 14 for "c"

Step 2. use a/b x c to get 15/25 x 14 = 8.4

Step 3. add the answer to the option price to get 31.4¢.

Do These: Find the Sept. "at the money" option price for each problem below.

1.

strike		
price	Sept.	Sept. future's price is $7.18
700	40	
725	30	

2.

strike		
price	Sept.	Sept. future's price is $7.07
700	43	
725	26	

Answers:
1. 32.8¢ (7/25 x 10 = 2.8, 30 + 2.8 = 32.8)
2. 38.24 or 38.2 rounded off (18/25 x 17 = 12.24 or 12.2, 26 + 12.2. = 38.2)

Do This: Below is a quote page as might be found in any newspaper. Find the "at the money" price for each of the option months.

Soybean Options — 5000 bu., cents per bu.

strike price	calls			
	Mar.	May	July	Soybean futures' closing prices
650	27	32	53	March is $6.75
675	15	26	46	May is $6.85
700	10	13	37	July is $7.09
725	6	10	32	

Answers: March is 15¢ (the future's and strike prices are identical)
May is 20.8¢ (15/25 x 13 = 7.8, 13 + 7.8 = 20.8)
July is 35.2¢ (16/25 x 5 = 3.2, 32 + 3.2 = 35.2)

The Interpolation Graph

This is a good place to introduce the interpolation graph. Some people prefer a quick method by graph, rather than do an arithmetic problem. Below is a reduced version of the interpolation graph. A full size graph is located near the back of the book.

Below are some problems to be done by graph. Use the larger graph at the back of the book. Read the instructions and examples on the graph, then proceed.

1.

strike		
price	Sept.	Sept. future's price is $7.15
700	27	
725	17	

2.

strike		
price	Sept.	Sept. future's price is $7.13
700	32	
725	21	

Answers: 1. 23¢ (17 + 6)   2. 26.3$ (21 + 5.3)

14

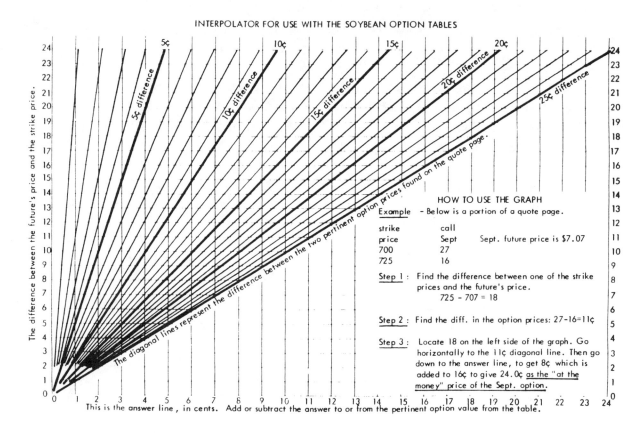

HOW TO USE THE GRAPH – Below is a portion of a quote page.

strike price	call Sept	
700	27	Sept. future price is $7.07
725	16	

Step 1: Find the difference between one of the strike prices and the future's price.
725 - 707 = 18

Step 2: Find the diff. in the option prices: 27-16=11¢

Step 3: Locate 18 on the left side of the graph. Go horizontally to the 11¢ diagonal line. Then go down to the answer line, to get 8¢ which is added to 16¢ to give 24.0¢ as the "at the money" price of the Sept. option.

The difference between the future's price and the strike price.

The diagonal lines represent the difference between the two pertinent option prices found on the quote page.

This is the answer line, in cents. Add or subtract the answer to or from the pertinent option value from the table.

That was a good workout. You should be good at finding the "at the money" price by now. You will see later that this practice was essential. The next important thing to learn is how to find the "weeks to expiration".

TIME TO EXPIRATION

You have seen the black strip at the bottom of each option table where it says, "Weeks to expiration". You will now learn how to find the number of weeks remaining in an option contract. As you have seen, time is one of the 3 market forces affecting an option's value.

At the back of this book, in Part 4, is a page titled *The Day Finder*. That page will enable you to find the number of days between two dates. Turn to that page now and read the directions.

Follow this example in The Day Finder. The date is Apr. 17th and you wish to buy a September call. Let's say the expiry date for the Sept. option is the 21st of Aug. Therefore, you wish to find the number of days between Apr. 17th and Aug. 21st. Follow This in The Day Finder. Locate Apr. 17th and you get 107 as its number. (Actually 107 represents the number of days in the year, up to and including Apr. 17th.) Locate Aug. 21st and you see 233 as its daily number. Subtract:233 - 107 = 126 as the number of days between those two dates.

But you want "weeks to expiration, so divide by 7: $126 \div 7 = 18$ weeks. Use the nearest week if there is a remainder after dividing. For leap year, add another day in February.

Do these: Use The Day Finder to find the number of days between the following dates.
    (1) Aug. 17 to Nov. 12   (2) Nov. 1 to Aug. 13, no leap year
    (3) Mar. 1 to June 14   (4) Dec. 6 to Apr. 1, a leap year
    Answers: (1) 87 (2) 285 (3) 105 (4) 117

This is a good place to introduce you to a graph which will quickly give you the weeks remaining to the expiration date. The graph is located near the back of the book in Part 4. Below is a reduced copy of the "weeks to expiration" graph.

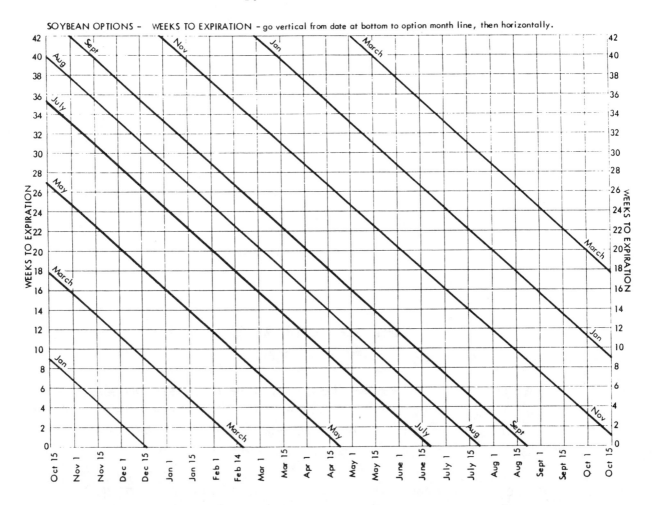

SOYBEAN OPTIONS – WEEKS TO EXPIRATION – go vertical from date at bottom to option month line, then horizontally.

Follow this example: The date is Jan. 15th and you are thinking of taking a bull spread in the May option. You wish to know how many weeks remain to the expiration date.

Method: Locate Jan. 15 on the bottom line of the graph. Go straight up to the May diagonal line, then go horizontally to the edge of the graph to get 14 weeks as the "weeks to expiration".

Another example: a more difficult one. Find the weeks to exp. from June 19th to the September contract.

16

Method: Look at the bottom line of the graph, and estimate where June 19th is located, just after June 15th. Move directly up to touch the Sept. diagonal line. Go horizontally to get ***9 weeks.***

You try some: Find the "weeks to expiration" for these dates and option months, to the nearest week.
1. from Apr. 1st for the Sept. option 2. from July 22nd for the Sept. option
3. From Aug. 6 for the Nov. contract 4. from March 7th for the July contract
Answers: 1. 20   2. 4   3. 11   4. 15

SELECTING THE APPROPRIATE TABLE

You have learned how to find (1) the "at the money" price (2) the "weeks to expiration" and now you will use that information to select the appropriate option table, the table which is best suited for your option position.

There are many option tables in Part 4 of this book, but only one of them is best suited to your trade. That suitability is determined by those 3 market variables (1) time (2) price (3) volatility. The problem, then, is to select the table which has the proper balance of these 3 market variables or forces, as pertains to your option trade.

Turn to the page which is titled ***Table Finder*** – located just in front of the option tables at the beginning of Part 4. Read the directions at the top of the page, then follow this example in the Table Finder.

Example problem: On Feb. 1st you decide to buy a May call. You will select the proper table.

Method: (1) By using the graph, you find that the ***"weeks to expiration" are 12 wks.***
(2) From the quote page, you calculate the ***"at the money" price is 30.1¢***
(3) Turn to the Table Finder page and locate column 12, the 12th week to expiration.
(4) Search in column 12 to locate 30.1¢, or to come as close to it as possible.
(5) The nearest you can get to 30.1¢ is 30.0. Use it.
(6) Look directly to the right, along the 30.0 row to the Table number column.
(7) You see Table 43 as the table best suited for your trade.
(8) Turn to Table 43 and you would use it to see if your trade was profitable.

The 3 market forces: time, price, and volatility (for the example above) were incorporated into the table by the selection of Table 43. Here is how it happened.
1. When you found the time to expiration was 12 weeks, and when you had used column 12 of the Table Finder page, you had taken ***time*** into account.
2. When you searched column 12 for the "at the money" price of 30.1¢ and used

30.0¢ as the closest to the actual price, you had taken **price** into account.

3. When you had selected Table 43, you had taken *volatility* into account. In the example, when you used the page of option data (from a newspaper or a quote screen) to find the "weeks to expiration" and the "at the money" price, then you had automatically instilled in those two figures, 12 wks. and 30.1¢, the volatility of that day's action. Table 43 reflected the volatility of that action expressed in the quote page. Table 42 would not have enough volatility, and Table 44 would have had too much. Table 43 is the one.

Part 2 of the book is now concluded. The real purpose of the book, the planning and trading of options, begins in Part 3.

PART 3

HOW TO PLAN and PROFIT WITH GRANDMILL'S OPTION TABLES

You have finally arrived at the most interesting section. Here you will use the skills which you learned in Part 2, to help form a winning option strategy. The tables will give you an amazing versatility in your planning. If you enjoy putting different option moves together in your search for a safer, more profitable trade, then you have hours of enjoyment ahead of you, thanks to the tables and the new type spreadsheet which you will see soon. But, first, let's look at the **conventional method** of graphing an option's profit or loss.

Below are the graphs of a call and a put. The graphs show the expected profit or loss **at the expiration date.** For example, if you bought a call at a strike price of 650 for a cost of 30¢ ($1500), then the graph will show you the profit or loss for a variety of strike prices, **at the expiration date.**

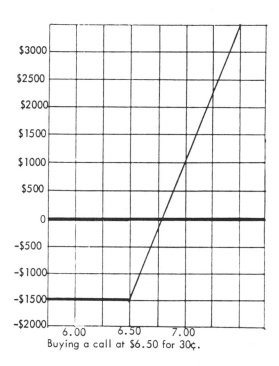

Buying a call at $6.50 for 30¢.

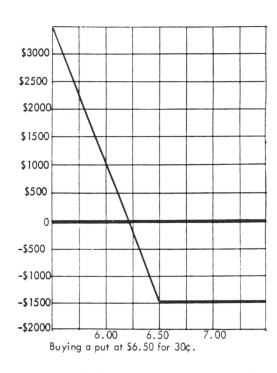

Buying a put at $6.50 for 30¢.

Look at the "buying a call" graph above. As you will remember, a call option makes money when prices rise and loses money when prices fall. You bought the call at a strike price of 650 and you paid $1500 for it. Do you see the heavy black line at the -$1500 level? The heavy black line extends horizontally to the left, signifying that the most money you can lose when prices decline, is $1500.

Look, now, at the rising graph line. As prices rise, so does the call's profit. You can see where the graph's line crosses the 0 horizontal line. This is the "break even" point, at $6.80, the point where you would have got your money back — and from there on is profit. You can see that when the future's price rises to $7.00, you will have earned a profit of $1000, **at the expiration date.**

Look at the "buying a put" graph. You will recall that you make money from buying a put only when the future's price declined after you had bought the put. That's why the graph line slants upward to the left — it shows profits increasing as the prices decline. The heavy black horizontal line shows you that the most money you can lose as prices rise, is the $1500 which you paid for the put. Once again, the two graphs show the profit or loss *at the expiration date only*.

Near the back of this book, in Part 4, are copies of blank graphs and spreadsheets which are suitable for copying. Run off some copies and try to make a graph of a call.

Selling a call or a put. The two graphs below depict the profit or loss at the expiration date only when you sell a call or a put.

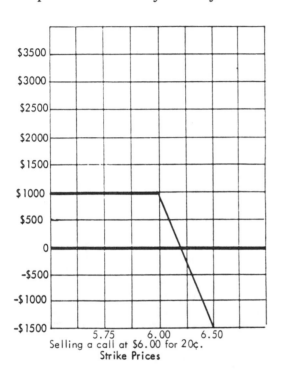

Selling a call at $6.00 for 20¢.
Strike Prices

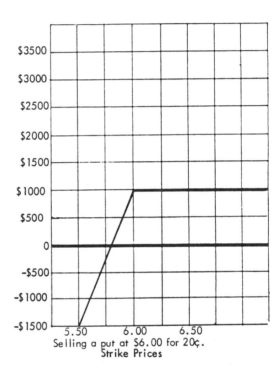

Selling a put at $6.00 for 20¢.
Strike Prices

Look at the "selling a call" graph. You will recall that when you sell a call (also called "writing a call") you receive the premium into your trading account from the unknown trader who bought your call. In this example, you sold the call at a strike price of 600, for a premium of 20¢ ($1000) which went straight into your account and it stays there until the end of the transaction. Recall, also, that you sold a call because you believed that prices would decline, thereby allowing you to keep all the premium as a profit. However, the other fellow who bought your call believes that prices will rise, and he is figuring on making a profit. So there is a clash of expectations, and only one of you is right.

Look at the "sell a call" graph again. Note the heavy horizontal line at the $1000 level, moving to the left. That indicates your profit which you have already collected when you sold the call. By extending the $1000 line to the left, it shows that all the profit (premium) is yours to keep as long as prices remain below $6.00. But look what happens when prices rise above $6.00 – down goes the graph into the losing area. Note that the break even point is $6.20 (not including commissions).

The "selling a put" graph is self explanatory. Remember, you sold a put because you believed prices would rise, thus preventing the other fellow from making a profit, and allowing you to keep all the premium. That's why the horizontal heavy line is above the higher prices.

A NEW TYPE OF PROFIT and LOSS SHEET IS NEEDED

The graphs shown a page or two back displayed the profit or loss **only at the date of expiration**. Thus, if you had bought a call at 12 weeks to expiration, those graphs would show you what to expect 12 weeks later at a variety of prices. In other words, the graphs told you nothing of what was happening between the time you bought the option and its expiration date. There were probably plenty of opportunities to get out of the trade with a good profit, long before it expired. But the graphs did not show those opportunities. That's not good enough. As traders, we need something which will show us the chances for a profit or the dangers of a loss, in the middle of the position, between the time the initial position is taken and its expiration.

It is said that fewer than 20% of traders keep their options right through to the expiration date. That means that 80% of us are traders willing to take a profit and exit long before expiration.

What an advantage it would be if we could look at the middle of an option trade and see what could happen to it, under a variety of conditions. Not only would it be nice to know what is our chance of success or failure during the course of the trade, but it would be even better to have that information **before we committed our money to the option position**.

The Spreadsheet

This is where you can turn to the tables for help. Remember, the option tables have the 3 option forces incorporated into them — time, price, volatility. Also, you learned in Part 2 to use the Table Finder to select the table which best reflects the volatility of the day you take the trade. Therefore, all that is needed now is some means of translating the information from the selected table to a convenient from which is easy to use by the trader. That convenient form is a new type spreadsheet, shown below.

Look at the spreadsheet below. Note the top row is for the weeks remaining to the expiration date. Look at the numbers on the left side of the sheet. These numbers represent **the amount of change in the underlying future's price**. For example, the +.25 means that the future's price has risen by 25¢ since the option position was originally taken. The -.25 means that the future's price has declined by 25¢ since the position was initiated. The 0 indicates that there has been no price change in the underlying future's price.

+$1									
+.75									
+.50									
+.25									
0									
-.25									
-.50									
-.75									
-$1									

changes in the soybean future's price (left vertical axis label)

The rectangular spaces in the spreadsheet will be filled in with the amount of profit or loss at a particular week to expiration. This will be clearly explained in the next chapter.

HOW TO USE THE SPREADSHEET

Buying a Call

"Buying a call" will be used to demonstrate how to complete the spreadsheet by calculating the profit or loss for each rectangular section. "Buying a call" was chosen for this example because everyone knows how to buy a call, and because it is familiar to everyone, you will understand better how the profits and losses were calculated. Actually, in real trading, it is doubtful that you need a spreadsheet for such a simple move as buying a call or a put.

Example – choosing the correct table

A scenario will be depicted here which will show the sequence of things you must do, to arrive at the point of actually filling in a spreadsheet.

The date is Dec. 23rd. Your charts and moving averages indicate that soybean futures prices will rise over the next few weeks. You decide to buy a March call at the money. Here are the steps you will take:

1. You will calculate the March option "at the money" price from the quote page. For this example, let's say it was 31¢.
2. You use the graph at the back of the book to find the weeks remaining from Dec. 23rd to the expiration date for March. You get 8 weeks.
3. Using the data from above i.e. 8 weeks, and the "at the money" price of 31.0¢, you turn to the Table Finder page. You search the 8th week column for 31.0 or as close to it as possible. You find it and look to the right to get the table

number which will best reflect the volatility of the market for Dec. 23rd. The table number is 55.

4. You run off a copy of the spreadsheet on your copier, turn to Table 55, and prepare to fill in the spreadsheet. Each rectangular section requires a complete calculation. It will take about 15 minutes to do a sheet, after you have done a few. The details for calculating the profit or loss for each section is printed below.

Filling in the spreadsheet

Below is the completed spreadsheet and a copy of Table 55. You will learn how each section of the spreadsheet was calculated. Follow the steps in Table 55 and in the spreadsheet.

	weeks to expiration				weeks to expiration			
	7	**6**	**5**	**4**	**3**	**2**	**1**	**0**
−$1	69.4	69.1	69.0	69.0	69.0	69.0	69.0	69.0
−.75	46.6	45.9	45.0	44.4	44.1	44.0	44.0	44.0
−.50	27.1	25.8	24.0	21.4	20.5	19.4	19.0	19.0
−.25	10.4	8.5	5.9	3.2	0.2	− 3.0	− 4.2	− 6.0
0	− 1.9	− 4.2	− 7.2	− 10.4	− 14.2	− 18.6	− 23.5	− 31.0
−.25	− 11.0	− 13.0	− 15.7	− 18.8	− 23.3	− 26.3	− 29.6	− 31.0
−.50	− 17.1	− 18.9	− 21.1	− 23.5	− 26.1	− 29.0	− 30.8	− 31.0
−.75	− 21.4	− 23.0	− 25.1	− 27.0	− 29.0	− 30.5	− 31.0	− 31.0
−$1	− 24.2	− 25.3	− 26.8	− 28.2	− 29.5	− 30.7	− 31.0	− 31.0

changes in the soybean future's price

Buying a soybean call, at the money, at a cost of 31¢, taken at the 8th week to expiration, Tab

BEAN FUTURES – Table No: 55

126.1	125.7	125.4	125.2	125.0	125.0	125.0	125.0	125.0	125.0	125.0	125.0	125.0	125.0	125.0	125.0	$1.25	IN THE MONEY
102.6	102.2	101.9	101.7	101.4	101.1	100.8	100.6	100.4	100.1	100.0	100.0	100.0	100.0	100.0	100.0	$1.00	
82.5	82.0	81.4	80.8	80.2	79.6	78.9	78.3	77.6	76.9	76.0	75.4	75.1	75.0	75.0	75.0	75¢	
66.3	65.5	64.6	63.7	62.7	61.6	60.5	59.4	58.1	56.8	55.0	53.4	51.5	50.4	50.0	50.0	50¢	
51.8	50.8	49.8	48.7	47.5	46.1	44.7	43.2	41.4	39.5	36.9	34.2	31.2	28.0	25.8	25.0	25¢	
40.6	39.6	38.4	37.2	35.8	34.3	32.7	31.0	29.1	26.8	23.8	20.6	16.8	12.4	7.5	0.0	AT THE MONEY	
31.3	30.3	29.2	28.0	26.6	25.1	23.6	21.9	20.0	18.0	15.3	12.2	8.7	4.7	1.4	0	25¢	OUT OF THE MONEY
23.6	22.6	21.6	20.5	19.3	18.1	16.8	15.5	13.9	12.1	9.9	7.5	4.9	2.0	0.2	0	50¢	
19.3	18.3	17.3	16.3	15.1	13.8	12.5	11.2	9.6	8.0	5.9	4.0	2.0	0.5	0	0	75¢	
14.0	13.3	12.5	11.7	10.8	9.9	8.8	8.0	6.8	5.7	4.2	2.8	1.5	0.3	0	0	$1.00	
9.8	9.3	8.7	8.1	7.4	6.6	5.8	5.1	4.3	3.4	2.3	1.5	0.5	0	0	0	$1.25	
15	14	13	12	11	10	9	8	7	6	5	4	3	2	1	0		

WEEKS TO EXPIRATION

ARE IN CENTS - to nearest tenth.

WM GRANDMILL (1985) LTD.

Step 1. **Find the cost.** You bought the call "at the money", in the 8th week to expiration. Look in Table 55, at the intersection of the 8th week column and the "at the money" line, and you will see 31.0¢ ($1550) as the cost of the call. This book will use cents rather than dollars to signify costs, profits and losses because cents are quicker and easier to use. Also, this book will use a + or a - sign to signify whether money is coming into your account or going out of your account. **Money in** uses a + sign. **Money out** uses a - sign. Therefore, **the cost of the call is --31.0**.

Step 2. **Filling in the spreadsheet**, section by section. Follow this carefully:

(a) As you know, you can get out of an option position any time you wish by giving your broker the order. In this example, you have bought a call. You can liquidate that call position by phoning your broker and saying, "Sell a Soybean March call at the market".

(b) **What happens next?** Well, you will get some money put back **into** your account because, if you exited early (before the expiration date) your call will still likely be worth something, no matter whether prices rose or fell. You can see the call's residual value in the table.

(c) **How much money will you get back?** That depends on the time remaining in the option position, and on whether prices have risen or fallen.

(d) **Here is an example of receiving money back** after you have liquidated your call. Keep in mind that you bought the call originally in the 8th week to exp., at a cost of **-31.0 cents** (a negative sign is used here to signify money "going out" of your account).

1. Suppose that **1 week has passed** and there has been **no price change**. You feel nervous about the position and decide to get out of it. You do so and you will get a partial "refund". You will receive back 29.1 cents. Where did that number come from? From the table, at the 7th week column, at the money (one week had passed and the price had not changed). This is expressed as +29.1 because it is money coming into your account (commissions are not included in the calculations — more on that later). How did you fare in the transaction? Here it is: -31.0 (the original cost) + 29.1 returned = -1.9¢ (a loss of $95).

Now look above at the completed spreadsheet. Look at that particular section (column 7, at the money) and you will see -1.9, the amount you would have lost if you had exited after only 1 week and with no price change.

Here's the point. Each rectangular space in the completed spreadsheet contains the amount of profit or loss which you would have sustained if you had liquidated your call position at each week to expiration, and at each price change.

24

2. **Another example.** Look at the spreadsheet above. Look at the section 6th week, +.50 (that means: the 6th week to expiration column, and the future's price has risen by 50 cents). You see 26.8¢. That amount represents the profit you would make if you liquidated your long call position at the 6th week to expiration, with a 50¢ future's price increase. So you can see that each section of the spreadsheet contains the profit or loss at each intersection of time and price. So the spreadsheet informs you what your call option would earn or lose under the various changes of time and price.

But how was it calculated? First we will need to look at the table. Look at Table 55, at the 6th week column, at the .50 "in the money" row. (Prices have risen by 50¢, so the call is now 50¢ "in the money".) You see 56.8 as the new value of the call at that juncture. That 56.8 represents the amount of money you would get back if you liquidate the call position at that juncture (the 6th week column and the +.50 row). If you had liquidated the position at that point, how would you have fared? Here's how to calculate it: -31.0¢ (your original cost of the call) +56.8¢ (received after liquidating the call) = +25.8¢ profit (commissions not included).

The point, again. The completed spreadsheet above shows you what to expect in the way of profit or loss, for every time change and price change.

Another example. This time, we will lose some of your money. Three weeks pass (which puts the trade in the 5th week to exp.) and the future's price has fallen by 50¢. This time, we will do the calculation first, then look at the spreadsheet.

(a) Look at Table 55, at the 5th week column, at the 50¢ "out of the money" row. You see 9.9 as the amount that you would get back if you liquidated the call at that point. (Remember, you paid -31.0 for the call at the beginning.) Here are the results, using the formula: - money out + money in = the profit or loss. -31.0 + 9.9 = -21.1 cents (a loss of $1055).

Check this calculation out with the spreadsheet. Look at the intersection of the 5th week column and -.50 row and yu see -21.1 as the loss which you would sustain if you liquidated your call position at that particular time and with that particular price change.

It's your turn. Find the profit or loss for the following sections of the spreadsheet. Use Table 55. When you have finished each problem below, check your answer with the spreadsheet. The calculations for each problem will also be printed at the end of the questions in case you get one wrong.

Find the profit or loss for each of the following — use Table 55. Remember, you took the call at the 8th week to expiration, at a cost of -31.0 cents.

(a) It is now 5 weeks since you took the call, and prices have risen 50¢.

(b) Four weeks have passed, and the future's price has fallen 25¢.

(c) 6 weeks later the prices are "at the money".

(d) After one week, the price rose by 25¢.

Answers: (a) -31.0 (the cost) + 51.5 (Table 55, 3rd week column, +.50 row) = +20.5 cents

(b) -31.0 + 12.2 (4th week column, at the -.25 row) = -18.8 cents

(c) -31.0 + 12.4 (2nd week column, at the money) = -18.6 cents

(d) -31.0 + 41.1 = +10.2 cents

Analysis:

Now that the calculations are taken care of, let's look at the spreadsheet itself to decide whether buying a call is a good deal. Calculating the profits and losses for the spreadsheet is laborious work for some, though it shouldn't take more than 15 minutes after you get used to it. But once that part is over, the satisfaction comes from taking an overall view of the sheet. It is like looking at a map laid out before you. And as you look at it, your mind begins to form a strategy to benefit by the best areas and to avoid the losing areas. But it must be admitted that you can't form much strategy with a call — it is fairly clear cut. The best moves lie ahead of you in this book and you will gain a real insight into option trading from the spreadsheets. But let's take a look at the spreadsheet of the long option call.

1. Note that the profit areas are in the top half of the sheet which emphasizes how important it is to have an upward price trend in the futures before you buy a call.

2. Note that even if prices rise 25¢ in your favor, you can still lose money after week 3.

3. Note that the worst loss is 31.0 cents, the price you paid for the call.

4. This option trade and the others which will be written in detail later in the book, will be rated with the words: poor, average, good, very good.

5. The long call (or the long put) position is rated as *average*.

6. **Here is a question for you.** What would you do if the future's price rose by 50¢ at the 6th week to expiration? Would you take the profit of 25.8¢ as shown in the spreadsheet at that place and get out? Or would you stay with your position, figuring that you can get the larger profit of 69.0 cents at expiration? Of course, the answer depends on the confidence and daring of the individual trader, but, mathematically speaking, you are usually better off if you take an early profit. In this example, by taking the 25.8¢ after being in the market only 2 weeks, you are earning at an annual rate of 2164%, whereas if you received the 69.0¢ after being in the market 8 weeks, you would be earning at an annual rate of 1447%. The point being made here is that sometimes it is better to take your money early rather than risk prices going against you later while seeking a greater profit.

7. **Selling a call.** Selling is the opposite of buying, so what does it do to the spreadsheet of the call, above? Look and visualize the following: all those minus numbers in the bottom half, 0 and +.25 rows now have + signs. All the profit numbers in the top half would now have minus signs, signifying losses.

The numbers themselves remain in the section they are in now, only the signs are reversed.

8. ***Rating "selling a call".*** You can visualize that if you took the "buying a call" and the "selling a call" positions ***in a neutral market***, then the "selling a call" trade would have an edge on the "buying a call" because you would have an extra row and a half of profit numbers (the 0 row and part of the +.25 row). But if you did as you were advised to do earlier in this book — which was to sell a call only when there were indications that prices would ***fall*** — then your chances of a profit are greatly enhanced. The same can be said for "selling a put" — but sell it when you think prices will rise. Therefore, if you sold a call when your indicators pointed to a price decline, then "selling a call" is rated as ***good.***

9. The option table and its spreadsheet will give you an edge in option trading. This was a simple spreadsheet. The real value of a spreadsheet comes later in the book when we do spreads, a strangle, a future with an option, etc.

10. An advantage of using these tables and spreadsheets, is that you can test a new method of trading or test a theory without having to commit any of your money. That is what will be done now.

   You have probably heard someone say the following, "If you think the future's price is going to go up, then the best place to buy a call is as far out of the money as possible. The price is dirt cheap when it is far from the "at the money" price, and it will take only a small price increase to double your money". That theory certainly sounds reasonable. Let's check it out.

   Below is the completed spreadsheet for this trade: buying a call at -$1.00 (a dollar "out of the money"), at the 8th week to expiration, using Table 55. The cost is only -8¢.

	weeks to expiration					weeks to expiration			
	7	6	5	4	3	2	1	0	
-$1	21.1	18.8	15.8	12.6	8.8	4.4	- 0.5	- 8.0	
-.75	12.0	10.0	7.3	4.2	0.7	- 3.3	- 6.6	- 8.0	
-.50	5.9	4.1	1.9	- 0.5	- 3.1	- 6.0	- 7.8	- 8.0	
-.25	1.6	0	- 2.1	- 4.0	- 6.0	- 7.5	- 8.0	- 8.0	
0	- 1.2	- 2.3	- 3.8	- 5.2	- 6.5	- 7.7	- 8.0	- 8.0	
-.25	- 3.7	- 4.6	- 5.7	- 6.5	- 7.5	- 8.0	- 8.0	- 8.0	
-.50									
-.75									
-$1									

changes in the soybean future's price

Buying a soybean call, at $1 out of the money, at a cost of 8¢, taken at the 8th week to expiration.

This trade is a loser. Look at those minus signs – even when the price rises by $1.00 the losses pile up just before the expiration date and at expiration. The only chance of success is for the prices to rise dramatically in the early weeks of the position. Now you know what will happen if that trade is taken.

COMMISSIONS

All profits and losses in the spreadsheet are calculated without taking commissions into account. The reason is clear — commissions vary from $15 to $125, depending on whether you trade with a discount broker or a full-service broker. Therefore, it is impossible to use a commission figure in the calculations.

But you should be aware of the commission costs, particularly when you do a spread. It is not uncommon to have 3 or 4 contracts in a complex spread — which means 3 or 4 commissions to be paid. A butterfly spread, for example, requires 4 positions and because it is a near neutral spread, it is possible to lose money because of the commission costs alone.

BULL CALL SPREAD

Now you will learn to complete a more complicated spreadsheet. It is vital that you become expert at completing a spreadsheet. The table and the spreadsheet operate as one. The bull call spread is a popular option trade. So you will reap double benefits here: you will learn more about completing the spreadsheet, and you will gain some important insights into this popular position.

The theory of the bull call spread. Here's how it works. Let's suppose your charts show a possible price rise coming up — but it looks like a weak rise which won't carry upward more than 25 or 30 cents by the future's price. Naturally you are hesitant to take a position here but there is a way to spread the risk and thus cut down the size of a potential loss. Also, it will cut in half the amount of your own money that you will need to use for this trade. Here's what to do.

Buy a call "at the money" and ***sell a call*** at 25¢ "out of the money". For example, you could buy a call at a strike price of 700 and sell a call at a strike price of 725, both in the same option month.

If prices rise this happens: your call will move into the "in the money" area whereas the other fellow's call will lag behind yours by 25¢ all the time. This means that your call will increase in value faster than the call which you sold because it is more "in the money".

If prices fall this happens: both your call and the other fellow's call will lose value, but your call will lose value faster than his. However, your call will always be worth more than his. Look back at Table 55 and you can see what happens as prices fall.

The bull spread has 3 advantages. (1) You won"t have much of your own money involved because you received the premium of the call which you sold. (2) This spread is less risky than just selling an ordinary call. Remember a few pages back that you were warned of the danger of selling a call — that, if prices did rise, the other fellow would earn a profit from the call he had bought from you — and that profit would come from your account. That's why margin is required when you sell a call or a put. But there is no danger of that happening here because your call is earning money faster than his. (3) In fact, this spread is so safe that most brokers do not require margin money, even though it is usual to put up margin when you sell a call. The most money you can lose is the amount you initially invested.

| weeks to expiration | | | | weeks to expiration | | | |
7	**6**	**5**	**4**	**3**	**2**	**1**	**0**
-$1	13.7	14.1	14.9	15.5	15.8	15.9	15.9	15.9

changes in the soybean future's price

	7	**6**	**5**	**4**	**3**	**2**	**1**	**0**
-$1	13.7	14.1	14.9	15.5	15.8	15.9	15.9	15.9
-.75	10.4	11.0	11.9	12.9	14.5	15.5	15.9	15.9
-.50	7.6	8.2	9.0	10.1	11.2	13.3	15.1	15.9
-.25	3.2	3.6	4.0	4.5	5.3	6.5	9.2	15.9
0	0	- 0.3	- 0.6	- 0.7	- 1.0	- 1.4	- 3.0	- 9.1
- .25	- 3.0	- 3.2	- 3.7	- 4.4	- 5.3	- 6.4	- 7.9	- 9.1
- .50	- 4.8	- 5.0	- 5.1	- 5.6	- 6.2	- 7.6	- 8.9	- 9.1
- .75	- 6.3	- 6.8	- 7.4	- 7.9	- 8.6	- 8.9	- 9.1	- 9.1
- $1	- 6.6	- 6.8	- 7.2	- 7.8	- 8.1	- 8.8	- 9.1	- 9.1

Bull spread. Buy a call at the money and sell a call at 25¢ out of the money, at a cost of 9.1¢.

BEAN FUTURES – Table No: 55

15	14	13	12	11	10	9	8	7	6	5	4	3	2	1	0		
126.1	125.7	125.4	125.2	125.0	125.0	125.0	125.0	125.0	125.0	125.0	125.0	125.0	125.0	125.0	125.0	$1.25	IN THE MONEY
102.6	102.2	101.9	101.7	101.4	101.1	100.8	100.6	100.4	100.1	100.0	100.0	100.0	100.0	100.0	100.0	$1.00	
82.5	82.0	81.4	80.8	80.2	79.6	78.9	78.3	77.6	76.9	76.0	75.4	75.1	75.0	75.0	75.0	75¢	
66.3	65.5	64.6	63.7	62.7	61.6	60.5	59.4	58.1	56.8	55.0	53.4	51.5	50.4	50.0	50.0	50¢	
51.8	50.8	49.8	48.7	47.5	46.1	44.7	43.2	41.4	39.5	36.9	34.2	31.2	28.0	25.8	25.0	25¢	
40.6	39.6	38.4	37.2	35.8	34.3	32.7	31.0	29.1	26.8	23.8	20.6	16.8	12.4	7.5	0.0	AT THE MONEY	
31.3	30.3	29.2	28.0	26.6	25.1	23.6	21.9	20.0	18.0	15.3	12.2	8.7	4.7	1.4	0	25¢	OUT OF THE MONEY
23.6	22.6	21.6	20.5	19.3	18.1	16.8	15.5	13.9	12.1	9.9	7.5	4.9	2.0	0.2	0	50¢	
19.3	18.3	17.3	16.3	15.1	13.8	12.5	11.2	9.6	8.0	5.9	4.0	2.0	0.5	0	0	75¢	
14.0	13.3	12.5	11.7	10.8	9.9	8.8	8.0	6.8	5.7	4.2	2.8	1.5	0.3	0	0	$1.00	
9.8	9.3	8.7	8.1	7.4	6.6	5.8	5.1	4.3	3.4	2.3	1.5	0.5	0	0	0	$1.25	
15	14	13	12	11	10	9	8	7	6	5	4	3	2	1	0		

WEEKS TO EXPIRATION

ARE IN CENTS - to nearest tenth.

WM GRANDMILL (1985) LTD.

How to complete a spreadsheet for a bull call spread.

The calculations for a bull call spread are a bit more complicated than for the call done a few pages back. Just remember the rule: - money paid out + money coming in = profit.

Above is a completed spreadsheet for the bull call spread. Again, **Table 55** was used. The position was taken at the **8th week** to expiration. You bought your call "*at the money*" and sold a call at **25¢ "*out of the money*"**.

We will calculate the profit or loss for each rectangular section of the spreadsheet. But the first step is **always** to calculate the initial cost.

Step 1 — Calculating the initial cost
(a) You bought your call at the 8th week to expiration, at the money. Look in Table 55, at the money, and you see 31.0¢. You paid it out of your account, **so it is written as -31.0.**

(b) You sold a call at the 8th week to expiration of the same option month, at 25¢ "out of the money" and you received 21.9¢ into your account. That's money in, so **it is written as +21.9.**

(c) Putting the two amounts together to get the final initial cost: -31.0 + 21.9 = **-9.1¢.** That's less than a third of what it would cost you to buy a call only.

Step 2 — Calculating the profit or loss for each section of the spreadsheet.
(a) Just as we did for the spreadsheet of the call which was done a few pages back, we assume that we will liquidate this spread at each section of the spreadsheet, so that we can calculate the profit or loss for each section. But this spread has an extra calculation to be made. When we liquidate, the unknown trader who had bought your call must receive some money back. This will be represented as "money paid out", so it will have a minus sign in front of it.

(b) **The first example.** Look at the complected spreadsheet above, for the bull spread. Look at the "at the money" section in the 7th week column. You see 0¢. Here is how it was calculated.

   1. Look at Table 55 above. Look at "at the money" in the 7th week column, and you see 29.1 which is the amount you would receive back if you liquidated the spread at that place. **Write it as +29.1** because it is money coming into your account.

   2. But you must pay back the trader who had bought your call which you had sold. He had bought it at 25¢ "out of the money". Look at the -.25 row, column 7 and you can see that his call is now worth 20.0¢. **Write it as -20.0** because it is money going out of your account.

   3. Here is the total calculation for that section of the spreadsheet:
-9.1 (the initial cost) + 29.1 (the money you get back) - 20.0 (paid out) = 0¢. The above showed how the calculation for the section column 7, row 0 was done.

(c) **The second example.** Look at the spreadsheet above. Look at the intersection of the 5th week column and the +.50 row. **There you see a profit of 9.0.** You will see how that number was calculated.

(1) Look in Table 55 at the 5th week column, at the +.50 row (the future's price has risen by 50¢). You see the new value of your call, 55.0¢. If you liquidated the call at this place, that 55.0 cents would go into your account. **Write it as +55.0**, money in.

(2) Now we have to consider the other fellow, the trader who had bought your call which you had originally sold at 25¢ "out of the money". But think about this. Prices have risen by 50¢, so his call's value has also increased. Where should we look for its new value? Answer: in column 5, at the +.25 row. Why? Because when the future's price rose by 50¢, the value of his call moved upward by two rows, in the table. We can see from the table that his call is now valued at 36.9¢. Do you see it? Because it is money being paid out, **write it as -36.9**.

(3) Now for the final calculation to find what the profit is for the section 5th week, row +.50: -9.1 (initial cost) + 55.0 - 36.9 = +9.0 cents profit.

(d) **The third example.** This time we will do one that shows a loss. Assume that 5 weeks have passed since the spread was taken. (That places the action in the 3rd week column). Let's assume that the future's price has fallen by 50¢. Therefore, your call's value will be located in column 3, at the -.50 row. The other fellow's call's value will be .25 lower in the table, at the -.75 row, column 3. Look in Table 55 for the new values.

(1) The new value of your call is 4.9¢.
(2) The new value of the other fellow's call is 2.0¢.
(3) Here is the final calculation for that section of the spreadsheet:
     -9.1 (initial cost) + 4.9 (for your call) - 2.0 (for his call) = -6.2 cents loss.
     Look at the appropriate section in the spreadsheet to confirm it.

You try some:
It's practice time! Do the following calculations for the bull spread. Then check your answer in the appropriate section of the spreadsheet, back a page or two. Remember the data so far: you took the spread at the 8th week to expiration, and your initial cost was -9.1¢.
(a) Calculate the profits for the 5th week to expiration, if prices have risen by 75¢.
(b) Calculate the loss at the 2nd week to expiration, with no change in the future's price.
(c) You have been holding the spread for 2 weeks. Prices have risen by 50¢. How much profit have you made?

Check your answers in the spreadsheet. But if you get one wrong, see the working below.
(a) -9.1 (initial cost) + 76.0 - 55.0 = + 11.9 cents profit

31

(b) -9.1 + 12.4 - 4.7 = - 1.4 cents loss

(c) -9.1 + 56.8 - 39.5 = +8.2 cents profit

Analysis of the Bull Call Spread

1. We will compare the spreadsheet of the bull spread with the spreadsheet of the "buying a call" a few pages back — to see if this spread is better than an ordinary call. Look back to the call's sheet.

2. Note that the losses for the spread are smaller than the call's losses — but so are the profits.

3. Less money is needed to initiate the spread than the call (-9.1 compared to -31).

4. The losses are less in the spread on 0 row and on row +.25. But these are minor advantages. Therefore, **the bull call spread is rated as average.**

5. Because the bull spread is so popular, it is disappointing that it is only average.

6. But wait. Let's experiment. We have tables and spreadsheets, so we can try different combinations of option positions, and it won't cost a cent to try them out. The theory for the bull call spread sounded logical — so let's try this combination: **Buy a call "at the money" and sell 2 calls at 25¢ "out of the money".** Selling an extra call should change something.

Another bull spread combination : Buy a call "at the money" and sell 2 calls at 25¢ "out of the money".

1. **Conditions:** Again we will use Table 55. Again we will take the spread at the 8th week to expiration. Again two or three of the completed spreadsheet sections will be calculated to show you how it was done.

2. **Finding the cost of taking the spread.**

   (a) Look at Table 55. Look at the 8th week column, at the money. There you see 31.0 as the cost of your call. It is money paid out, so **write it as --31.0.**

   (b) Now to find out how much you will receive from the trader who will buy those 2 calls at 25¢ "out of the money" which you are putting up for sale. Look in column 8th week, at the -.25 row, and you see 21.9 as the cost of each. You are selling 2 of them, so **you will receive into your account +21.9 + 21.9.**

   (c) Here is the calculation for the initial spread cost: -31.0 + 21.9 + 21.9 = **+12.8**. Note that you are starting the spread with a profit of 12.8¢. The trick is to keep it.

3. **First Example.** Look at the completed spreadsheet below. Look at the intersection of the 4th week column and the +.25 row. There we see a profit of 5.8 cents. . Here is how it was calculated.

   (a) Looking at Table 55, at the 4th week column, at the 25¢ "in the money" row, we see 34.2 which is the amount you would get back from your call, if it was liquidated at this point. It is money in, so **write it as +34.2.**

   (b) The other trader's 2 calls which he bought from you, are located 25¢ below your call. So his new value for each call is 20.6. each. (See col. 4, at the money.) Because you will be paying the money out for them if you liquidated the spread at this point, **write tham -20.6 -20.6.**

32

(c) The final calculation: +12.8 (the initial credit) + 34.2 (from your call) - 20.6 - 20.6)paid to the trader who had bought your 2 calls) = **+5.8 profit.** That's how the section was done.

		7	6	5	4	3	2	1	0
		weeks to expiration				weeks to expiration			
changes in the soybean future's price	-$1	- 42.0	- 40.9	- 39.2	- 38.0	- 37.4	- 37.2	- 37.2	- 37.2
	-.75	- 25.8	- 23.9	- 21.2	- 18.6	- 15.1	- 13.0	- 12.2	- 12.2
	-.50	- 11.9	- 8.4	- 6.0	- 2.2	1.9	7.2	11.2	12.8
	-.25	- 4.0	- 1.3	2.1	5.8	10.4	16.0	23.6	37.8
	0	1.9	3.6	6.0	9.0	12.2	15.8	17.5	12.8
	- .25	5.0	6.7	8.3	10.0	11.7	13.5	13.8	12.8
	- .50	7.5	8.9	10.9	12.3	13.7	13.8	13.0	12.8
	- .75	8.8	9.4	10.3	11.2	11.8	12.7	12.8	12.8
	- $1	11.0	11.7	12.4	12.6	13.3	13.1	12.8	12.8

Bull spread. Buy a call at the money and sell 2 calls at 25¢ out of the money, for a credit 12.8¢.

4. **Second example.** Look at the spreadsheet above. Look at the intersection of the 5th week column and the -.50 row. There you see a profit of 10.9. Here are the calculations for it. **member, the initial "cost" is a +12.8 credit.**

(a) The -.50 row in the spreadsheet means that the future's price has fallen by 50¢. That means that when you look in Table 55 for the new option values, you will find the new value of your call at 50¢ "out of the money" in the 5th week column. The new value is 9.9. Because it is money into your account if you liquidated the spread here, **is written as +9.9.**

(b) Because you initially sold the 2 calls at 25¢ "out of the money", then the new value for the other fellow's 2 calls will be located on the line below yours. Look there, at the 5th week column, at 75¢ "out of the money" in Table 55, you see a value of 5.9 for each call. It is money being paid out, so **write it as -5.9 - 5.9.**

(c) **The final calculation:** +12.8 (initial credit) + 9.9 - 5.9 - 5.9 = +10.9 for that section of the spreadsheet.

Analysis:

1. This bull spread is quite different from the first one, a couple of pages back. For one thing, all the bottom half of the spreadsheet shows profits – compared to the first spread which had nothing but losses in the lower half. This is unusual in a bull spread.

2. The top half of the spreadsheet is disappointing because there are far too many losses in that half to make it worthwhile to take. *As a bull spread, it is rated as poor.*

33

3. But there is another way to look at this unusual spreadsheet. Look at all those profits in the bottom half – not a minus sign in sight, and the profits get better the farther the prices decline. Surely we could take advantage of this situation. We usually take a bull spread when we believe the future's price will rise. but, in this case, one could change that pattern to take advantage of those profits which occur when the prices declined. Here is a plan which should work: Take this bull spread of buying a call "at the money" and selling 2 calls at 25¢ "out of the money", *only when your price charts indicate a neutral or a slightly bearish trend.* This way, you would be deliberately steering the spread toward the profit area as shown by the bottom half of the spreadsheet.

   There is a further thing you could do. As you can see in the spreadsheet, nearly all of row +.25 is profit. This profit row could act as a cushion in case you misjudged the bearish trend from your charts. In other words, you could make a note to liquidate the spread if the future's price should *rise* by 25¢. By doing this you would be almost completely protected against a loss. It is something to think about. *By using the spread in this way, it is rated as good.*

4. As mentioned before, one of the advantages of using these new soybean option table is this: you can experiment and search for the perfect trade, without spending a cent of your money. Let's try one more type of bull spread.

Buy a call "at the money" and see 2 calls at 50¢ "out of the money".
   This time we will sell the 2 calls a little farther out of the money.

		weeks to expiration				weeks to expiration		
	7	6	5	4	3	2	1	0
-$1	- 15.8	- 15.5	- 10.0	- 6.8	- 3.0	- 0.8	0	0
+.75	- 5.2	- 2.1	2.2	7.0	12.7	19.0	23.4	25.0
-.50	- 0.1	4.2	8.2	12.2	17.9	25.6	35.0	50.0
-.25	1.4	3.5	6.3	9.8	13.8	18.6	23.0	25.0
0	1.3	2.6	4.0	5.6	7.0	8.4	7.1	0
- .25	0.8	2.0	3.5	4.2	4.7	3.7	1.4	0
- .50	0.3	0.7	1.5	1.9	1.9	1.4	0.2	0
- .75	1.0	1.2	1.3	1.0	1.0	0.5	0	0
- $1	1.7	1.7	1.8	1.3	1.3	0.3	0	0

changes in the soybean future's price

Bull spread. Buy a call at the money and sell 2 calls at 50¢ out of the money, at a cost of 0¢,

34

Analysis:

1. Look at the spreadsheet above! What a beautiful sight! It looks like a trader's dream come true.

2. As a bull spread is supposed to do, it can make a good sized profit when prices go up.

3. But look at the bottom half of the spreadsheet! It shows that you will not lose money if prices decline. The profits there are not large – but that's not the point. The point is that there are no losses on the downside.

4. So what we have here shown by the spreadsheet, is good profits on the upside and no losses on the downside.

5. The only weak point is the top, left corner. It means that if prices were to rise rapidly in the first week of the spread, you could lose.

6. Here is a plan for this spread which should be very safe under normal conditions:

    Take this spread when your charts indicate a bullish or a neutral price trend ahead. Then make a note to liquidate the spread if the future's price should rise more than 75¢. This way, Any loss in the first week or two (as shown in the upper, left corner at the +.75 row), would be very small and would change into a profit after a couple of weeks. Also, this will catch all the profits which are in the first 3 rows above the 0 row.

7. ***This spread is rated as very good.***

THE STRADDLE

Buy a call and buy a put, both "at the market"

This spread is mentioned in most book as being suitable to use when you think the market is about to make a substantial move, but you are not sure of the direction, up or down.

The theory is that if the future's price should rise, then the call will make profits while the value of the put will diminish. On the other hand, if prices should fall, then the put will earn the profits while the value of the call will diminish.

You are probably thinking, "Wait a minute! If one option gains while the other option is losing, then you are getting nowhere! The losses will cancel out the gains."

Wrong! Strange as it may seem, if the future's price is rising, then the call option will earn more money faster than the put will lose money. Also, if prices are falling, the put will earn more money faster than the call will lose money.

It's true. An option table will prove it. Look at Table 55, in the 8th week column, at the money. You see 31.0 cents. Suppose you bought both a call and a put here, for 31.0¢ each – you are doing what is known as "a straddle". It is actually a spread. Follow this in the table. Suppoose the future's price rose by 50¢. Let's see what will happen to both the call and the put, as regards their new values. For the call, it's new value is 59.4¢ – **an increase of 28.4¢.** For the put, it's new value is 15.5¢ – **a decrease of 15.5¢.** So you see, the call earned more than the put lost. Likewise, if prices declined, the put would earn more than the call lost. That's the principle behind the straddle.

	7	6	5	4	3	2	1	0
-$1	45.2	43.8	42.2	40.8	39.5	38.3	38.0	38.0
-.75	25.2	22.9	19.9	17.4	15.1	13.5	13.0	13.0
-.50	10.0	7.9	2.9	-1.1	-5.6	-9.6	-11.8	-12.0
-.25	-0.6	-4.5	-9.8	-15.6	-22.1	-29.3	-34.8	-37.0
0	-3.8	-8.4	-14.4	-20.8	-28.4	-37.2	-47.0	-62.0
-.25	-0.6	-4.5	-9.8	-15.6	-22.1	-29.3	-34.8	-37.0
-.50	10.0	7.9	2.9	-1.1	-5.6	-9.6	-11.8	-12.0
-.75	25.2	22.9	19.9	17.4	15.1	13.5	13.0	13.0
-$1	45.2	43.8	42.2	40.8	39.7	38.3	38.0	38.0

weeks to expiration   weeks to expiration

changes in the soybean future's price

Straddle. Buy a call and buy a put, both at the money, for a cost of 62.0¢.

You can see that the theory is sound but let's see how it works out in real option trading. Above is a completed spreadsheet for a straddle spread. ***Buy both a call and a put, at the money, at the 8th week to expiration.***

One of the profit areas will be worked out to show you how it was done. Follow this in Table 55. Look at the intersection of the 5th week column and the +.50 row. You see a profit of 2.9 cents. Here is how that 2.9 was calculated. Let's assume that the future's price has ***risen by 50¢.***

    (a) The first step is always to find the initial cost. Both the call and the put cost 31.0 each. It was money paid out so ***the total initial cost is written as -62.0.***

    (b) The future's price rose by 50¢, which means the call gained in value while the put lost in value. Looking in Table 55 for the call's new value, in the 5th week column, we see the new value is 55.0. If we liquidated the position at this point, it would be money coming into the account, so it is ***written as +55.0.*** Meanwhile the put has declined by 50¢. It's new value in the 5th week column is 9.9. That money would go back into your account on liquidation, so ***it is written as +9.9.***

    (c) The final calculation is: -62.0 + 55.0 + 9.9 = +2.9 cents profit.

Analysis. Rated average to good to very good, depending on the situation.
1. Look at the spreadsheet above. Note that there are 5 lines of losses altogether, in the middle of the spreadsheet. That means that prices would have to change by more than 50¢ in order to earn a profit.
2. If the future's price would have to rise or fall by more than 50¢ before you could make a profit, then you would need a lively market where uncertainty exists – like a weather scare where you wouldn't know whether prices will continue to rise or whether a heavy rain might come and cause prices to fall rapidly.
3. This is an ideal position to take for a weather scare because you are protected both ways for a big price move, either up or down. You should not use this straddle in a quiet market.

Selling a straddle. Rated good if used in a quiet market.
    This kind of position would be a good one to sell when prices are going nowhere. You would make a note to liquidate the straddle when prices rise by 30¢ – thus ensuring an almost perfect chance for a profit. After the 5th week has passed, one could extend that limit to 50¢ and still be safe from loss.

    To visualize your profits, look at the straddle spreadsheet above. Just reverse the signs in front of the numbers. Where you see minuses now when you ***buy*** the straddle, will become pluses when you ***sell*** the straddle. Likewise, the profits now would become losses when you sell the straddle, as shown in the spreadsheet of the straddle above.

THE STRANGLE

Buy a call and buy a put, both at 25¢ out of the money.

First a few words to tell you what the difference is between a **straddle** and a **strangle**. Both are spreads, using a call and a put. The straddle is taken "at the money", whereas the strangle is the named used for this spread when it is taken "out of the money".

Here's the theory behind the strangle. Because the strangle is taken "out of the money", it will cost less money to take it, than taking a straddle. True. Also, the theory goes on to say, if there is a big price move from a weather scare, you will catch that big move anyway and it will have cost you less. That theory certainly sounds reasonable. Let's see how it will work out in practice.

Below is a spreadsheet for a strangle. Both the call and the put were bought at 25¢ "out of the money". Compare this spreadsheet with the one for the straddle.

	7	**6**	**5**	**4**	**3**	**2**	**1**	**0**
-$1	38.1	36.5	34.5	33.1	31.8	31.2	31.2	31.2
-.75	21.1	18.7	15.4	12.4	9.2	6.9	6.2	6.2
-.50	7.2	3.7	-1.0	-5.6	-10.6	-15.0	-18.0	-18.8
-.25	-0.8	-4.9	-10.1	-15.7	-22.1	-29.4	-36.1	-43.8
0	-3.8	-7.8	-13.2	-19.4	-26.4	-34.4	-41.0	-43.8
-.25	-0.8	-4.9	-10.1	-15.7	-22.1	-29.4	-36.1	-43.8
-.50	7.2	3.7	-1.0	-5.6	-10.6	-15.0	-18.0	-18.8
-.75	21.1	18.7	15.4	12.4	9.2	6.9	6.2	6.2
-$1	38.1	36.5	34.5	33.1	31.8	31.2	31.2	31.2

(left axis label: changes in the soybean future's price)

Strangle. Buy a call and a put, both at 25¢ out of the money, at a cost of 43.8¢.

Analysis: Rated average to good.
1. The cost for this strangle was -43.8¢, compared to -62.0¢ for the straddle.
2. The profits are smaller for the strangle.
3. It appears that nothing has been gained by doing a strangle. True, it costs less, but the profits are less, too. It seem to be in proportion to the money spent as the initial cost.
4. Both the strangle and the straddle are ideal "weather market" positions.

MIXING OPTIONS and FUTURES

Buy a future and sell 2 calls at 50¢ "out of the money".

    This is a different kind of option position. This book is attempting to show you the different kinds of option positions – but there are also about a dozen varieties of each kind which you can discover for yourself by using the tables and spreadsheets. Experiment. Test out models by using the tables. You are limited only by your imagination. Someday you could discover a very safe and very profitable option trade.

    Because a future's position is used here, it is worthwhile to review the difference between a fture's and an option's move. The main difference is this: If the future's price rises by 25¢, and if you were long a future's position at the time, then you would have earned 25¢ profit ($1250). But that is not the case with an option – its value increase would be much less. You can see it in the tables. Look at Table 55, in the 8th week column at the money and you see a value of 31.0. The future's price rises by 25¢. Now look at the new option value and you see 43.2, an increase of only 12.2, about half the future's increase. That fact just described is the basis of using options and futures together.

    Here's the theory. Because a future earns more money than an option, then you could sell a couple of options without risk, and thus have some money put into your account from the sale. For example, if you went long a future and sold 2 calls, then you would have the money from the sale to start with, and the future will gain as fast or faster than the 2 calls so you could maybe make more money on the upside, whereas, if prices went against you, the money you had made from the sale would soften the loss from the declining future's position. And, also, it would be a good idea to sell the 2 call "out of the money" because when prices rise (as you expect them to do because you are long a future), the 2 calls will increase at a lesser rate when sold "out of the money". It sounds reasonable. Let's see how it works in practice.

    Therefore, when you calculate the profits and losses for the spreadsheet, you must keep in mind that the future's position will increase by the full price change, where as a long call position will benefit by only a fraction of the price increase. There is no need of a table to find the increased value for the future's position — it will increase by the price amount. But you do need a table to give you the option values. Again, a couple of examples will be explained in detail so you can see how each section of the spreadsheet was done.

Example. One of the sections from the spreadsheet above will be calculated so that you can see how it was done. Look at the intersection of the 5th week column and the +.50 row, and you will see 33.4. Here is how that number was calculated. Follow it in Table 55.

    (a) The first task is to find the initial cost or credit. ***We are buying a future and selling 2 calls at 50¢ out of the money.*** This position was taken at the 8th week to expiration. Looking in Table 55, column 8, at the row of 50¢ out of the money, you see 15.5. You sold 2 calls so you will receive into your account +15.5 +15.5 = ***+31.0 cents credit.***

(b) Looking now at the 5th week, with prices having risen by 50¢, you can see that the calls are now worth 23.8 each. If you had liquidated the position here, this money would have to be paid to the fellow who had bought your calls, so it is money out, so it is written as -23.8 - 23.8 = **-47.6.**

(c) Meanwhile your long future has gained 50¢, and it gains all of it, so **it is written as +50.0.**

(d) **The final calculation:** +31.0 - 47.6 + 50.0 = +33.4, the number in the section that we checked.

changes in the soybean future's price	7	6	5	4	3	2	1	0
+$1	14.8	17.4	21.0	24.2	28.0	30.2	31.0	31.0
+.75	23.2	27.0	32.2	37.6	43.6	50.0	54.4	56.0
+.50	22.8	27.4	33.4	39.8	47.4	56.2	66.0	81.0
+.25	16.0	20.0	25.4	31.6	38.6	46.6	53.2	56.0
0	3.2	6.8	11.2	16.0	21.2	27.0	30.6	31.0
-.25	-13.2	-10.0	-5.8	-2.0	2.0	5.0	5.6	6.0
-.50	-32.6	-30.4	-27.4	-24.6	-22.0	-19.6	-19.0	-19.0
-.75	-52.6	-50.8	-48.6	-47.0	-45.0	-44.0	-44.0	-44.0
-$1								

Buy a future and sell 2 calls at 50¢ out of the money, for a credit of 31¢, taken at the 8th week

BEAN FUTURES – Table No: 55

15	14	13	12	11	10	9	8	7	6	5	4	3	2	1	0		
126.1	125.7	125.4	125.2	125.0	125.0	125.0	125.0	125.0	125.0	125.0	125.0	125.0	125.0	125.0	125.0	$1.25	IN THE MONEY
102.6	102.2	101.9	101.7	101.4	101.1	100.8	100.6	100.4	100.1	100.0	100.0	100.0	100.0	100.0	100.0	$1.00	
82.5	82.0	81.4	80.8	80.2	79.6	78.9	78.3	77.6	76.9	76.0	75.4	75.1	75.0	75.0	75.0	75¢	
66.3	65.5	64.6	63.7	62.7	61.6	60.5	59.4	58.1	56.8	55.0	53.4	51.5	50.4	50.0	50.0	50¢	
51.8	50.8	49.8	48.7	47.5	46.1	44.7	43.2	41.4	39.5	36.9	34.2	31.2	28.0	25.8	25.0	25¢	
40.6	39.6	38.4	37.2	35.8	34.3	32.7	31.0	29.1	26.8	23.8	20.6	16.8	12.4	7.5	0.0	AT THE MONEY	
31.3	30.3	29.2	28.0	26.6	25.1	23.6	21.9	20.0	18.0	15.3	12.2	8.7	4.7	1.4	0	25¢	OUT OF THE MONEY
23.6	22.6	21.6	20.5	19.3	18.1	16.8	15.5	13.9	12.1	9.9	7.5	4.9	2.0	0.2	0	50¢	
19.3	18.3	17.3	16.3	15.1	13.8	12.5	11.2	9.6	8.0	5.9	4.0	2.0	0.5	0	0	75¢	
14.0	13.3	12.5	11.7	10.8	9.9	8.8	8.0	6.8	5.7	4.2	2.8	1.5	0.3	0	0	$1.00	
9.8	9.3	8.7	8.1	7.4	6.6	5.8	5.1	4.3	3.4	2.3	1.5	0.5	0	0	0	$1.25	
15	14	13	12	11	10	9	8	7	6	5	4	3	2	1	0		

WEEKS TO EXPIRATION

ARE IN CENTS - to nearest tenth.

WM GRANDMILL (1985) LTD.

Analysis.

1. The purpose of taking this position in the first place was to cut down your losses in case the prices went against you, and to start off with some extra money into your account. It does that.

2. But some people would say, "I would be better off to just take the long future and to use a stop". Perhaps, because your upside earnings would be much greater with a future only. But there is a plus side to this position: (1) Note the 0 row. It has a profit, whereas with a future only, you have nothing in this row. (2) If the future fell by 25¢, would would lose 25¢, whereas, with the options, you could lose a little or gain a little in the -.25 row.

3. But there is a kind of market where this position would perform well. It is best in a slow market. Suppose that your charts indicated a slow market ahead for the next 8 weeks, with maybe a neutral or a 25¢ upmove at the most. It is doubtful that you would consider a future only. It would be better to sell the 2 calls. Look at the spreadsheet. See, you make good money in row +.25. You do well if there is no price change, row 0. And you don't lose much or you could make a bit in case you had misjudged the price trend, row -.25. A comfortable situation.

4. This trade, buy a future and sell 2 calls at 50¢ out of the money, **is rated very good** for a slow market.

5. **Note this:** you should make a list of trades which you can do under different situations. Some people think one kind of position works for soybeans, all the time. Not so. You must employ various tactics. Make a list headed "slow market", and under it you could put this trade and selling a straddle or a strangle, etc. Under a heading "weather markets", you could list "buy a straddle", etc. and so on. This book is attempting to prove in black and white, how the different types of positions work in different situations.

Using a put instead of a stop on a long future.

Have you ever had this happen to you? You bought a future and placed a stop at 12¢ under your entry price, then suddenly, "for no reason at all", the price descended, touched your stop, and putting you out of the market it climbed back up where it had started – leaving you aghast. Most future's traders have had that happen to them.

But, if you had used a put instead of a stop, then, when the prices recovered, you would still be in the market. A price dip like that would be no problem.

But you are probably unaware how a put affects a future, so the following spreadsheet was made to show you what happens.

Analysis:

1. A long future's position was taken and a put was bought "at the money" in the 8th week to expiration, for 31.0¢.

2. First, note that the most money the position can lose is the cost of 31¢, no matter whether the future's price fell 25¢ or $1.

3. Note that the upside profit is reduced from what you would have without using a put.
4. The advantages are: (1) You can't be put out of the market by a price reversal. (2) Your loss is limited to the cost of the put.

		7	6	5	4	3	2	1	0
	-$1	75.8	74.7	73.2	71.8	70.5	69.3	69.0	69.0
	-.75	53.6	52.0	49.9	48.0	46.0	44.5	44.0	44.0
	-.50	32.9	31.1	28.9	26.2	23.9	21.0	19.2	19.0
	-.25	14.0	12.0	9.3	6.2	2.7	-1.3	-4.6	-6.0
	0	-1.9	-4.2	-7.2	-10.4	-14.2	-18.6	-23.5	-31.0
	-.25	-14.6	-16.5	-19.1	-21.8	-24.8	-28.0	-30.2	-31.0
	-.50	-22.9	-24.2	-26.0	-27.6	-29.5	-30.6	-31.0	-31.0
	-.75	-28.4	-29.1	-30.0	-30.6	-30.9	-31.0	-31.0	-31.0
	-$1	-30.6	-30.9	-31.0	-31.0	-31.0	-31.0	-31.0	-31.0

changes in the soybean future's price (left axis label)

Buy a future and buy a put as a substitute for a stop, at a cost of 31¢. Taken at the 8th week.

THE TIME SPREAD

This is a different kind of spread from any you have seen so far. Sometimes it is called a "horizontal spread". The kinds of spreads you have done so far are called "vertical spreads" because you calculated the profits or losses for the spreadsheet by using the numbers which were in the same week's column. That is why it is called "vertical". But this new type spread is calculated horizontally as you will see soon.

Up until now you have used the same month in a spread. For example, when you did a bull spread, you may have said, "Buy a March call at the money, and sell a March call at 25 cents out of the money". You used the same month. Similarly, you used the same month for the straddle.

But a **time spread** is different — it uses two different months. A vertical spread made its profit from a difference in prices. A time spread makes its profit from a difference in time. An example will show you what is meant.

Example: Buy a May soybean call and sell a March soybean call, both at the money.

Assume that this spread was initiated on Dec. 23rd – which would give the March option an expiry time of 8 weeks and 17 weeks for the May option. Both options were taken at the money. Follow this example in Table 55 below.

42

1. The expiry dates for March and May are 9 weeks apart.
2. Therefore, in this example, we buy the March call at the 8th week and buy the May call at the 17th week to expiration — 9 weeks apart.
3. They were both taken "at the money".
4. **What is the initial cost?** Look "at the money" in the 17th week column and you see 42.6¢ as the cost of the May call. **Write it as -42.6.** For the March

		weeks to expiration				weeks to expiration		
		16&7	15&6	14&5	13&4	12&3	11&2	10&1	9&0
	+$1	- 8.9	- 9.0	- 9.4	- 9.7	- 9.9	- 10.2	- 10.5	- 10.8
	+.75	- 6.2	- 6.0	- 5.6	- 5.6	- 5.9	- 6.4	- 7.0	- 7.7
	+.50	- 2.6	- 2.1	- 1.1	- 0.4	0.6	0.7	0	- 1.1
	+.25	- 0.3	0.7	2.3	4.0	5.9	7.9	8.7	8.1
	0	0.9	2.2	4.2	6.2	8.8	11.8	15.2	21.1
	-.25	0.7	1.7	3.4	5.4	7.7	10.3	12.1	12.0
	-.50	- 1.0	- 0.1	1.1	2.5	4.0	5.7	6.3	5.2
	-.75	- 1.0	- 0.3	0.8	1.7	2.7	3.0	2.2	0.9
	-$1	- 3.7	- 3.6	- 2.5	- 1.9	- 1.4	- 1.1	- 1.7	- 2.8

changes in the soybean future's price (left axis label)

Time spread. Bought a May call and sold a March call, both at the money, for a cost of 11.6¢.

BEAN FUTURES – Table No: 55

126.1	125.7	125.4	125.2	125.0	125.0	125.0	125.0	125.0	125.0	125.0	125.0	125.0	125.0	125.0	125.0	$1.25	IN THE MONEY
102.6	102.2	101.9	101.7	101.4	101.1	100.8	100.6	100.4	100.1	100.0	100.0	100.0	100.0	100.0	100.0	$1.00	
82.5	82.0	81.4	80.8	80.2	79.6	78.9	78.3	77.6	76.9	76.0	75.4	75.1	75.0	75.0	75.0	75¢	
66.3	65.5	64.6	63.7	62.7	61.6	60.5	59.4	58.1	56.8	55.0	53.4	51.5	50.4	50.0	50.0	50¢	
51.8	50.8	49.8	48.7	47.5	46.1	44.7	43.2	41.4	39.5	36.9	34.2	31.2	28.0	25.8	25.0	25¢	
40.6	39.6	38.4	37.2	35.8	34.3	32.7	31.0	29.1	26.8	23.8	20.6	16.8	12.4	7.5	0.0	AT THE MONEY	
31.3	30.3	29.2	28.0	26.6	25.1	23.6	21.9	20.0	18.0	15.3	12.2	8.7	4.7	1.4	0	25¢	OUT OF THE MONEY
23.6	22.6	21.6	20.5	19.3	18.1	16.8	15.5	13.9	12.1	9.9	7.5	4.9	2.0	0.2	0	50¢	
19.3	18.3	17.3	16.3	15.1	13.8	12.5	11.2	9.6	8.0	5.9	4.0	2.0	0.5	0	0	75¢	
14.0	13.3	12.5	11.7	10.8	9.9	8.8	8.0	6.8	5.7	4.2	2.8	1.5	0.3	0	0	$1.00	
9.8	9.3	8.7	8.1	7.4	6.6	5.8	5.1	4.3	3.4	2.3	1.5	0.5	0	0	0	$1.25	
15	14	13	12	11	10	9	8	7	6	5	4	3	2	1	0	WEEKS TO EXPIRATION	

ARE IN CENTS - to nearest tenth.

WM GRANDMILL (1985) LTD.

call, look in the 8th week column and you will see 31.0¢ – which is money in because you sold it, so **write it as +31.0.** Putting the two values together, you get: -42.6 + 31.0 = **-11.6, as the initial cost.**

Above is the completed spreadsheet for the example above.

5. Leave the information above for a moment while the theory of the time spread is expounded.

6. **The Theory**

   (a) You know that the nearer an option is to the expiry date, the faster its value is eroded by the passage of time.

   (b) Here you have 2 options — one at 17 weeks and the other at 8 weeks. The latter will have a greater erosion of its value because it is closer to its expiration date.

   (c) As time passes, the two options move week by week closer to March's expiration.

   (d) The move onward in lock step — always 9 weeks apart. When March finally expires, the May option is located in the 9th week column.

   (e) March lost its value rapidly as it approached its expiration date, whereas May lost its value slowly because it is farther from its expiration date.

   (f) The profit results from the difference in the rate of value loss of the two months and this will occur no matter whether prices rise or fall.

   (g) The rule for taking a time spread is: **Always buy the farther away month and sell the month nearest to its expiration date.**

7. One of the sections in the spreadsheet will be calculated here to show you how it is done. But, first, notice how the weeks to expiration are printed in the top row. It is best to put the weeks for both option months together. Look at the intersection of the +.25 row and the 12&3 column. You see 5.9 at that place. Here is how it was calculated.

   12&3 means that May is in the 12th week column and March is in the 3rd week column, using Table 55. Looking in the 12th week column, at +.25 row, in Table 55, you see 48.7 as the value of the May call. If you liquidated here, it would be money in, so **write it as +48.7.**

   The March call which you sold is located in the +.25 row, 3rd week column. You see a value of 31.2 for it. It will be money paid out on liquidation, so **write it as -31.2.**

   Putting all the numbers together: -11.6 + 48.7 - 31.2 = **+5.9.**

Analysis:

1. At first glance, it seems that this spread may have some promise of success but when you look closely you see that most of the profits are small, and most of the losses are small. By the time you had paid two full commissions, there would be very little left for yourself.

2. With reluctance, **this spread is rated as poor.**

3. But the theory seems plausible, so let's try it another way. Let's sell the call or calls "out of the money".

4. Below is the spreadsheet for this Time Spread: **Buy a May call at the money, and sell 2 March calls at 50¢ "out of the money".** Again, the spread was taken at the 17th and 8th weeks.

		weeks to expiration				weeks to expiration			
		16&7	15&6	14&5	13&4	12&3	11&2	10&1	9&0	
	+$1	− 24.2	− 22.6	− 19.4	− 16.5	− 12.9	− 11.0	− 10.5	− 10.8	
	+.75	− 13.9	− 8.1	− 3.4	1.4	6.8	12.6	16.4	16.4	
	+.50	− 3.5	1.1	6.3	11.6	18.5	26.3	35.0	48.9	
	+.25	1.1	4.2	8.6	13.8	19.7	26.5	31.7	33.1	
	0	2.2	4.8	8.2	11.8	15.8	20.2	22.3	21.1	
	− .25	1.5	3.7	6.9	9.6	12.4	14.0	13.5	12.0	
	− .50	− 0.7	0.6	2.6	4.4	5.9	7.1	6.5	5.2	
	− .75	0	0.9	2.1	2.7	3.7	3.5	2.2	0.9	
	− $1									

changes in the soybean future's price (left axis label)

Time spread. Bought a May call at the money and sold 2 March calls at 50¢ out of money, cost 11.6¢.

Analysis.

1. It looks as if we have found a winner. Look at those plus numbers, 3 rtows of them on each side of the 0 row.
2. Look at the bottom 3 rows of values in the spreadsheet. That's your safety net in case you misjudged the upward price trend. Even if prices went against you by as much as 75¢, you still wouldn't lose money. That's real protection.
3. But there is a weak spot in the upper, left corner. Do you see those minuses there? That means that if prices rose rapidly in the first week or two of the spread, you could lose some money. But, as you can see, those losses turn into profits for two of the rows, as time passes. That's a break because mostly time works against you – but here it is working for you.
4. Now that the weak spot is known, one should have a plan made in advance to handle it. For example, one could do this: make a note to liquidate the spread if the future's price rises by 75¢ in the first 2 weeks of the spread.
5. The size of the profits are good. The cost is 11.6¢ and the maximum profit is 48.9¢. That's a good ratio of profit to investment for a period of only 8 weeks.
6. If one takes precautions against that weak left corner, then **this spread is rated as very good.**

You may need 2 option tables for the Time Spread.

The examples of the Time Spread above used only one option table — Table 55. But this is not likely to happen in real trading. Only one table was used in the examples above because it was easier to put across the ideas involved in the Time Spread, with one table. It was done to keep things simple. But, in fact, there is better than a 50-50 chance that you will need 2 different option tables to complete the spreadsheet for a Time Spread.

Here's why you may need two different option tables. (1) Every time you decide to use an option month, you must go through the routine of selecting the appropriate option table by using the Table Finder page. This is done so that you will be using the table which best reflects the volatility of the day. (2) When you take a Time Spread, you will always be using 2 option months. In the example above, the months of March and May were used. Therefore, if you are using 2 different months, you will have to use the Table Finder page for each one — and in so doing, you will likely finish up with two different able numbers, one table for each option month. (3) There is not much extra work involved when you use two tables.

In the example worked out above where you **bought** the May call and **sold** the March call, just suppose that after using the Table Finder page, you found that May would use Table 57 and March would use Table 55. Then, when you calculated the initial cost, you would find May's cost in Table 57 and March's cost in Table 55. Then you would follow the formula - + to calculate the final cost.

While we are on the subject of using different option tables, one should always use the Table Finder page whenever one is taking a new option position. This applies to buying call and puts as well as spreads. For example, suppose you bought a call one day, then on the following day you had second thoughts and liquidated it, and immediately bought a put. Don't automatically use the same option table you used for the call — instead, go through the routine and use the quote page on your screen or newspaper to find the put's "at the money" price, and then use the Table Finder page to select the new table number. It is likely to be a different table number than was used on the call.

WHAT HAPPENS WHEN THE VOLATILITY RATE CHANGES?

Picture this scenario. The markets are quiet and normal. You think you will take a bull spread, by "buying a call at the money and selling 2 call at 50 cents out of the money". You fill in a spreadsheet first to see what likely lies ahead. You like what you see, and you take the spread. But 4 weeks later there is a drought scare , the markets here react, and volatility for the Soybean Options increase. Here's the problem: because of the increased rate of volatility, are the remaining calculations on your spreadsheet now obsolete? The answer is **no.** But they will be altered by a small amount. For example, you may find that the profits will be a bit larger under the new rate of volatility than you had previously calculated for the spreadsheet — maybe by a cent or two.

What does a volatility change do? If there is an increase in the rate of volatility after you have completed the spreadsheet and taken your spread, then sizes of both the estimated profits and losses will increase by a small amount. On the other hand, if the rate of volatility decreases, then the sizes of the estimated profits and losses will decrease a bit.

What can you do about it? The answer: **nothing.** You can do nothing in advance to prepare for a change in volatility because no one yet has yet exhibited the ability to forecast it in advance. It's like trying to forecast the weather a couple of months away.

If you waited to take an option position until you were sure of the economic conditions which affect volatility — then you would never take a position. It's like a farmer planting his crop in the spring. He doesn't know what the weather will be in the summer — but he plants the crop anyway.

And so when you construct the spreadsheet to show whether your contemplated option position will be profitable, you will have to use the data which is pertinent at that time — and you will have done all you can do. Anyway, if you have estimated the price trend correctly, then a volatility increase would benefit you by a small amount.

BUYING AT THE STRIKE PRICE

All the examples in this book have been done by buying a call "at the money" or selling a call at 50¢ "out of the money", and so on. In other words, the buys and sells which were made in the examples were made at 25 cent increments to correspond to the rows in the table and spreadsheet.

But it isn't always that easy in real trading. If you have traded options before, you will know that you must buy or sell an option at a **strike price** and only at a strike price. In other words, you cannot buy an option **between** strike prices.

Let's Review the Situation – This is information mainly for the new option trader.
  1. The option tables are based on the future's price.
  2. The future's price is the "at the money" price. For example, if May's future's price is $6.67, then May's "at the money" option price is $6.67.
  3. But the Soybean Option exchange in Chicago cannot let us buy "at the money" because there would have to be thousands of price levels to accomodate the multitude of "at the money" prices.
  4. So the simple and efficient system of buying an option only at certain prices, was instituted. We can buy an option only at certain designated prices, like . . . 675, 700, 725 . . . etc. in increments of 25 cents. Those designated prices are called **strike prices.**
  5. **The question** that is probably in your mind is this. "In this book we constructed many spreadsheets of straddles **"at the money"**, Time Spreads at 50¢ **"out of the money",** etc. Are those spreadsheets still valid, considering that we have to buy at a strike price?" **The answwer is Yes.** An option trade which was rated **very good** using the "at the money" methods will still be rated "very good" when you use a strike price. Also, an option trade which was rated **poor** is still rated "poor" when a strike price is used.
  6. Therefore, when you buy a call at a strike price, you will likely be buying the call either "in the money" or "out of the money" when you use the option table. Here are some examples.

(a) If the future's price is $6.65 and if you buy a call at a strike of 675, then you are buying a call at 10¢ "out of the money".

(b) If the future's price is $6.75 and if you buy a call at a strike price of 675, then you are buying the call "at the money".

(c) If the future's price is $6.85 and if you buy a call at a strike price of 675, then you are buying the call at 10¢ "in the money".

Can you make a spreadsheet for a strike price?

The answer is **Yes,** but it is more work than the spreadsheets done so far. Here is how it is done.

Example: Suppose the future's price is ¢6.60 and you wish to buy a call at a strike price of 675. But first, you want to make a spreadsheet for the call at strike 675, to see what the profit prospects are. Here's how to do it.

Step 1: Make a spreadsheet for the "at the money" price of $6.60, as was done many times in this book.

Step 2: Make a spreadsheet for 25¢ "out of the money" as was done many times in this book. That would be equivalent to a future's price of ¢6.85 ($6+ .25).

Step 3: Now you have 2 spreadsheets and the strike price of 675 is between them. So a third spreadsheet for 675 will be made by interpolating between the 660 spreadsheet and the 685 spreadsheet already done. Interpolate between the values in each section.

Step 4: That seems like alot of work, and it is. But it is not necessary to be so precise if all you want to know is if the intended option position is feasible. In the example above, if you used the table which you had made for the 25¢ "out of the money" future's price, it would tell you if your option position, taken at the strike price of 675, would be worthwhile to take. But, if you are after precision, then interpolate.

CONCLUSION

At the beginning of this book, it was stated that one of the principal objectives was to give you the means to test an option trade for its profitability **before you had committed your money.** The introduction of the option table and its spreadsheet has enabled you to do that. It is hoped that you have gained a new insight into your options by using this new concept for trading soybean options.

All of the most popular option positions have been tested and rated. Out of the testing have come a few which seem to be safe and profitable under a variety of changes in time and price. These are the ones upon which you should concentrate. Safety of your working capital is more important than taking an unnecessary risk just to gain a higher rate of profit.

You also learned that you could experiment with many of the popular option trades by testing to achieve more safety and profit, by constructing spreadsheets using a variety of times to expiration and positions in and out of the money. Continue to experiment and search for that elusive option trade which is both safe and profitable.

A note about the tables. It was mentioned earlier in the book that the tables were based on soybean option prices as they actually occurred in daily trading. But now that is not entirely true. Here's what happened. In late May 1988, as the tables were being completed, it became evident that a threatened drought condition was going to push soybean prices to new highs. If that was likely to be the case, then the purchasers of this book would need some additional tables to handle the expected high prices. So additional new tables were added. But the new tables could not be based on actual trading because those prices had not yet occurred. Therefore the additional tables were made by extrapolation – extending the prevailing value trends. It is hoped these additional tables will handle any price surge. When you use tables 94 and over, it may be necessary to interpolate between them.

It should be mentioned that if you have to use a table over Table 90, then you are trading in a very volatile and dangerously wild market where the option prices are seriously overpriced. A prudent trader would cease trading in such an expensive, erratic market.

PART 4
TABLES and GRAPHS

Table Finder

Option tables begin

Time to expiration graph

Day Finder

Interpolation graph

Blank spreadsheets for copying

TABLE FINDER

It is important that you select the appropriate table of option values – the table which best reflects the implied volatility of the option month you are using. To select the table, do this:

1. Find the "Weeks to Expiration" of the option month you are using.
2. Find the "at the money" option price.
3. Look vertically in the selected "weeks to expiration" column until you come as close as possible to the "at the money" price found in (2.) above.
4. Look to the right to find the Table number.

18	17	16	15	14	13	12	11	10	9	8	7	6	5	4	3	2	Table
5.6	5.5	5.4	5.2	5.1	5.0	4.8	4.6	4.4	4.2	4.0	3.7	3.5	3.2	2.7	2.2	1.6	1
6.3	6.2	6.0	5.9	5.7	5.6	5.4	5.2	5.0	4.8	4.5	4.2	3.9	3.6	3.0	2.4	1.8	2
7.0	6.9	6.8	6.6	6.4	6.2	6.0	5.8	5.6	5.3	5.0	4.7	4.4	4.0	3.4	2.7	2.0	3
7.7	7.6	7.4	7.2	7.0	6.8	6.6	6.4	6.1	5.8	5.5	5.2	4.8	4.3	3.7	3.0	2.2	4
8.5	8.3	8.1	7.9	7.7	7.5	7.2	6.9	6.6	6.3	6.0	5.6	5.2	4.7	4.0	3.2	2.4	5
9.2	8.9	8.7	8.5	8.3	8.1	7.8	7.5	7.2	6.9	6.5	6.1	5.6	5.1	4.4	3.5	2.6	6
9.9	9.6	9.4	9.2	9.0	8.7	8.4	8.1	7.9	7.4	7.0	6.6	6.1	5.5	4.7	3.5	2.8	7
10.6	10.3	10.1	9.8	9.6	9.3	9.0	8.7	8.3	7.9	7.5	7.0	6.5	5.8	5.0	4.1	3.0	8
11.3	11.0	10.8	10.5	10.2	9.9	9.6	9.2	8.8	8.4	8.0	7.5	7.0	6.3	5.4	4.3	3.2	9
12.0	11.7	11.4	11.1	10.8	10.5	10.2	9.8	9.4	9.0	8.5	8.0	7.4	6.7	5.7	4.6	3.4	10
12.7	12.4	12.1	11.8	11.5	11.2	10.8	10.4	10.0	9.5	9.0	8.4	7.8	7.1	6.0	4.9	3.6	11
13.4	13.1	12.8	12.5	12.1	11.8	11.4	11.0	10.5	10.0	9.5	8.9	8.3	7.5	6.4	5.1	3.8	12
14.1	13.8	13.5	13.1	12.8	12.4	12.0	11.6	11.1	10.6	10.0	9.4	8.6	7.7	6.7	5.4	4.0	13
14.8	14.5	14.2	13.8	13.4	13.0	12.6	12.1	11.6	11.1	10.5	9.8	9.0	8.1	7.0	5.7	4.2	14
15.5	15.2	14.8	14.4	14.0	13.6	13.2	12.7	12.2	11.6	11.0	10.3	9.4	8.5	7.3	6.0	4.4	15
16.2	15.8	15.5	15.1	14.7	14.3	13.8	13.3	12.7	12.1	11.5	10.8	9.9	8.9	7.6	6.2	4.6	16
16.9	16.5	16.2	15.7	15.3	14.9	14.4	13.9	13.3	12.7	12.0	11.2	10.3	9.3	8.0	6.5	4.8	17
17.6	17.2	16.8	16.4	16.0	15.5	15.0	14.4	13.8	13.2	12.5	11.7	10.8	9.7	8.3	6.8	5.0	18
18.3	17.9	17.5	17.0	16.6	16.1	15.6	15.0	14.4	13.7	13.0	12.2	11.2	10.0	8.6	7.0	5.2	19
18	17	16	15	14	13	12	11	10	9	8	7	6	5	4	3	2	

WEEKS TO EXPIRATION

18	17	16	15	14	13	12	11	10	9	8	7	6	5	4	3	2	Table
19.0	18.6	18.1	17.7	17.2	16.7	16.2	15.6	14.9	14.2	13.5	12.7	11.7	10.4	9.0	7.3	5.4	20
19.7	19.3	18.8	18.3	17.9	17.4	16.8	16.2	15.5	14.8	14.0	13.1	12.1	10.8	9.3	7.6	5.6	21
20.4	20.0	19.5	19.0	18.5	18.0	17.4	16.7	16.0	15.3	14.5	13.6	12.5	11.1	9.6	7.8	5.8	22
21.1	20.6	20.2	19.7	19.2	18.6	18.0	17.3	16.6	15.8	15.0	14.0	13.0	11.5	10.0	8.1	6.0	23
21.8	21.3	20.8	20.3	19.8	19.2	18.6	17.9	17.2	16.4	15.5	14.5	13.4	11.9	10.3	8.4	6.2	24
22.5	22.0	21.5	21.0	20.4	19.8	19.2	18.5	17.7	16.9	16.0	15.0	13.8	12.3	10.7	8.7	6.4	25
23.2	22.7	22.2	21.6	21.1	20.5	19.8	19.1	18.3	17.4	16.5	15.5	14.3	12.7	11.0	8.9	6.6	26
24.0	23.4	22.8	22.3	21.7	21.1	20.4	19.6	18.8	18.0	17.0	15.9	14.7	13.1	11.3	9.4	6.8	27
24.7	24.1	23.5	22.9	22.3	21.7	21.0	20.2	19.4	18.5	17.5	16.4	15.1	13.5	11.7	9.5	7.0	28
25.4	24.8	24.2	23.6	23.0	22.3	21.6	20.8	19.9	19.0	18.0	16.9	15.6	13.8	12.0	9.7	7.2	29
26.1	25.5	24.9	24.2	23.6	22.9	22.2	21.4	20.5	19.5	18.5	17.2	16.0	14.2	12.3	10.0	7.4	30
26.8	26.2	25.5	24.9	24.3	23.6	22.8	21.9	21.0	20.1	19.0	17.8	16.4	14.6	12.7	10.3	7.6	31
27.5	26.9	26.2	25.6	24.9	24.2	23.4	22.5	21.6	20.6	19.5	18.3	16.8	15.0	13.0	10.6	7.8	32
28.2	27.5	26.9	26.2	25.5	24.8	24.0	23.1	22.1	21.1	20.0	18.7	17.4	15.8	13.4	10.8	8.0	33
28.9	28.2	27.6	26.9	26.2	25.4	24.6	23.7	22.7	21.6	20.5	19.2	17.7	15.7	13.7	11.1	8.2	34
29.6	28.9	28.2	27.5	26.8	26.0	25.2	24.2	23.3	22.2	21.0	19.7	18.1	16.1	14.0	11.4	8.4	35
30.3	29.6	28.9	28.2	27.5	26.7	25.8	24.8	23.8	22.7	21.5	20.1	18.6	16.5	14.3	11.6	8.6	36
31.0	30.3	29.6	28.8	28.1	27.3	26.4	25.4	24.4	23.2	22.0	20.6	19.0	16.9	14.7	11.9	8.8	37
31.7	31.0	30.3	29.5	28.7	27.9	27.0	26.0	24.9	23.8	22.5	21.1	19.5	17.8	15.1	12.2	9.0	38
32.4	31.7	30.9	30.1	29.4	28.5	27.6	26.6	25.5	24.3	23.0	21.6	19.9	17.8	15.3	12.4	9.2	39
33.1	32.4	31.6	30.8	30.0	29.1	28.2	27.1	26.0	24.8	23.5	22.0	20.3	18.0	15.7	12.7	9.4	40
33.8	33.0	32.2	31.4	30.6	29.8	28.8	27.7	26.6	25.3	24.0	22.5	20.7	18.4	16.0	13.0	9.6	41
34.5	33.7	32.9	32.1	31.3	30.4	29.4	28.3	27.1	25.9	24.5	23.0	21.2	18.8	16.3	13.3	9.8	42
35.2	34.4	33.6	32.8	31.9	31.0	30.0	28.9	27.7	26.4	25.0	23.8	21.6	19.2	16.7	13.5	10.0	43
35.9	35.1	34.3	33.4	32.5	31.6	30.6	29.4	28.2	26.9	25.5	23.9	22.0	19.6	17.0	13.5	10.2	44
36.6	35.8	35.0	34.1	33.2	32.2	31.2	30.0	28.8	27.5	26.0	24.4	22.5	20.0	17.3	14.1	10.4	45
37.3	36.5	35.6	34.7	33.8	32.8	31.8	30.6	29.4	28.0	26.5	24.8	22.9	20.4	17.6	14.3	10.6	46
38.0	37.2	36.3	35.4	34.5	33.5	32.4	31.2	29.9	28.5	27.0	25.3	23.3	20.7	18.0	14.6	10.8	47
38.7	37.9	37.0	36.1	35.1	34.1	33.0	31.8	30.5	29.0	27.5	25.8	23.8	21.1	18.3	14.9	11.0	48
39.4	38.5	37.6	36.7	35.7	34.7	33.6	32.3	31.0	29.6	28.0	26.3	24.2	21.5	18.6	15.2	11.2	49
40.2	39.3	38.4	37.4	36.4	35.3	34.2	32.9	31.6	30.1	28.5	26.7	24.6	21.9	19.0	15.4	11.4	50
40.9	40.0	39.0	38.0	37.0	35.9	34.8	33.5	32.1	30.6	29.0	27.2	25.1	22.3	19.3	15.7	11.6	51
41.5	40.6	39.7	38.7	37.7	36.6	35.4	34.1	32.7	31.2	29.5	27.6	25.5	22.7	19.6	16.0	11.8	52
18	17	16	15	14	13	12	11	10	9	8	7	6	5	4	3	2	

WEEKS TO EXPIRATION

18	17	16	15	14	13	12	11	10	9	8	7	6	5	4	3	2	Table
42.3	41.3	40.3	39.3	38.3	37.2	36.0	34.6	33.2	31.7	30.0	28.1	25.9	23.0	20.0	16.2	12.0	53
42.9	42.0	41.0	40.0	38.9	37.8	36.6	35.2	33.8	32.2	30.5	28.6	26.4	23.4	20.3	16.2	12.2	54
43.6	42.6	41.6	40.6	39.6	38.4	37.2	35.8	34.3	32.7	31.0	29.1	26.8	23.8	20.6	16.8	12.4	55
44.3	43.4	42.4	41.3	40.2	39.0	37.8	36.4	34.9	33.3	31.4	29.5	27.2	24.2	21.0	17.0	12.5	56
45.1	44.1	43.1	41.9	40.9	39.7	38.4	36.9	35.4	33.8	31.0	30.0	27.6	24.6	21.3	17.3	12.7	57
45.8	44.8	43.7	42.6	41.5	40.3	39.0	37.5	36.0	34.3	42.4	30.5	28.1	25.0	21.6	17.6	12.9	58
46.5	45.4	44.3	43.2	42.1	40.9	39.6	38.1	36.6	34.8	32.9	30.9	28.5	25.3	22.0	17.9	13.1	59
47.2	46.1	45.0	43.9	42.8	41.5	40.2	38.7	37.1	35.4	33.4	31.4	28.9	25.7	22.3	18.1	13.3	60
47.9	46.8	45.7	44.6	43.4	42.2	40.8	39.3	37.7	35.9	33.9	31.9	29.4	26.1	22.6	18.4	13.5	61
48.5	47.5	46.4	45.2	44.0	42.8	41.4	39.8	38.2	36.4	34.4	32.3	29.8	26.5	23.0	18.7	13.7	62
49.3	42.8	47.1	45.9	44.7	43.4	42.0	40.4	38.8	37.0	34.9	32.8	30.2	26.9	23.3	18.9	13.9	63
50.0	48.9	47.7	46.5	45.3	44.0	42.6	41.0	39.3	37.5	35.4	33.3	30.7	27.3	23.6	19.2	14.1	64
50.7	49.6	48.4	47.2	46.0	44.6	43.2	41.6	39.9	38.0	35.9	33.7	31.1	27.6	24.0	19.5	14.3	65
51.4	50.3	49.1	47.9	46.6	45.2	43.8	42.1	40.4	38.5	36.4	34.2	31.5	28.0	24.3	19.8	14.5	66
52.1	50.9	49.7	48.5	47.2	45.9	44.4	42.7	41.0	39.1	36.9	34.7	32.0	28.4	24.6	20.0	14.7	67
52.8	51.6	50.4	49.2	47.9	46.5	45.0	43.3	41.5	39.6	37.4	35.1	32.4	28.8	25.0	20.3	14.9	68
53.5	52.3	51.1	49.8	48.5	47.1	45.6	43.9	42.1	40.1	37.6	35.6	32.8	29.2	25.3	20.6	15.1	69
54.2	53.0	51.7	50.4	49.1	47.7	46.2	44.4	42.6	40.7	38.4	36.1	33.3	29.6	25.6	20.8	15.3	70
54.9	53.7	52.4	51.1	49.8	48.3	46.8	45.0	43.2	41.2	38.9	36.6	33.7	30.0	26.0	21.1	15.5	71
55.6	54.4	53.1	51.8	50.4	49.0	47.4	45.6	43.8	41.7	39.4	37.0	34.1	30.3	26.3	21.4	15.7	72
56.3	55.1	53.8	52.4	51.1	49.6	48.0	46.2	44.3	42.2	39.9	37.5	34.6	30.7	26.6	21.6	15.9	73
57.0	55.7	54.4	53.1	51.7	50.2	48.6	46.8	44.9	42.8	40.4	38.0	35.0	31.1	26.9	21.9	16.1	74
57.7	56.5	55.1	53.7	52.3	50.8	49.2	47.3	45.4	43.3	41.0	38.4	35.4	31.5	27.3	22.2	16.3	75
58.4	57.1	55.8	54.4	53.0	51.4	49.8	47.9	46.0	43.8	41.5	38.9	35.9	31.9	27.6	22.5	16.5	76
59.1	57.8	56.4	55.0	53.6	52.1	50.4	48.5	46.5	44.4	42.0	39.4	36.3	32.3	28.0	22.7	16.7	77
59.8	58.5	57.1	55.7	54.3	52.7	51.0	49.1	47.1	44.9	42.4	39.8	36.7	32.6	28.3	23.0	16.9	78
60.5	59.2	57.8	56.4	54.9	53.3	51.6	49.6	47.6	45.4	43.0	40.3	37.1	33.0	28.6	23.3	17.1	79
61.3	59.9	58.5	57.1	55.6	54.0	52.2	50.2	48.2	45.9	43.5	40.8	37.6	33.4	29.0	23.5	17.3	80
61.9	60.6	59.2	57.7	56.2	54.6	52.8	50.8	48.7	46.4	44.0	41.2	38.0	33.8	29.3	23.8	17.5	81
62.8	61.3	59.9	58.4	56.9	55.2	53.4	51.4	49.3	47.0	44.5	41.7	38.4	34.2	29.6	24.1	17.7	82
63.4	62.0	60.5	59.0	57.5	55.8	54.0	51.9	49.8	47.5	45.0	42.2	38.9	34.6	30.0	24.4	17.9	83
64.1	62.7	61.2	59.7	58.2	56.5	54.6	52.5	50.4	48.0	45.5	42.6	39.3	34.9	30.3	24.6	18.1	84
18	17	16	15	14	13	12	11	10	9	8	7	6	5	4	3	2	

WEEKS TO EXPIRATION

If you are trading in an area which indicates that you should use tables 85 to 92, then you are trading options which are overpriced and speculative . The market is erratic here , and often the future's price will make limit moves, either up or down.   A prudent trader would withdraw from the market here, and wait for the situation to cool down.

If you are using tables 93 and up, then you are trading in a very seriously overpriced market and speculative to the extreme.

Up until now, you have chosen the table number which is closest to the "at the money" price. But, here, you may have to interpolate between tables to get the values you need if there is a big difference between the "at the money" price and the nearest option value in the selected column.

18	17	16	15	14	13	12	11	10	9	8	7	6	5	4	3	2	Table
66.2	64.7	63.2	61.7	60.1	58.3	56.4	54.3	52.1	49.6	47.0	44.0	40.6	36.1	31.3	25.4	18.7	85
68.0	66.5	65.0	63.5	61.8	60.0	58.0	55.8	53.5	51.0	48.3	45.3	41.8	37.1	32.2	26.2	19.3	86
70.4	68.8	67.2	65.6	63.9	62.0	60.0	57.7	55.4	52.8	50.0	46.9	43.2	38.4	33.3	27.1	19.9	87
72.7	71.1	69.5	67.8	66.0	64.1	62.0	59.6	57.2	54.6	51.6	48.4	44.6	39.7	34.4	28.0	20.6	88
75.1	73.4	71.7	70.0	68.2	66.2	64.0	61.6	59.1	56.3	53.3	50.0	46.1	41.0	35.5	28.9	21.2	89
77.4	75.7	74.0	72.2	70.3	68.2	66.0	63.5	60.9	58.1	55.0	51.5	47.5	42.2	36.6	29.8	21.9	90
79.7	77.9	76.1	74.3	72.4	70.3	68.0	65.4	62.8	59.8	56.6	53.1	49.0	43.5	37.7	30.7	22.6	91
82.1	80.2	78.4	76.6	74.6	72.4	70.0	67.3	64.6	61.6	58.3	54.7	50.4	44.8	38.9	31.6	23.2	92
88.0	86.0	84.0	82.0	79.9	77.6	75.0	72.2	69.2	66.0	62.5	58.6	54.0	48.0	41.6	33.8	24.9	93
93.8	91.7	89.6	87.4	85.2	82.7	80.0	77.0	73.8	70.4	66.6	62.5	57.6	51.2	44.4	36.1	26.6	94
105.6	103.1	100.8	98.4	95.8	93.1	90.0	86.6	83.1	79.2	75.0	70.3	64.8	57.6	50.0	40.6	29.9	95
117.3	114.6	112.0	109.3	106.5	103.4	100.0	96.2	92.3	88.0	83.3	78.1	72.0	64.0	55.5	45.1	33.2	96
18	17	16	15	14	13	12	11	10	9	8	7	6	5	4	3	2	

WEEKS TO EXPIRATION

OPTION VALUES on SOYBEAN FUTURES – Table No: 2

	30	29	28	27	26	25	24	23	22	21	20	19	18	17	16	15	14	13	12	11	10	9	8	7	6	5	4	3	2	1	0
IN THE MONEY																															
$1.25	125.0	125.0	125.0	125.0	125.0	125.0	125.0	125.0	125.0	125.0	125.0	125.0	125.0	125.0	125.0	125.0	125.0	125.0	125.0	125.0	125.0	125.0	125.0	125.0	125.0	125.0	125.0	125.0	125.0	125.0	125.0
$1.00	100.0	100.0	100.0	100.0	100.0	100.0	100.0	100.0	100.0	100.0	100.0	100.0	100.0	100.0	100.0	100.0	100.0	100.0	100.0	100.0	100.0	100.0	100.0	100.0	100.0	100.0	100.0	100.0	100.0	100.0	100.0
75¢	75.0	75.0	75.0	75.0	75.0	75.0	75.0	75.0	75.0	75.0	75.0	75.0	75.0	75.0	75.0	75.0	75.0	75.0	75.0	75.0	75.0	75.0	75.0	75.0	75.0	75.0	75.0	75.0	75.0	75.0	75.0
50¢	50.0	50.0	50.0	50.0	50.0	50.0	50.0	50.0	50.0	50.0	50.0	50.0	50.0	50.0	50.0	50.0	50.0	50.0	50.0	50.0	50.0	50.0	50.0	50.0	50.0	50.0	50.0	50.0	50.0	50.0	50.0
25¢	25.8	25.8	25.7	25.7	25.7	25.6	25.6	25.6	25.6	25.6	25.5	25.5	25.5	25.5	25.4	25.4	25.4	25.4	25.4	25.3	25.3	25.3	25.3	25.3	25.2	25.2	25.1	25.1	25.1	25.0	25.0
AT THE MONEY																															
25¢	7.6	7.5	7.4	7.3	7.2	7.1	7.0	6.9	6.8	6.7	6.6	6.5	6.3	6.2	6.0	5.9	5.7	5.6	5.4	5.2	5.0	4.8	4.5	4.2	3.9	3.6	3.0	2.4	1.8	1.1	0.0
OUT OF THE MONEY																															
25¢	1.4	1.4	1.4	1.3	1.3	1.3	1.2	1.2	1.2	1.1	1.1	1.1	1.0	1.0	1.0	0.9	0.9	0.9	0.8	0.8	0.7	0.7	0.6	0.6	0.5	0.4	0.3	0.2	0.1	0.1	0.0
50¢	0.3	0.2	0.2	0.2	0.2	0.2	0.2	0.2	0.2	0.1	0.1	0.1	0.1	0.1	0.1	0	0	0	0	0	0	0	0	0	0	0	0	0	0	0	0
75¢	0	0	0	0	0	0	0	0	0	0	0	0	0	0	0	0	0	0	0	0	0	0	0	0	0	0	0	0	0	0	0
$1.00	0	0	0	0	0	0	0	0	0	0	0	0	0	0	0	0	0	0	0	0	0	0	0	0	0	0	0	0	0	0	0
$1.25	0	0	0	0	0	0	0	0	0	0	0	0	0	0	0	0	0	0	0	0	0	0	0	0	0	0	0	0	0	0	0

WEEKS TO EXPIRATION

OPTION VALUES ARE IN CENTS – to nearest tenth.

WM GRANDMILL (1985) LTD.

OPTION VALUES on SOYBEAN FUTURES – Table No: 1

	30	29	28	27	26	25	24	23	22	21	20	19	18	17	16	15	14	13	12	11	10	9	8	7	6	5	4	3	2	1	0
IN THE MONEY																															
$1.25	125.0	125.0	125.0	125.0	125.0	125.0	125.0	125.0	125.0	125.0	125.0	125.0	125.0	125.0	125.0	125.0	125.0	125.0	125.0	125.0	125.0	125.0	125.0	125.0	125.0	125.0	125.0	125.0	125.0	125.0	125.0
$1.00	100.0	100.0	100.0	100.0	100.0	100.0	100.0	100.0	100.0	100.0	100.0	100.0	100.0	100.0	100.0	100.0	100.0	100.0	100.0	100.0	100.0	100.0	100.0	100.0	100.0	100.0	100.0	100.0	100.0	100.0	100.0
75¢	75.0	75.0	75.0	75.0	75.0	75.0	75.0	75.0	75.0	75.0	75.0	75.0	75.0	75.0	75.0	75.0	75.0	75.0	75.0	75.0	75.0	75.0	75.0	75.0	75.0	75.0	75.0	75.0	75.0	75.0	75.0
50¢	50.0	50.0	50.0	50.0	50.0	50.0	50.0	50.0	50.0	50.0	50.0	50.0	50.0	50.0	50.0	50.0	50.0	50.0	50.0	50.0	50.0	50.0	50.0	50.0	50.0	50.0	50.0	50.0	50.0	50.0	50.0
25¢	25.8	25.8	25.6	25.6	25.5	25.5	25.5	25.5	25.5	25.4	25.4	25.4	25.4	25.4	25.4	25.3	25.3	25.3	25.3	25.3	25.2	25.2	25.2	25.2	25.2	25.2	25.1	25.1	25.0	25.0	25.0
AT THE MONEY																															
25¢	6.8	6.7	6.6	6.5	6.4	6.3	6.2	6.1	6.0	5.9	5.8	5.7	5.6	5.5	5.4	5.2	5.1	5.0	4.8	4.6	4.4	4.2	4.0	3.7	3.5	3.2	2.7	2.2	1.6	1.0	0.0
OUT OF THE MONEY																															
25¢	1.2	1.1	1.1	1.1	1.0	1.0	1.0	1.0	0.9	0.9	0.9	0.9	0.8	0.8	0.8	0.8	0.7	0.7	0.7	0.6	0.6	0.6	0.5	0.5	0.4	0.4	0.3	0.2	0.1	0.1	0.0
50¢	0.2	0.1	0.1	0.1	0.1	0.1	0.1	0.1	0.1	0.1	0.1	0.1	0	0	0	0	0	0	0	0	0	0	0	0	0	0	0	0	0	0	0
75¢	0	0	0	0	0	0	0	0	0	0	0	0	0	0	0	0	0	0	0	0	0	0	0	0	0	0	0	0	0	0	0
$1.00	0	0	0	0	0	0	0	0	0	0	0	0	0	0	0	0	0	0	0	0	0	0	0	0	0	0	0	0	0	0	0
$1.25	0	0	0	0	0	0	0	0	0	0	0	0	0	0	0	0	0	0	0	0	0	0	0	0	0	0	0	0	0	0	0

WEEKS TO EXPIRATION

OPTION VALUES ARE IN CENTS – to nearest tenth.

WM GRANDMILL (1985) LTD.

OPTION VALUES on SOYBEAN FUTURES – Table No: 4

WM GRANDMILL (1985) LTD.

	WEEKS TO EXPIRATION	30	29	28	27	26	25	24	23	22	21	20	19	18	17	16	15	14	13	12	11	10	9	8	7	6	5	4	3	2	1	0
IN THE MONEY	$1.25	125.0	125.0	125.0	125.0	125.0	125.0	125.0	125.0	125.0	125.0	125.0	125.0	125.0	125.0	125.0	125.0	125.0	125.0	125.0	125.0	125.0	125.0	125.0	125.0	125.0	125.0	125.0	125.0	125.0	125.0	125.0
	$1.00	100.0	100.0	100.0	100.0	100.0	100.0	100.0	100.0	100.0	100.0	100.0	100.0	100.0	100.0	100.0	100.0	100.0	100.0	100.0	100.0	100.0	100.0	100.0	100.0	100.0	100.0	100.0	100.0	100.0	100.0	100.0
	75¢	75.0	75.0	75.0	75.0	75.0	75.0	75.0	75.0	75.0	75.0	75.0	75.0	75.0	75.0	75.0	75.0	75.0	75.0	75.0	75.0	75.0	75.0	75.0	75.0	75.0	75.0	75.0	75.0	75.0	75.0	75.0
	50¢	50.0	50.0	50.0	50.0	50.0	50.0	50.0	50.0	50.0	50.0	50.0	50.0	50.0	50.0	50.0	50.0	50.0	50.0	50.0	50.0	50.0	50.0	50.0	50.0	50.0	50.0	50.0	50.0	50.0	50.0	50.0
	25¢	26.4	26.4	26.3	26.3	26.2	26.1	26.1	26.1	26.0	26.0	26.0	25.9	25.9	25.8	25.8	25.7	25.7	25.6	25.6	25.5	25.5	25.4	25.4	25.3	25.3	25.2	25.2	25.1	25.1	25.0	25.0
AT THE MONEY		9.3	9.2	9.1	9.0	8.8	8.7	8.6	8.5	8.4	8.2	8.1	7.9	7.7	7.6	7.4	7.2	7.0	6.8	6.6	6.4	6.1	5.8	5.5	5.2	4.8	4.3	3.7	3.0	2.2	1.3	0.0
OUT OF THE MONEY	25¢	2.0	2.0	1.9	1.9	1.8	1.8	1.8	1.7	1.7	1.6	1.6	1.5	1.5	1.4	1.4	1.3	1.2	1.2	1.1	1.0	1.0	0.9	0.8	0.8	0.7	0.6	0.5	0.3	0.2	0	0
	50¢	0.5	0.5	0.5	0.4	0.4	0.4	0.4	0.4	0.4	0.3	0.3	0.3	0.3	0.3	0.2	0.2	0.2	0.2	0.1	0.1	0.1	0	0	0	0	0	0	0	0	0	0
	75¢	0	0	0	0	0	0	0	0	0	0	0	0	0	0	0	0	0	0	0	0	0	0	0	0	0	0	0	0	0	0	0
	$1.00	0	0	0	0	0	0	0	0	0	0	0	0	0	0	0	0	0	0	0	0	0	0	0	0	0	0	0	0	0	0	0
	$1.25	0	0	0	0	0	0	0	0	0	0	0	0	0	0	0	0	0	0	0	0	0	0	0	0	0	0	0	0	0	0	0

OPTION VALUES on SOYBEAN FUTURES – Table No: 3

WM GRANDMILL (1985) LTD.

	WEEKS TO EXPIRATION	30	29	28	27	26	25	24	23	22	21	20	19	18	17	16	15	14	13	12	11	10	9	8	7	6	5	4	3	2	1	0
IN THE MONEY	$1.25	125.0	125.0	125.0	125.0	125.0	125.0	125.0	125.0	125.0	125.0	125.0	125.0	125.0	125.0	125.0	125.0	125.0	125.0	125.0	125.0	125.0	125.0	125.0	125.0	125.0	125.0	125.0	125.0	125.0	125.0	125.0
	$1.00	100.0	100.0	100.0	100.0	100.0	100.0	100.0	100.0	100.0	100.0	100.0	100.0	100.0	100.0	100.0	100.0	100.0	100.0	100.0	100.0	100.0	100.0	100.0	100.0	100.0	100.0	100.0	100.0	100.0	100.0	100.0
	75¢	75.0	75.0	75.0	75.0	75.0	75.0	75.0	75.0	75.0	75.0	75.0	75.0	75.0	75.0	75.0	75.0	75.0	75.0	75.0	75.0	75.0	75.0	75.0	75.0	75.0	75.0	75.0	75.0	75.0	75.0	75.0
	50¢	50.0	50.0	50.0	50.0	50.0	50.0	50.0	50.0	50.0	50.0	50.0	50.0	50.0	50.0	50.0	50.0	50.0	50.0	50.0	50.0	50.0	50.0	50.0	50.0	50.0	50.0	50.0	50.0	50.0	50.0	50.0
	25¢	26.1	26.0	26.0	26.0	25.9	25.9	25.9	25.8	25.8	25.8	25.7	25.7	25.7	25.6	25.6	25.6	25.5	25.5	25.4	25.4	25.4	25.3	25.3	25.3	25.2	25.2	25.2	25.1	25.0	25.0	25.0
AT THE MONEY		8.4	8.3	8.2	8.1	8.0	7.9	7.8	7.7	7.6	7.5	7.3	7.2	7.0	6.9	6.8	6.6	6.4	6.2	6.0	5.8	5.6	5.3	5.0	4.7	4.4	4.0	3.4	2.7	2.0	1.2	0.0
OUT OF THE MONEY	25¢	1.7	1.7	1.6	1.6	1.6	1.5	1.5	1.5	1.4	1.4	1.3	1.3	1.2	1.2	1.1	1.1	1.0	1.0	0.9	0.9	0.8	0.8	0.7	0.7	0.6	0.5	0.4	0.3	0.2	0.1	0
	50¢	0.4	0.4	0.3	0.3	0.3	0.3	0.3	0.3	0.3	0.2	0.2	0.2	0.2	0.2	0.2	0.1	0.1	0.1	0.1	0	0	0	0	0	0	0	0	0	0	0	0
	75¢	0	0	0	0	0	0	0	0	0	0	0	0	0	0	0	0	0	0	0	0	0	0	0	0	0	0	0	0	0	0	0
	$1.00	0	0	0	0	0	0	0	0	0	0	0	0	0	0	0	0	0	0	0	0	0	0	0	0	0	0	0	0	0	0	0
	$1.25	0	0	0	0	0	0	0	0	0	0	0	0	0	0	0	0	0	0	0	0	0	0	0	0	0	0	0	0	0	0	0

OPTION VALUES on SOYBEAN FUTURES – Table No: 6

	WEEKS TO EXPIRATION	30	29	28	27	26	25	24	23	22	21	20	19	18	17	16	15	14	13	12	11	10	9	8	7	6	5	4	3	2	1	0
IN THE MONEY	$1.25	125.0	125.0	125.0	125.0	125.0	125.0	125.0	125.0	125.0	125.0	125.0	125.0	125.0	125.0	125.0	125.0	125.0	125.0	125.0	125.0	125.0	125.0	125.0	125.0	125.0	125.0	125.0	125.0	125.0	125.0	125.0
	$1.00	100.0	100.0	100.0	100.0	100.0	100.0	100.0	100.0	100.0	100.0	100.0	100.0	100.0	100.0	100.0	100.0	100.0	100.0	100.0	100.0	100.0	100.0	100.0	100.0	100.0	100.0	100.0	100.0	100.0	100.0	100.0
	75¢	75.0	75.0	75.0	75.0	75.0	75.0	75.0	75.0	75.0	75.0	75.0	75.0	75.0	75.0	75.0	75.0	75.0	75.0	75.0	75.0	75.0	75.0	75.0	75.0	75.0	75.0	75.0	75.0	75.0	75.0	75.0
	50¢	50.2	50.2	50.2	50.2	50.2	50.2	50.1	50.1	50.1	50.1	50.1	50.1	50.1	50.0	50.0	50.0	50.0	50.0	50.0	50.0	50.0	50.0	50.0	50.0	50.0	50.0	50.0	50.0	50.0	50.0	50.0
	25¢	27.1	27.1	27.0	27.0	27.0	26.9	26.8	26.8	26.7	26.6	26.5	26.4	26.4	26.3	26.2	26.1	26.0	26.0	25.9	25.8	25.7	25.6	25.5	25.5	25.4	25.3	25.3	25.2	25.1	25.0	25.0
AT THE MONEY	25¢	11.0	10.8	10.7	10.6	10.5	10.3	10.2	10.0	9.9	9.7	9.6	9.4	9.2	8.9	8.7	8.5	8.3	8.1	7.8	7.5	7.2	6.9	6.5	6.1	5.6	5.1	4.4	3.5	2.6	1.6	0.0
OUT OF THE MONEY	25¢	3.3	3.1	3.0	2.9	2.8	2.7	2.6	2.5	2.4	2.3	2.2	2.1	2.0	1.9	1.8	1.7	1.7	1.6	1.5	1.4	1.3	1.2	1.1	1.0	0.9	0.8	0.6	0.4	0.2	0.1	0
	50¢	1.0	0.9	0.9	0.8	0.8	0.7	0.7	0.6	0.6	0.6	0.5	0.5	0.5	0.4	0.4	0.4	0.3	0.3	0.3	0.2	0.2	0.2	0.1	0.1	0	0	0	0	0	0	0
	75¢	0.2	0.2	0.2	0.1	0.1	0.1	0.1	0.1	0.1	0	0	0	0	0	0	0	0	0	0	0	0	0	0	0	0	0	0	0	0	0	0
	$1.00	0	0	0	0	0	0	0	0	0	0	0	0	0	0	0	0	0	0	0	0	0	0	0	0	0	0	0	0	0	0	0
	$1.25	0	0	0	0	0	0	0	0	0	0	0	0	0	0	0	0	0	0	0	0	0	0	0	0	0	0	0	0	0	0	0

OPTION VALUES ARE IN CENTS - to nearest tenth.

WM GRANDMILL (1985) LTD.

OPTION VALUES on SOYBEAN FUTURES – Table No: 5

	WEEKS TO EXPIRATION	30	29	28	27	26	25	24	23	22	21	20	19	18	17	16	15	14	13	12	11	10	9	8	7	6	5	4	3	2	1	0
IN THE MONEY	$1.25	125.0	125.0	125.0	125.0	125.0	125.0	125.0	125.0	125.0	125.0	125.0	125.0	125.0	125.0	125.0	125.0	125.0	125.0	125.0	125.0	125.0	125.0	125.0	125.0	125.0	125.0	125.0	125.0	125.0	125.0	125.0
	$1.00	100.0	100.0	100.0	100.0	100.0	100.0	100.0	100.0	100.0	100.0	100.0	100.0	100.0	100.0	100.0	100.0	100.0	100.0	100.0	100.0	100.0	100.0	100.0	100.0	100.0	100.0	100.0	100.0	100.0	100.0	100.0
	75¢	75.0	75.0	75.0	75.0	75.0	75.0	75.0	75.0	75.0	75.0	75.0	75.0	75.0	75.0	75.0	75.0	75.0	75.0	75.0	75.0	75.0	75.0	75.0	75.0	75.0	75.0	75.0	75.0	75.0	75.0	75.0
	50¢	50.1	50.1	50.1	50.1	50.1	50.1	50.1	50.1	50.1	50.1	50.0	50.0	50.0	50.0	50.0	50.0	50.0	50.0	50.0	50.0	50.0	50.0	50.0	50.0	50.0	50.0	50.0	50.0	50.0	50.0	50.0
	25¢	26.8	26.7	26.6	26.6	26.5	26.5	26.4	26.4	26.3	26.3	26.2	26.1	26.1	26.0	26.0	25.9	25.8	25.8	25.7	25.6	25.6	25.5	25.4	25.4	25.3	25.3	25.2	25.1	25.1	25.0	25.0
AT THE MONEY	25¢	10.1	10.0	9.9	9.8	9.6	9.5	9.4	9.3	9.1	9.0	8.8	8.6	8.5	8.3	8.1	7.9	7.7	7.5	7.2	6.9	6.6	6.3	6.0	5.6	5.2	4.7	4.0	3.2	2.4	1.4	0.0
OUT OF THE MONEY	25¢	2.6	2.5	2.4	2.3	2.2	2.1	2.1	2.0	1.9	1.9	1.8	1.8	1.7	1.7	1.6	1.5	1.5	1.4	1.3	1.2	1.1	1.0	0.9	0.9	0.8	0.7	0.5	0.4	0.2	0.1	0
	50¢	0.7	0.6	0.6	0.6	0.6	0.5	0.5	0.5	0.5	0.5	0.4	0.4	0.4	0.3	0.3	0.3	0.3	0.2	0.2	0.2	0.1	0.1	0.1	0	0	0	0	0	0	0	0
	75¢	0.1	0.1	0.1	0	0	0	0	0	0	0	0	0	0	0	0	0	0	0	0	0	0	0	0	0	0	0	0	0	0	0	0
	$1.00	0	0	0	0	0	0	0	0	0	0	0	0	0	0	0	0	0	0	0	0	0	0	0	0	0	0	0	0	0	0	0
	$1.25	0	0	0	0	0	0	0	0	0	0	0	0	0	0	0	0	0	0	0	0	0	0	0	0	0	0	0	0	0	0	0

OPTION VALUES ARE IN CENTS - to nearest tenth.

WM GRANDMILL (1985) LTD.

OPTION VALUES on SOYBEAN FUTURES – Table No: 8

OPTION VALUES ARE IN CENTS – to nearest tenth.

		WEEKS TO EXPIRATION																													
		30	29	28	27	26	25	24	23	22	21	20	19	18	17	16	15	14	13	12	11	10	9	8	7	6	5	4	3	2	1	0
IN THE MONEY	$1.25	125.0	125.0	125.0	125.0	125.0	125.0	125.0	125.0	125.0	125.0	125.0	125.0	125.0	125.0	125.0	125.0	125.0	125.0	125.0	125.0	125.0	125.0	125.0	125.0	125.0	125.0	125.0	125.0	125.0	125.0	125.0
	$1.00	100.0	100.0	100.0	100.0	100.0	100.0	100.0	100.0	100.0	100.0	100.0	100.0	100.0	100.0	100.0	100.0	100.0	100.0	100.0	100.0	100.0	100.0	100.0	100.0	100.0	100.0	100.0	100.0	100.0	100.0	100.0
	75¢	75.0	75.0	75.0	75.0	75.0	75.0	75.0	75.0	75.0	75.0	75.0	75.0	75.0	75.0	75.0	75.0	75.0	75.0	75.0	75.0	75.0	75.0	75.0	75.0	75.0	75.0	75.0	75.0	75.0	75.0	75.0
	50¢	50.4	50.4	50.4	50.4	50.4	50.3	50.3	50.3	50.3	50.3	50.2	50.2	50.2	50.1	50.1	50.1	50.1	50.1	50.1	50.0	50.0	50.0	50.0	50.0	50.0	50.0	50.0	50.0	50.0	50.0	50.0
	25¢	28.2	28.1	28.0	27.9	27.8	27.7	27.6	27.5	27.4	27.3	27.2	27.1	27.0	26.8	26.7	26.6	26.5	26.4	26.3	26.2	26.0	25.9	25.8	25.6	25.5	25.4	25.3	25.2	25.1	25.0	25.0
AT THE MONEY		12.7	12.5	12.4	12.2	12.1	11.9	11.7	11.6	11.4	11.2	11.0	10.8	10.6	10.3	10.1	9.8	9.6	9.3	9.0	8.7	8.3	7.9	7.5	7.0	6.5	5.8	5.0	4.1	3.0	1.8	0.0
OUT OF THE MONEY	25¢	5.0	4.8	4.7	4.5	4.4	4.2	4.0	3.9	3.7	3.5	3.3	3.1	2.9	2.7	2.5	2.3	2.2	2.0	1.9	1.8	1.7	1.5	1.4	1.2	1.1	0.9	0.7	0.5	0.3	0.1	0.0
	50¢	2.2	2.0	1.9	1.8	1.7	1.6	1.4	1.3	1.2	1.1	1.0	0.9	0.8	0.7	0.6	0.6	0.6	0.5	0.5	0.4	0.3	0.3	0.2	0.2	0.1	0	0	0	0	0	0
	75¢	0.6	0.6	0.5	0.5	0.4	0.4	0.4	0.3	0.3	0.3	0.2	0.2	0.1	0.1	0.1	0	0	0	0	0	0	0	0	0	0	0	0	0	0	0	0
	$1.00	0.3	0.3	0.3	0.2	0.2	0.2	0.1	0.1	0.1	0.1	0.1	0	0	0	0	0	0	0	0	0	0	0	0	0	0	0	0	0	0	0	0
	$1.25	0	0	0	0	0	0	0	0	0	0	0	0	0	0	0	0	0	0	0	0	0	0	0	0	0	0	0	0	0	0	0

WM GRANDMILL (1985) LTD.

OPTION VALUES on SOYBEAN FUTURES – Table No: 7

OPTION VALUES ARE IN CENTS – to nearest tenth.

		WEEKS TO EXPIRATION																													
		30	29	28	27	26	25	24	23	22	21	20	19	18	17	16	15	14	13	12	11	10	9	8	7	6	5	4	3	2	1	0
IN THE MONEY	$1.25	125.0	125.0	125.0	125.0	125.0	125.0	125.0	125.0	125.0	125.0	125.0	125.0	125.0	125.0	125.0	125.0	125.0	125.0	125.0	125.0	125.0	125.0	125.0	125.0	125.0	125.0	125.0	125.0	125.0	125.0	125.0
	$1.00	100.0	100.0	100.0	100.0	100.0	100.0	100.0	100.0	100.0	100.0	100.0	100.0	100.0	100.0	100.0	100.0	100.0	100.0	100.0	100.0	100.0	100.0	100.0	100.0	100.0	100.0	100.0	100.0	100.0	100.0	100.0
	75¢	75.0	75.0	75.0	75.0	75.0	75.0	75.0	75.0	75.0	75.0	75.0	75.0	75.0	75.0	75.0	75.0	75.0	75.0	75.0	75.0	75.0	75.0	75.0	75.0	75.0	75.0	75.0	75.0	75.0	75.0	75.0
	50¢	50.3	50.3	50.3	50.3	50.3	50.2	50.2	50.2	50.2	50.2	50.2	50.1	50.1	50.1	50.1	50.1	50.1	50.0	50.0	50.0	50.0	50.0	50.0	50.0	50.0	50.0	50.0	50.0	50.0	50.0	50.0
	25¢	27.7	27.6	27.5	27.4	27.3	27.2	27.2	27.1	27.0	26.9	26.8	26.7	26.6	26.5	26.4	26.3	26.2	26.1	26.0	25.9	25.8	25.7	25.6	25.5	25.4	25.3	25.2	25.1	25.0	25.0	25.0
AT THE MONEY		11.8	11.7	11.5	11.4	11.3	11.1	11.0	10.8	10.6	10.5	10.3	10.1	9.9	9.6	9.4	9.2	9.0	8.7	8.4	8.1	7.9	7.4	7.0	6.6	6.1	5.5	4.7	3.5	2.8	1.7	0.0
OUT OF THE MONEY	25¢	4.2	4.0	3.8	3.7	3.6	3.4	3.3	3.1	2.9	2.8	2.7	2.5	2.4	2.2	2.1	2.0	1.9	1.8	1.7	1.6	1.5	1.4	1.2	1.1	1.0	0.8	0.7	0.5	0.3	0.1	0.0
	50¢	1.6	1.4	1.3	1.2	1.2	1.1	1.0	0.9	0.8	0.8	0.7	0.7	0.6	0.6	0.5	0.5	0.4	0.4	0.4	0.3	0.3	0.2	0.2	0.2	0.1	0	0	0	0	0	0
	75¢	0.4	0.3	0.3	0.3	0.2	0.2	0.2	0.2	0.1	0.1	0.1	0.1	0	0	0	0	0	0	0	0	0	0	0	0	0	0	0	0	0	0	0
	$1.00	0.2	0.1	0.1	0.1	0.1	0.1	0	0	0	0	0	0	0	0	0	0	0	0	0	0	0	0	0	0	0	0	0	0	0	0	0
	$1.25	0	0	0	0	0	0	0	0	0	0	0	0	0	0	0	0	0	0	0	0	0	0	0	0	0	0	0	0	0	0	0

WM GRANDMILL (1985) LTD.

OPTION VALUES on SOYBEAN FUTURES – Table No: 10

OPTION VALUES ARE IN CENTS – to nearest tenth.

																WEEKS TO EXPIRATION															
	30	29	28	27	26	25	24	23	22	21	20	19	18	17	16	15	14	13	12	11	10	9	8	7	6	5	4	3	2	1	0
IN THE MONEY																															
$1.25	125.0	125.0	125.0	125.0	125.0	125.0	125.0	125.0	125.0	125.0	125.0	125.0	125.0	125.0	125.0	125.0	125.0	125.0	125.0	125.0	125.0	125.0	125.0	125.0	125.0	125.0	125.0	125.0	125.0	125.0	125.0
$1.00	100.0	100.0	100.0	100.0	100.0	100.0	100.0	100.0	100.0	100.0	100.0	100.0	100.0	100.0	100.0	100.0	100.0	100.0	100.0	100.0	100.0	100.0	100.0	100.0	100.0	100.0	100.0	100.0	100.0	100.0	100.0
75¢	75.0	75.0	75.0	75.0	75.0	75.0	75.0	75.0	75.0	75.0	75.0	75.0	75.0	75.0	75.0	75.0	75.0	75.0	75.0	75.0	75.0	75.0	75.0	75.0	75.0	75.0	75.0	75.0	75.0	75.0	75.0
50¢	50.7	50.7	50.6	50.6	50.6	50.6	50.5	50.5	50.5	50.4	50.4	50.4	50.3	50.3	50.3	50.2	50.2	50.2	50.1	50.1	50.1	50.1	50.0	50.0	50.0	50.0	50.0	50.0	50.0	50.0	50.0
25¢	29.4	29.3	29.2	29.0	28.9	28.7	28.6	28.5	28.4	28.2	28.1	27.9	27.8	27.6	27.4	27.2	27.1	26.9	26.8	26.6	26.4	26.3	26.1	25.9	25.7	25.6	25.4	25.3	25.2	25.1	25.0
AT THE MONEY	14.4	14.2	14.0	13.8	13.7	13.5	13.3	13.1	12.9	12.7	12.5	12.2	12.0	11.7	11.4	11.1	10.8	10.5	10.2	9.8	9.4	9.0	8.5	8.0	7.4	6.7	5.7	4.6	3.4	2.1	0.0
OUT OF THE MONEY																															
25¢	6.5	6.3	6.2	6.0	5.9	5.7	5.5	5.3	5.2	5.0	4.8	4.5	4.3	4.0	3.7	3.4	3.1	2.8	2.6	2.3	2.1	1.9	1.7	1.6	1.4	1.1	0.9	0.6	0.4	0.1	0
50¢	3.2	3.1	3.0	2.9	2.8	2.7	2.5	2.4	2.3	2.2	2.0	1.8	1.6	1.4	1.2	1.1	0.9	0.8	0.7	0.6	0.5	0.4	0.4	0.3	0.2	0.1	0	0	0	0	0
75¢	1.2	1.1	1.1	1.0	1.0	0.9	0.8	0.8	0.7	0.6	0.6	0.5	0.4	0.3	0.3	0.2	0.2	0.1	0.1	0	0	0	0	0	0	0	0	0	0	0	0
$1.00	0.7	0.6	0.6	0.5	0.5	0.5	0.4	0.4	0.4	0.3	0.3	0.2	0.2	0.1	0.1	0.1	0	0	0	0	0	0	0	0	0	0	0	0	0	0	0
$1.25	0.2	0.2	0.2	0.1	0.1	0.1	0.1	0.1	0.1	0.1	0.1	0	0	0	0	0	0	0	0	0	0	0	0	0	0	0	0	0	0	0	0

WM GRANDMILL (1985) LTD.

OPTION VALUES on SOYBEAN FUTURES – Table No: 9

OPTION VALUES ARE IN CENTS – to nearest tenth.

																WEEKS TO EXPIRATION															
	30	29	28	27	26	25	24	23	22	21	20	19	18	17	16	15	14	13	12	11	10	9	8	7	6	5	4	3	2	1	0
IN THE MONEY																															
$1.25	125.0	125.0	125.0	125.0	125.0	125.0	125.0	125.0	125.0	125.0	125.0	125.0	125.0	125.0	125.0	125.0	125.0	125.0	125.0	125.0	125.0	125.0	125.0	125.0	125.0	125.0	125.0	125.0	125.0	125.0	125.0
$1.00	100.0	100.0	100.0	100.0	100.0	100.0	100.0	100.0	100.0	100.0	100.0	100.0	100.0	100.0	100.0	100.0	100.0	100.0	100.0	100.0	100.0	100.0	100.0	100.0	100.0	100.0	100.0	100.0	100.0	100.0	100.0
75¢	75.0	75.0	75.0	75.0	75.0	75.0	75.0	75.0	75.0	75.0	75.0	75.0	75.0	75.0	75.0	75.0	75.0	75.0	75.0	75.0	75.0	75.0	75.0	75.0	75.0	75.0	75.0	75.0	75.0	75.0	75.0
50¢	50.6	50.5	50.5	50.5	50.5	50.4	50.4	50.4	50.4	50.3	50.3	50.3	50.3	50.2	50.2	50.2	50.1	50.1	50.1	50.1	50.0	50.0	50.0	50.0	50.0	50.0	50.0	50.0	50.0	50.0	50.0
25¢	28.7	28.7	28.6	28.5	28.4	28.2	28.1	28.0	27.9	27.8	27.6	27.4	27.3	27.2	27.1	26.9	26.8	26.6	26.5	26.4	26.2	26.1	25.9	25.8	25.6	25.5	25.4	25.2	25.1	25.0	25.0
AT THE MONEY	13.5	13.4	13.2	13.0	12.9	12.7	12.5	12.3	12.2	12.0	11.8	11.5	11.3	11.0	10.8	10.5	10.2	9.9	9.6	9.2	8.8	8.4	8.0	7.5	7.0	6.3	5.4	4.3	3.2	1.9	0.0
OUT OF THE MONEY																															
25¢	5.7	5.6	5.4	5.3	5.2	5.0	4.8	4.6	4.5	4.3	4.1	3.8	3.6	3.3	3.1	2.8	2.6	2.4	2.2	2.0	1.8	1.7	1.6	1.4	1.2	1.0	0.8	0.6	0.4	0.1	0
50¢	2.7	2.6	2.5	2.4	2.3	2.2	2.0	1.9	1.8	1.7	1.5	1.3	1.2	1.0	0.9	0.8	0.7	0.6	0.6	0.5	0.4	0.4	0.3	0.2	0.2	0.1	0	0	0	0	0
75¢	0.9	0.9	0.8	0.7	0.7	0.6	0.6	0.5	0.5	0.4	0.4	0.3	0.3	0.2	0.2	0.1	0.1	0.1	0	0	0	0	0	0	0	0	0	0	0	0	0
$1.00	0	0	0	0	0	0	0	0	0	0	0	0	0	0	0	0	0	0	0	0	0	0	0	0	0	0	0	0	0	0	0
$1.25	0	0	0	0	0	0	0	0	0	0	0	0	0	0	0	0	0	0	0	0	0	0	0	0	0	0	0	0	0	0	0

WM GRANDMILL (1985) LTD.

OPTION VALUES on SOYBEAN FUTURES – Table No:12

WEEKS TO EXPIRATION

	30	29	28	27	26	25	24	23	22	21	20	19	18	17	16	15	14	13	12	11	10	9	8	7	6	5	4	3	2	1	0
IN THE MONEY																															
$1.25	125.0	125.0	125.0	125.0	125.0	125.0	125.0	125.0	125.0	125.0	125.0	125.0	125.0	125.0	125.0	125.0	125.0	125.0	125.0	125.0	125.0	125.0	125.0	125.0	125.0	125.0	125.0	125.0	125.0	125.0	125.0
$1.00	100.0	100.0	100.0	100.0	100.0	100.0	100.0	100.0	100.0	100.0	100.0	100.0	100.0	100.0	100.0	100.0	100.0	100.0	100.0	100.0	100.0	100.0	100.0	100.0	100.0	100.0	100.0	100.0	100.0	100.0	100.0
75¢	75.0	75.0	75.0	75.0	75.0	75.0	75.0	75.0	75.0	75.0	75.0	75.0	75.0	75.0	75.0	75.0	75.0	75.0	75.0	75.0	75.0	75.0	75.0	75.0	75.0	75.0	75.0	75.0	75.0	75.0	75.0
50¢	51.2	51.2	51.1	51.1	51.0	51.0	50.9	50.8	50.7	50.7	50.6	50.6	50.5	50.5	50.4	50.4	50.3	50.3	50.2	50.2	50.2	50.1	50.1	50.0	50.0	50.0	50.0	50.0	50.0	50.0	50.0
25¢	30.6	30.5	30.3	30.1	30.0	29.9	29.8	29.6	29.5	29.3	29.2	28.9	28.7	28.5	28.3	28.1	27.8	27.6	27.4	27.2	26.9	26.7	26.5	26.3	26.0	25.8	25.5	25.3	25.2	25.1	25.0
AT THE MONEY	16.0	15.9	15.7	15.5	15.3	15.1	14.9	14.7	14.4	14.2	14.0	13.7	13.4	13.1	12.8	12.5	12.1	11.8	11.4	11.0	10.5	10.0	9.5	8.9	8.3	7.5	6.4	5.1	3.8	2.3	0.0
OUT OF THE MONEY																															
25¢	8.0	7.9	7.7	7.5	7.3	7.1	7.0	6.8	6.5	6.3	6.1	5.9	5.6	5.3	5.1	4.8	4.4	4.1	3.7	3.3	2.8	2.5	2.2	1.9	1.7	1.4	1.1	0.8	0.5	0.2	0.0
50¢	4.4	4.3	4.1	3.9	3.8	3.7	3.6	3.4	3.2	3.1	3.0	2.8	2.6	2.4	2.2	2.0	1.7	1.5	1.2	1.0	0.8	0.6	0.5	0.4	0.3	0.2	0.1	0	0	0	0
75¢	1.7	1.6	1.6	1.5	1.4	1.4	1.3	1.3	1.2	1.1	1.1	1.0	0.9	0.8	0.7	0.6	0.5	0.4	0.3	0.2	0.1	0.1	0	0	0	0	0	0	0	0	0
$1.00	1.2	1.2	1.1	1.0	1.0	0.9	0.9	0.8	0.7	0.6	0.6	0.5	0.5	0.4	0.3	0.3	0.2	0.2	0.1	0.1	0.1	0	0	0	0	0	0	0	0	0	0
$1.25	0.4	0.4	0.3	0.3	0.3	0.3	0.2	0.2	0.2	0.2	0.2	0.1	0.1	0.1	0	0	0	0	0	0	0	0	0	0	0	0	0	0	0	0	0

OPTION VALUES ARE IN CENTS – to nearest tenth.

WM GRANDMILL (1985) LTD.

OPTION VALUES on SOYBEAN FUTURES – Table No:11

WEEKS TO EXPIRATION

	30	29	28	27	26	25	24	23	22	21	20	19	18	17	16	15	14	13	12	11	10	9	8	7	6	5	4	3	2	1	0
IN THE MONEY																															
$1.25	125.0	125.0	125.0	125.0	125.0	125.0	125.0	125.0	125.0	125.0	125.0	125.0	125.0	125.0	125.0	125.0	125.0	125.0	125.0	125.0	125.0	125.0	125.0	125.0	125.0	125.0	125.0	125.0	125.0	125.0	125.0
$1.00	100.0	100.0	100.0	100.0	100.0	100.0	100.0	100.0	100.0	100.0	100.0	100.0	100.0	100.0	100.0	100.0	100.0	100.0	100.0	100.0	100.0	100.0	100.0	100.0	100.0	100.0	100.0	100.0	100.0	100.0	100.0
75¢	75.0	75.0	75.0	75.0	75.0	75.0	75.0	75.0	75.0	75.0	75.0	75.0	75.0	75.0	75.0	75.0	75.0	75.0	75.0	75.0	75.0	75.0	75.0	75.0	75.0	75.0	75.0	75.0	75.0	75.0	75.0
50¢	51.0	50.9	50.9	50.8	50.8	50.7	50.7	50.6	50.6	50.6	50.5	50.5	50.4	50.4	50.4	50.3	50.3	50.2	50.2	50.2	50.1	50.1	50.1	50.0	50.0	50.0	50.0	50.0	50.0	50.0	50.0
25¢	30.0	29.9	29.7	29.6	29.5	29.4	29.2	29.1	28.9	28.7	28.6	28.4	28.2	28.0	27.8	27.6	27.4	27.3	27.1	26.9	26.7	26.5	26.3	26.1	25.9	25.7	25.4	25.3	25.2	25.1	25.0
AT THE MONEY	15.2	15.0	14.8	14.7	14.5	14.3	14.1	13.9	13.7	13.5	13.2	13.0	12.7	12.4	12.1	11.8	11.5	11.2	10.8	10.4	10.0	9.5	9.0	8.4	7.8	7.1	6.0	4.9	3.6	2.2	0.0
OUT OF THE MONEY																															
25¢	7.2	7.1	6.9	6.8	6.6	6.4	6.2	6.1	5.9	5.7	5.5	5.3	5.0	4.7	4.4	4.1	3.8	3.5	3.1	2.8	2.5	2.1	1.9	1.7	1.5	1.3	1.0	0.7	0.5	0.2	0.0
50¢	3.8	3.7	3.5	3.4	3.3	3.2	3.1	3.0	2.8	2.7	2.5	2.4	2.2	2.0	1.7	1.5	1.3	1.1	0.9	0.8	0.6	0.5	0.4	0.4	0.3	0.2	0.1	0	0	0	0
75¢	1.4	1.4	1.3	1.3	1.2	1.2	1.1	1.0	1.0	0.9	0.8	0.7	0.6	0.5	0.4	0.4	0.3	0.2	0.2	0.1	0.1	0	0	0	0	0	0	0	0	0	0
$1.00	0.9	0.9	0.8	0.8	0.7	0.7	0.6	0.6	0.5	0.5	0.4	0.4	0.3	0.3	0.2	0.2	0.1	0.1	0.1	0	0	0	0	0	0	0	0	0	0	0	0
$1.25	0.3	0.3	0.2	0.2	0.2	0.2	0.2	0.1	0.1	0.1	0.1	0	0	0	0	0	0	0	0	0	0	0	0	0	0	0	0	0	0	0	0

OPTION VALUES ARE IN CENTS – to nearest tenth.

WM GRANDMILL (1985) LTD.

OPTION VALUES on SOYBEAN FUTURES – Table No: 14

	30	29	28	27	26	25	24	23	22	21	20	19	18	17	16	15	14	13	12	11	10	9	8	7	6	5	4	3	2	1	0
IN THE MONEY $1.25	125.0	125.0	125.0	125.0	125.0	125.0	125.0	125.0	125.0	125.0	125.0	125.0	125.0	125.0	125.0	125.0	125.0	125.0	125.0	125.0	125.0	125.0	125.0	125.0	125.0	125.0	125.0	125.0	125.0	125.0	125.0
$1.00	100.0	100.0	100.0	100.0	100.0	100.0	100.0	100.0	100.0	100.0	100.0	100.0	100.0	100.0	100.0	100.0	100.0	100.0	100.0	100.0	100.0	100.0	100.0	100.0	100.0	100.0	100.0	100.0	100.0	100.0	100.0
75¢	75.2	75.2	75.1	75.1	75.1	75.1	75.1	75.1	75.1	75.0	75.0	75.0	75.0	75.0	75.0	75.0	75.0	75.0	75.0	75.0	75.0	75.0	75.0	75.0	75.0	75.0	75.0	75.0	75.0	75.0	75.0
50¢	51.9	51.8	51.7	51.6	51.5	51.5	51.4	51.3	51.2	51.1	51.0	51.0	50.9	50.8	50.7	50.6	50.5	50.5	50.4	50.4	50.3	50.2	50.2	50.1	50.1	50.0	50.0	50.0	50.0	50.0	50.0
25¢	31.9	31.7	31.5	31.4	31.3	31.1	30.9	30.7	30.5	30.3	30.1	29.9	29.7	29.5	29.3	29.0	28.7	28.5	28.2	27.8	27.5	27.2	26.9	26.6	26.3	26.0	25.6	25.4	25.2	25.1	25.0
AT THE MONEY	17.7	17.5	17.3	17.1	16.9	16.7	16.5	16.2	16.0	15.7	15.4	15.1	14.8	14.5	14.2	13.8	13.4	13.0	12.6	12.1	11.6	11.1	10.5	9.8	9.0	8.1	7.0	5.7	4.2	2.5	0.0
OUT OF THE MONEY 25¢	9.5	9.3	9.1	8.9	8.8	8.6	8.4	8.2	8.0	7.7	7.4	7.1	6.9	6.6	6.3	6.0	5.6	5.3	4.9	4.4	3.9	3.4	2.8	2.3	1.9	1.6	1.2	0.9	0.6	0.2	0
50¢	5.5	5.3	5.2	5.1	5.0	5.0	4.8	4.6	4.4	4.3	4.1	3.9	3.7	3.5	3.3	3.1	2.9	2.6	2.4	2.1	1.7	1.4	1.1	0.8	0.6	0.4	0.3	0.2	0	0	0
75¢	2.4	2.3	2.2	2.1	2.0	1.9	1.8	1.7	1.7	1.6	1.5	1.4	1.3	1.2	1.1	1.0	0.9	0.7	0.6	0.4	0.3	0.2	0.1	0	0	0	0	0	0	0	0
$1.00	1.8	1.7	1.7	1.6	1.5	1.4	1.4	1.3	1.2	1.1	1.0	0.9	0.8	0.7	0.6	0.5	0.5	0.4	0.3	0.2	0.1	0.1	0.1	0	0	0	0	0	0	0	0
$1.25	0.6	0.6	0.5	0.5	0.5	0.4	0.4	0.4	0.4	0.3	0.3	0.3	0.2	0.2	0.2	0.1	0.1	0.1	0.1	0	0	0	0	0	0	0	0	0	0	0	0.0

WEEKS TO EXPIRATION

OPTION VALUES ARE IN CENTS - to nearest tenth.

WM GRANDMILL (1985) LTD.

OPTION VALUES on SOYBEAN FUTURES – Table No: 13

	30	29	28	27	26	25	24	23	22	21	20	19	18	17	16	15	14	13	12	11	10	9	8	7	6	5	4	3	2	1	0
IN THE MONEY $1.25	125.0	125.0	125.0	125.0	125.0	125.0	125.0	125.0	125.0	125.0	125.0	125.0	125.0	125.0	125.0	125.0	125.0	125.0	125.0	125.0	125.0	125.0	125.0	125.0	125.0	125.0	125.0	125.0	125.0	125.0	125.0
$1.00	100.0	100.0	100.0	100.0	100.0	100.0	100.0	100.0	100.0	100.0	100.0	100.0	100.0	100.0	100.0	100.0	100.0	100.0	100.0	100.0	100.0	100.0	100.0	100.0	100.0	100.0	100.0	100.0	100.0	100.0	100.0
75¢	75.1	75.1	75.1	75.1	75.1	75.1	75.0	75.0	75.0	75.0	75.0	75.0	75.0	75.0	75.0	75.0	75.0	75.0	75.0	75.0	75.0	75.0	75.0	75.0	75.0	75.0	75.0	75.0	75.0	75.0	75.0
50¢	51.5	51.5	51.4	51.3	51.3	51.2	51.1	51.1	51.0	51.0	50.9	50.8	50.7	50.6	50.6	50.5	50.5	50.4	50.3	50.3	50.2	50.2	50.1	50.1	50.0	50.0	50.0	50.0	50.0	50.0	50.0
25¢	31.3	31.1	30.9	30.8	30.6	30.5	30.3	30.1	30.0	29.9	29.6	29.4	29.2	29.0	28.7	28.5	28.3	28.0	27.8	27.5	27.2	27.0	26.7	26.4	26.1	25.8	25.6	25.4	25.2	25.1	25.0
AT THE MONEY	16.9	16.7	16.5	16.3	16.1	15.9	15.7	15.5	15.2	15.0	14.7	14.4	14.1	13.8	13.5	13.1	12.8	12.4	12.0	11.6	11.1	10.6	10.0	9.4	8.6	7.7	6.7	5.4	4.0	2.4	0.0
OUT OF THE MONEY 25¢	8.8	8.6	8.4	8.2	8.0	7.9	7.7	7.5	7.3	7.1	6.8	6.5	6.2	6.0	5.7	5.3	5.1	4.7	4.3	3.9	3.4	2.9	2.5	2.1	1.8	1.5	1.1	0.8	0.5	0.2	0
50¢	5.0	4.8	4.6	4.5	4.4	4.3	4.1	3.9	3.8	3.7	3.5	3.3	3.1	2.9	2.7	2.4	2.2	2.0	1.7	1.4	1.1	0.8	0.6	0.5	0.4	0.3	0.1	0	0	0	0
75¢	20.0	1.9	1.8	1.8	1.7	1.6	1.6	1.5	1.4	1.4	1.3	1.2	1.1	1.0	0.9	0.8	0.7	0.5	0.4	0.3	0.2	0.1	0.1	0	0	0	0	0	0	0	0
$1.00	1.5	1.4	1.4	1.3	1.2	1.2	1.1	1.0	0.9	0.9	0.8	0.7	0.6	0.5	0.5	0.4	0.3	0.3	0.2	0.1	0.1	0	0	0	0	0	0	0	0	0	0
$1.25	0.5	0.4	0.4	0.4	0.4	0.4	0.3	0.3	0.3	0.3	0.2	0.2	0.2	0.1	0.1	0.1	0	0	0	0	0	0	0	0	0	0	0	0	0	0	0.0

WEEKS TO EXPIRATION

OPTION VALUES ARE IN CENTS - to nearest tenth.

WM GRANDMILL (1985) LTD.

OPTION VALUES on SOYBEAN FUTURES – Table No: 16

		30	29	28	27	26	25	24	23	22	21	20	19	18	17	16	15	14	13	12	11	10	9	8	7	6	5	4	3	2	1	0
IN THE MONEY	$1.25	125.0	125.0	125.0	125.0	125.0	125.0	125.0	125.0	125.0	125.0	125.0	125.0	125.0	125.0	125.0	125.0	125.0	125.0	125.0	125.0	125.0	125.0	125.0	125.0	125.0	125.0	125.0	125.0	125.0	125.0	125.0
	$1.00	100.0	100.0	100.0	100.0	100.0	100.0	100.0	100.0	100.0	100.0	100.0	100.0	100.0	100.0	100.0	100.0	100.0	100.0	100.0	100.0	100.0	100.0	100.0	100.0	100.0	100.0	100.0	100.0	100.0	100.0	100.0
	75¢	75.3	75.3	75.3	75.3	75.2	75.2	75.2	75.2	75.2	75.1	75.1	75.1	75.1	75.0	75.0	75.0	75.0	75.0	75.0	75.0	75.0	75.0	75.0	75.0	75.0	75.0	75.0	75.0	75.0	75.0	75.0
	50¢	52.8	52.7	52.6	52.5	52.4	52.3	52.1	52.0	51.8	51.7	51.5	51.4	51.3	51.2	51.1	51.0	50.8	50.7	50.6	50.5	50.4	50.4	50.3	50.2	50.1	50.0	50.0	50.0	50.0	50.0	50.0
	25¢	33.2	33.1	33.0	32.8	32.6	32.4	32.2	32.0	31.7	31.5	31.3	31.0	30.7	30.4	30.1	29.9	29.6	29.3	29.0	28.6	28.2	27.8	27.4	27.1	26.6	26.3	25.8	25.5	25.3	25.1	25.0
AT THE MONEY		19.4	19.2	19.0	18.8	18.5	18.3	18.0	17.8	17.5	17.2	16.9	16.6	16.2	15.8	15.5	15.1	14.7	14.3	13.8	13.3	12.7	12.1	11.5	10.8	9.9	8.9	7.6	6.2	4.6	2.8	0.0
OUT OF THE MONEY	25¢	11.1	10.9	10.7	10.5	10.2	10.0	9.8	9.6	9.3	9.0	8.8	8.5	8.1	7.8	7.5	7.1	6.8	6.4	6.0	5.5	5.0	4.4	3.8	3.1	2.4	1.9	1.4	1.0	0.6	0.3	0
	50¢	6.7	6.6	6.5	6.3	6.1	5.9	5.8	5.6	5.4	5.2	5.0	4.7	4.5	4.2	3.9	3.7	3.4	3.2	2.9	2.5	2.2	1.7	1.3	0.9	0.6	0.4	0.2	0.1	0	0	0
	75¢	3.4	3.3	3.2	3.0	2.8	2.7	2.6	2.5	2.3	2.2	2.0	1.9	1.7	1.6	1.5	1.4	1.3	1.2	1.0	0.8	0.6	0.4	0.3	0.2	0.1	0	0	0	0	0	0
	$1.00	2.4	2.3	2.2	2.2	2.1	2.0	1.9	1.8	1.7	1.6	1.5	1.4	1.3	1.1	1.0	0.9	0.8	0.7	0.5	0.4	0.3	0.2	0.1	0	0	0	0	0	0	0	0
	$1.25	1.1	1.0	1.0	0.9	0.8	0.7	0.7	0.6	0.6	0.5	0.5	0.4	0.4	0.3	0.3	0.3	0.2	0.2	0.1	0.1	0.1	0.2	0.1	0	0	0	0	0	0	0	0

WEEKS TO EXPIRATION

OPTION VALUES ARE IN CENTS – to nearest tenth.

WM GRANDMILL (1985) LTD.

OPTION VALUES on SOYBEAN FUTURES – Table No: 15

		30	29	28	27	26	25	24	23	22	21	20	19	18	17	16	15	14	13	12	11	10	9	8	7	6	5	4	3	2	1	0
IN THE MONEY	$1.25	125.0	125.0	125.0	125.0	125.0	125.0	125.0	125.0	125.0	125.0	125.0	125.0	125.0	125.0	125.0	125.0	125.0	125.0	125.0	125.0	125.0	125.0	125.0	125.0	125.0	125.0	125.0	125.0	125.0	125.0	125.0
	$1.00	100.0	100.0	100.0	100.0	100.0	100.0	100.0	100.0	100.0	100.0	100.0	100.0	100.0	100.0	100.0	100.0	100.0	100.0	100.0	100.0	100.0	100.0	100.0	100.0	100.0	100.0	100.0	100.0	100.0	100.0	100.0
	75¢	75.2	75.2	75.2	75.2	75.2	75.2	75.1	75.1	75.1	75.1	75.1	75.0	75.0	75.0	75.0	75.0	75.0	75.0	75.0	75.0	75.0	75.0	75.0	75.0	75.0	75.0	75.0	75.0	75.0	75.0	75.0
	50¢	52.4	52.3	52.1	52.0	51.9	51.8	51.7	51.6	51.5	51.4	51.3	51.2	51.1	51.0	50.9	50.8	50.7	50.6	50.5	50.4	50.5	50.3	50.2	50.1	50.1	50.0	50.0	50.0	50.0	50.0	50.0
	25¢	32.5	32.3	32.2	32.1	31.9	31.7	31.5	31.3	31.1	30.8	30.6	30.4	30.2	30.0	29.7	29.4	29.2	28.8	28.6	28.2	27.9	27.5	27.2	26.8	26.4	26.1	25.7	25.5	25.3	25.1	25.0
AT THE MONEY		18.5	18.3	18.1	17.9	17.7	17.5	17.2	17.0	16.7	16.4	16.1	15.8	15.5	15.2	14.8	14.4	14.0	13.6	13.2	12.7	12.2	11.6	11.0	10.3	9.4	8.5	7.3	6.0	4.4	2.7	0.0
OUT OF THE MONEY	25¢	10.2	10.0	9.8	9.7	9.5	9.3	9.1	8.9	8.6	8.3	8.0	7.8	7.5	7.2	6.9	6.5	6.2	5.8	5.4	5.0	4.5	3.9	3.3	2.7	2.1	1.7	1.3	0.9	0.6	0.3	0
	50¢	6.0	5.9	5.8	5.7	5.5	5.3	5.2	5.0	4.8	4.6	4.4	4.2	4.0	3.8	3.5	3.2	3.0	2.7	2.5	2.2	1.8	1.4	1.0	0.7	0.5	0	0	0	0	0	0
	75¢	2.8	2.7	2.6	2.5	2.4	2.3	2.2	2.1	1.9	1.8	1.7	1.6	1.5	1.4	1.3	1.2	1.1	0.9	0.8	0.6	0.5	0.3	0.2	0	0	0	0	0	0	0	0
	$1.00	2.1	2.0	1.9	1.9	1.8	1.7	1.6	1.5	1.3	1.3	1.2	1.1	1.0	0.9	0.8	0.7	0.6	0.5	0.4	0.3	0.2	0.1	0	0	0	0	0	0	0	0	0
	$1.25	0.8	0.7	0.7	0.6	0.6	0.6	0.5	0.5	0.4	0.4	0.4	0.3	0.3	0.2	0.2	0.1	0.1	0.1	0	0	0	0	0	0	0	0	0	0	0	0	0

WEEKS TO EXPIRATION

OPTION VALUES ARE IN CENTS – to nearest tenth.

WM GRANDMILL (1985) LTD.

OPTION VALUES on SOYBEAN FUTURES – Table No: 18

OPTION VALUES ARE IN CENTS – to nearest tenth.

WEEKS TO EXPIRATION

	30	29	28	27	26	25	24	23	22	21	20	19	18	17	16	15	14	13	12	11	10	9	8	7	6	5	4	3	2	1	0
IN THE MONEY																															
$1.25	125.0	125.0	125.0	125.0	125.0	125.0	125.0	125.0	125.0	125.0	125.0	125.0	125.0	125.0	125.0	125.0	125.0	125.0	125.0	125.0	125.0	125.0	125.0	125.0	125.0	125.0	125.0	125.0	125.0	125.0	125.0
$1.00	100.0	100.0	100.0	100.0	100.0	100.0	100.0	100.0	100.0	100.0	100.0	100.0	100.0	100.0	100.0	100.0	100.0	100.0	100.0	100.0	100.0	100.0	100.0	100.0	100.0	100.0	100.0	100.0	100.0	100.0	100.0
75¢	75.5	75.5	75.4	75.4	75.4	75.4	75.3	75.3	75.3	75.2	75.2	75.2	75.2	75.1	75.1	75.1	75.1	75.0	75.0	75.0	75.0	75.0	75.0	75.0	75.0	75.0	75.0	75.0	75.0	75.0	75.0
50¢	53.6	53.5	53.4	53.3	53.1	53.0	52.9	52.7	52.6	52.5	52.3	52.1	51.9	51.7	51.5	51.4	51.2	51.1	50.9	50.7	50.6	50.5	50.4	50.3	50.2	50.1	50.0	50.0	50.0	50.0	50.0
25¢	34.6	34.4	34.2	34.0	33.8	33.6	33.4	33.2	33.0	32.7	32.4	32.1	31.8	31.5	31.2	30.8	30.5	30.1	29.8	29.4	29.0	28.6	28.1	27.6	27.1	26.5	26.0	25.6	25.3	25.1	25.0
AT THE MONEY	21.1	20.9	20.6	20.4	20.1	19.9	19.6	19.3	19.0	18.7	18.4	18.0	17.6	17.2	16.8	16.4	16.0	15.5	15.0	14.4	13.8	13.2	12.5	11.7	10.8	9.7	8.3	6.5	5.0	3.0	0.0
OUT OF THE MONEY																															
25¢	12.6	12.4	12.2	12.0	11.8	11.6	11.3	11.0	10.7	10.4	10.1	9.8	9.4	9.0	8.7	8.3	8.0	7.5	7.1	6.5	6.0	5.4	4.8	4.0	3.1	2.3	1.7	1.2	0.7	0.3	0.0
50¢	7.9	7.8	7.6	7.4	7.2	7.0	6.8	6.6	6.4	6.2	6.0	5.8	5.5	5.2	4.9	4.6	4.3	3.9	3.6	3.2	2.9	2.5	2.0	1.4	0.9	0.6	0.4	0.2	0	0	0
75¢	4.3	4.2	4.0	3.9	3.7	3.6	3.5	3.3	3.1	2.9	2.8	2.6	2.4	2.2	2.0	1.8	1.7	1.5	1.4	1.2	1.0	0.8	0.6	0.3	0.1	0	0	0	0	0	0
$1.00	3.0	2.9	2.8	2.7	2.6	2.5	2.4	2.3	2.2	2.1	2.0	1.9	1.8	1.6	1.5	1.3	1.2	1.0	0.9	0.7	0.5	0.4	0.3	0.1	0	0	0	0	0	0	0
$1.25	1.6	1.6	1.5	1.4	1.3	1.2	1.1	1.0	1.0	0.9	0.8	0.7	0.6	0.5	0.4	0.3	0.3	0.2	0.2	0.1	0.1	0	0	0	0	0	0	0	0	0	0

WM GRANDMILL (1985) LTD.

OPTION VALUES on SOYBEAN FUTURES – Table No: 17

OPTION VALUES ARE IN CENTS – to nearest tenth.

WEEKS TO EXPIRATION

	30	29	28	27	26	25	24	23	22	21	20	19	18	17	16	15	14	13	12	11	10	9	8	7	6	5	4	3	2	1	0
IN THE MONEY																															
$1.25	125.0	125.0	125.0	125.0	125.0	125.0	125.0	125.0	125.0	125.0	125.0	125.0	125.0	125.0	125.0	125.0	125.0	125.0	125.0	125.0	125.0	125.0	125.0	125.0	125.0	125.0	125.0	125.0	125.0	125.0	125.0
$1.00	100.0	100.0	100.0	100.0	100.0	100.0	100.0	100.0	100.0	100.0	100.0	100.0	100.0	100.0	100.0	100.0	100.0	100.0	100.0	100.0	100.0	100.0	100.0	100.0	100.0	100.0	100.0	100.0	100.0	100.0	100.0
75¢	75.4	75.4	75.4	75.4	75.3	75.3	75.3	75.2	75.2	75.2	75.2	75.1	75.1	75.1	75.1	75.0	75.0	75.0	75.0	75.0	75.0	75.0	75.0	75.0	75.0	75.0	75.0	75.0	75.0	75.0	75.0
50¢	53.2	53.1	53.0	52.9	52.7	52.6	52.5	52.4	52.2	52.0	51.9	51.7	51.5	51.4	51.1	51.0	50.9	50.7	50.6	50.4	50.3	50.2	50.1	50.1	50.0	50.0	50.0	50.0	50.0	50.0	50.0
25¢	33.9	33.8	33.6	33.4	33.2	33.0	32.8	32.5	32.3	32.1	31.8	31.5	31.2	30.9	30.6	30.3	30.0	29.7	29.4	29.1	28.6	28.2	27.8	27.3	26.8	26.4	25.9	25.5	25.3	25.1	25.0
AT THE MONEY	20.2	20.0	19.8	19.6	19.3	19.1	18.8	18.5	18.2	17.9	17.6	17.3	16.9	16.5	16.2	15.7	15.3	14.9	14.4	13.9	13.3	12.7	12.0	11.2	10.3	9.3	8.0	6.5	4.8	2.9	0.0
OUT OF THE MONEY																															
25¢	11.8	11.7	11.5	11.3	11.0	10.8	10.5	10.2	9.9	9.7	9.4	9.1	8.8	8.4	8.1	7.7	7.3	7.0	6.6	6.1	5.5	4.9	4.3	3.5	2.7	2.1	1.6	1.1	0.7	0.3	0.0
50¢	7.3	7.2	7.0	6.8	6.6	6.5	6.3	6.1	5.9	5.7	5.4	5.2	5.0	4.7	4.4	4.1	3.8	3.5	3.2	3.0	2.6	2.2	1.7	1.2	0.7	0.5	0.3	0.1	0	0	0
75¢	3.8	3.7	3.6	3.5	3.4	3.3	3.0	2.8	2.7	2.5	2.4	2.2	2.0	1.8	1.7	1.6	1.4	1.3	1.2	1.0	0.8	0.6	0.4	0.2	0.1	0	0	0	0	0	0
$1.00	2.6	2.6	2.5	2.4	2.3	2.3	2.2	2.1	2.0	1.9	1.8	1.7	1.5	1.4	1.3	1.1	1.0	0.9	0.7	0.6	0.4	0.3	0.2	0.1	0	0	0	0	0	0	0
$1.25	1.3	1.3	1.2	1.1	1.0	1.0	0.9	0.8	0.7	0.6	0.6	0.5	0.5	0.4	0.4	0.3	0.3	0.2	0.2	0.1	0.1	0	0	0	0	0	0	0	0	0	0

WM GRANDMILL (1985) LTD.

OPTION VALUES on SOYBEAN FUTURES – Table No: 20

OPTION VALUES ARE IN CENTS - to nearest tenth.

	30	29	28	27	26	25	24	23	22	21	20	19	18	17	16	15	14	13	12	11	10	9	8	7	6	5	4	3	2	1	0
IN THE MONEY																															
$1.25	125.0	125.0	125.0	125.0	125.0	125.0	125.0	125.0	125.0	125.0	125.0	125.0	125.0	125.0	125.0	125.0	125.0	125.0	125.0	125.0	125.0	125.0	125.0	125.0	125.0	125.0	125.0	125.0	125.0	125.0	125.0
$1.00	100.0	100.0	100.0	100.0	100.0	100.0	100.0	100.0	100.0	100.0	100.0	100.0	100.0	100.0	100.0	100.0	100.0	100.0	100.0	100.0	100.0	100.0	100.0	100.0	100.0	100.0	100.0	100.0	100.0	100.0	100.0
75¢	75.8	75.8	75.7	75.7	75.6	75.6	75.5	75.5	75.4	75.4	75.4	75.3	75.3	75.2	75.2	75.2	75.1	75.1	75.1	75.0	75.0	75.0	75.0	75.0	75.0	75.0	75.0	75.0	75.0	75.0	75.0
50¢	54.5	54.3	54.2	54.1	53.9	53.8	53.6	53.5	53.3	53.2	53.0	52.8	52.6	52.4	52.1	51.9	51.7	51.5	51.3	51.1	50.9	50.7	50.6	50.4	50.3	50.2	50.1	50.0	50.0	50.0	50.0
25¢	36.0	35.7	35.5	35.3	35.1	34.8	34.6	34.4	34.1	33.9	33.6	33.3	33.0	32.6	32.2	31.9	31.5	31.1	30.7	30.2	29.8	29.3	28.7	28.2	27.6	26.9	26.3	25.7	25.4	25.1	25.0
AT THE MONEY	22.8	22.5	22.2	22.0	21.7	21.4	21.1	20.8	20.5	20.2	19.8	19.4	19.0	18.6	18.1	17.7	17.2	16.7	16.2	15.6	14.9	14.2	13.5	12.7	11.7	10.4	9.0	7.3	5.4	3.3	0.0
OUT OF THE MONEY																															
25¢	14.2	13.9	13.6	13.4	13.2	12.9	12.6	12.4	12.1	11.8	11.5	11.1	10.7	10.3	9.8	9.5	9.0	8.6	8.1	7.6	7.0	6.3	5.7	5.0	4.0	2.7	1.9	1.3	0.8	0.4	0.0
50¢	9.1	8.9	8.7	8.5	8.3	8.1	7.9	7.7	7.5	7.3	7.0	6.7	6.4	6.1	5.8	5.5	5.2	4.8	4.5	4.0	3.6	3.1	2.7	2.2	1.4	0.8	0.4	0.2	0	0	0
75¢	5.3	5.1	5.0	4.9	4.7	4.5	4.3	4.1	3.9	3.8	3.6	3.4	3.2	2.9	2.6	2.4	2.2	1.9	1.7	1.5	1.3	1.1	0.9	0.6	0.3	0.1	0	0	0	0	0
$1.00	3.7	3.6	3.5	3.4	3.3	3.3	3.1	3.0	2.9	2.8	2.6	2.5	2.4	2.2	2.1	1.9	1.8	1.6	1.4	1.3	1.1	0.9	0.7	0.5	0.3	0.1	0	0	0	0	0
$1.25	2.0	1.9	1.8	1.8	1.7	1.6	1.6	1.5	1.4	1.3	1.2	1.1	1.0	0.8	0.7	0.6	0.5	0.4	0.4	0.3	0.2	0.2	0.1	0.1	0.1	0	0	0	0	0	0

WEEKS TO EXPIRATION

WM GRANDMILL (1985) LTD.

OPTION VALUES on SOYBEAN FUTURES – Table No: 19

OPTION VALUES ARE IN CENTS - to nearest tenth.

	30	29	28	27	26	25	24	23	22	21	20	19	18	17	16	15	14	13	12	11	10	9	8	7	6	5	4	3	2	1	0
IN THE MONEY																															
$1.25	125.0	125.0	125.0	125.0	125.0	125.0	125.0	125.0	125.0	125.0	125.0	125.0	125.0	125.0	125.0	125.0	125.0	125.0	125.0	125.0	125.0	125.0	125.0	125.0	125.0	125.0	125.0	125.0	125.0	125.0	125.0
$1.00	100.0	100.0	100.0	100.0	100.0	100.0	100.0	100.0	100.0	100.0	100.0	100.0	100.0	100.0	100.0	100.0	100.0	100.0	100.0	100.0	100.0	100.0	100.0	100.0	100.0	100.0	100.0	100.0	100.0	100.0	100.0
75¢	75.7	75.6	75.6	75.5	75.5	75.4	75.4	75.4	75.3	75.3	75.3	75.2	75.2	75.2	75.2	75.1	75.1	75.1	75.0	75.0	75.0	75.0	75.0	75.0	75.0	75.0	75.0	75.0	75.0	75.0	75.0
50¢	54.0	53.9	53.8	53.7	53.5	53.4	53.2	53.1	52.9	52.8	52.6	52.5	52.3	52.0	51.8	51.6	51.4	51.3	51.1	50.9	50.7	50.6	50.5	50.4	50.2	50.1	50.0	50.0	50.0	50.0	50.0
25¢	35.3	35.1	34.9	34.7	34.5	34.2	33.9	33.7	33.5	33.2	33.0	32.7	32.4	32.1	31.7	31.4	31.0	30.6	30.2	29.9	29.4	28.9	28.5	27.9	27.3	26.7	26.1	25.6	25.3	25.1	25.0
AT THE MONEY	21.9	21.7	21.4	21.2	20.9	20.6	20.3	20.0	19.7	19.4	19.1	18.7	18.3	17.9	17.5	17.0	16.6	16.1	15.6	15.0	14.4	13.7	13.0	12.2	11.2	10.0	8.6	7.0	5.2	3.1	0.0
OUT OF THE MONEY																															
25¢	13.4	13.2	12.9	12.7	12.5	12.2	11.9	11.7	11.4	11.1	10.8	10.4	10.0	9.7	9.3	8.9	8.5	8.0	7.6	7.1	6.5	5.9	5.3	4.5	3.5	2.5	1.8	1.2	0.8	0.4	0.0
50¢	8.5	8.3	8.1	8.0	7.8	7.5	7.3	7.1	6.9	6.7	6.5	6.2	5.9	5.6	5.3	5.0	4.7	4.4	4.0	3.7	3.2	2.8	2.4	1.8	1.1	0.6	0.4	0.2	0	0	0
75¢	4.8	4.6	4.5	4.4	4.2	4.0	3.8	3.7	3.5	3.4	3.2	2.9	2.7	2.5	2.3	2.1	1.9	1.7	1.5	1.4	1.2	1.0	0.7	0.5	0.2	0	0	0	0	0	0
$1.00	3.4	3.3	3.2	3.1	3.0	2.8	2.7	2.6	2.5	2.4	2.3	2.1	2.0	1.9	1.7	1.6	1.4	1.2	1.1	0.9	0.7	0.5	0.4	0.2	0.1	0	0	0	0	0	0
$1.25	1.7	1.7	1.6	1.6	1.5	1.5	1.4	1.3	1.2	1.1	1.0	0.9	0.8	0.7	0.6	0.5	0.4	0.4	0.3	0.3	0.2	0.1	0.1	0	0	0	0	0	0	0	0

WEEKS TO EXPIRATION

WM GRANDMILL (1985) LTD.

OPTION VALUES on SOYBEAN FUTURES – Table No:22

	30	29	28	27	26	25	24	23	22	21	20	19	18	17	16	15	14	13	12	11	10	9	8	7	6	5	4	3	2	1	0
IN THE MONEY $1.25	125.0	125.0	125.0	125.0	125.0	125.0	125.0	125.0	125.0	125.0	125.0	125.0	125.0	125.0	125.0	125.0	125.0	125.0	125.0	125.0	125.0	125.0	125.0	125.0	125.0	125.0	125.0	125.0	125.0	125.0	125.0
$1.00	100.0	100.0	100.0	100.0	100.0	100.0	100.0	100.0	100.0	100.0	100.0	100.0	100.0	100.0	100.0	100.0	100.0	100.0	100.0	100.0	100.0	100.0	100.0	100.0	100.0	100.0	100.0	100.0	100.0	100.0	100.0
75¢	76.2	76.1	76.1	76.0	75.9	75.9	75.8	75.8	75.7	75.6	75.6	75.5	75.4	75.4	75.3	75.3	75.2	75.2	75.2	75.1	75.1	75.0	75.0	75.0	75.0	75.0	75.0	75.0	75.0	75.0	75.0
50¢	55.3	55.2	55.0	54.9	54.7	54.6	54.4	54.3	54.1	53.9	53.7	53.5	53.3	53.1	52.8	52.6	52.4	52.1	51.8	51.5	51.2	51.0	50.8	50.6	50.4	50.2	50.1	50.0	50.0	50.0	50.0
25¢	37.4	37.1	36.9	36.6	36.3	36.1	35.9	35.6	35.3	35.1	34.8	34.5	34.1	33.8	33.4	33.0	32.6	32.2	31.6	31.1	30.6	30.0	29.5	28.8	28.1	27.2	26.5	25.9	25.4	25.2	25.0
AT THE MONEY	24.5	24.2	23.9	23.6	23.3	23.0	22.7	22.4	22.0	21.7	21.3	20.9	20.4	20.0	19.5	19.0	18.5	18.0	17.4	16.7	16.0	15.3	14.5	13.6	12.5	11.1	9.6	7.8	5.8	3.5	0.0
OUT OF THE MONEY 25¢	15.8	15.5	15.2	14.9	14.6	14.3	14.0	13.8	13.5	13.2	12.8	12.4	12.0	11.6	11.2	10.7	10.2	9.7	9.2	8.6	8.0	7.3	6.6	5.8	4.8	3.4	2.2	1.5	0.9	0.5	0.0
50¢	10.4	10.2	10.0	9.7	9.5	9.3	9.0	8.8	8.6	8.3	8.0	7.7	7.4	7.1	6.8	6.4	6.0	5.7	5.3	4.9	4.4	3.8	3.3	2.7	2.0	1.1	0.6	0.3	0	0	0
75¢	6.3	6.2	6.0	5.8	5.6	5.4	5.2	5.1	4.9	4.6	4.4	4.2	3.9	3.7	3.4	3.1	2.8	2.6	2.3	2.0	1.7	1.4	1.2	0.9	0.6	0.2	0	0	0	0	0
$1.00	4.5	4.4	4.2	4.1	3.9	3.8	3.7	3.6	3.4	3.3	3.1	3.0	2.8	2.6	2.4	2.2	2.1	1.9	1.7	1.4	1.2	1.0	0.7	0.5	0.3	0.1	0	0	0	0	0
$1.25	2.6	2.5	2.4	2.3	2.2	2.1	2.0	1.9	1.8	1.7	1.6	1.5	1.4	1.3	1.1	1.0	0.8	0.7	0.5	0.4	0.4	0.3	0.2	0.1	0	0	0	0	0	0	0

WEEKS TO EXPIRATION

OPTION VALUES ARE IN CENTS – to nearest tenth.

WM GRANDMILL (1985) LTD.

OPTION VALUES on SOYBEAN FUTURES – Table No:21

	30	29	28	27	26	25	24	23	22	21	20	19	18	17	16	15	14	13	12	11	10	9	8	7	6	5	4	3	2	1	0
IN THE MONEY $1.25	125.0	125.0	125.0	125.0	125.0	125.0	125.0	125.0	125.0	125.0	125.0	125.0	125.0	125.0	125.0	125.0	125.0	125.0	125.0	125.0	125.0	125.0	125.0	125.0	125.0	125.0	125.0	125.0	125.0	125.0	125.0
$1.00	100.0	100.0	100.0	100.0	100.0	100.0	100.0	100.0	100.0	100.0	100.0	100.0	100.0	100.0	100.0	100.0	100.0	100.0	100.0	100.0	100.0	100.0	100.0	100.0	100.0	100.0	100.0	100.0	100.0	100.0	100.0
75¢	76.0	76.0	75.9	75.8	75.8	75.8	75.7	75.7	75.6	75.6	75.5	75.4	75.4	75.3	75.3	75.2	75.2	75.1	75.1	75.1	75.0	75.0	75.0	75.0	75.0	75.0	75.0	75.0	75.0	75.0	75.0
50¢	54.9	54.8	54.6	54.5	54.3	54.2	54.0	53.9	53.7	53.5	53.3	53.1	52.9	52.7	52.5	52.3	52.0	51.8	51.5	51.3	51.1	50.9	50.7	50.5	50.4	50.2	50.1	50.0	50.0	50.0	50.0
25¢	36.6	36.4	36.2	36.0	35.7	35.5	35.3	35.0	34.7	34.4	34.1	33.8	33.5	33.1	32.8	32.4	32.1	31.6	31.2	30.7	30.1	29.7	29.2	28.5	27.8	27.1	26.4	25.8	25.4	25.2	25.0
AT THE MONEY	23.6	23.4	23.1	22.8	22.5	22.2	21.9	21.6	21.3	20.9	20.5	20.1	19.7	19.3	18.8	18.3	17.9	17.4	16.8	16.2	15.5	14.8	14.0	13.1	12.1	10.8	9.3	7.6	5.6	3.4	0.0
OUT OF THE MONEY 25¢	14.9	14.7	14.4	14.2	13.9	13.6	13.4	13.1	12.8	12.5	12.1	11.7	11.4	11.0	10.5	10.0	9.6	9.2	8.7	8.1	7.5	6.9	6.2	5.3	4.4	3.1	2.0	1.4	0.9	0.4	0.0
50¢	9.7	9.5	9.3	9.1	8.9	8.7	8.5	8.2	8.0	7.8	7.5	7.2	6.9	6.6	6.3	6.0	5.7	5.3	4.9	4.5	3.9	3.5	3.0	2.4	1.7	0.9	0.5	0.3	0	0	0
75¢	5.9	5.7	5.5	5.3	5.1	5.0	4.8	4.6	4.4	4.2	4.0	3.7	3.5	3.3	3.0	2.7	2.5	2.3	2.0	1.8	1.5	1.3	1.1	0.8	0.4	0.2	0	0	0	0	0
$1.00	4.1	4.0	3.8	3.7	3.6	3.5	3.4	3.2	3.1	3.0	2.8	2.6	2.5	2.3	2.2	2.0	1.9	1.7	1.6	1.3	1.0	0.8	0.6	0.4	0.2	0	0	0	0	0	0
$1.25	2.2	2.1	2.0	2.0	1.9	1.8	1.7	1.7	1.6	1.5	1.4	1.3	1.2	1.0	0.9	0.7	0.6	0.5	0.5	0.4	0.3	0.2	0.2	0.1	0	0	0	0	0	0	0

WEEKS TO EXPIRATION

OPTION VALUES ARE IN CENTS – to nearest tenth.

WM GRANDMILL (1985) LTD.

OPTION VALUES on SOYBEAN FUTURES – Table No: 24

WEEKS TO EXPIRATION	30	29	28	27	26	25	24	23	22	21	20	19	18	17	16	15	14	13	12	11	10	9	8	7	6	5	4	3	2	1	0
IN THE MONEY $1.25	125.0	125.0	125.0	125.0	125.0	125.0	125.0	125.0	125.0	125.0	125.0	125.0	125.0	125.0	125.0	125.0	125.0	125.0	125.0	125.0	125.0	125.0	125.0	125.0	125.0	125.0	125.0	125.0	125.0	125.0	125.0
$1.00	100.0	100.0	100.0	100.0	100.0	100.0	100.0	100.0	100.0	100.0	100.0	100.0	100.0	100.0	100.0	100.0	100.0	100.0	100.0	100.0	100.0	100.0	100.0	100.0	100.0	100.0	100.0	100.0	100.0	100.0	100.0
75¢	76.7	76.6	76.5	76.4	76.3	76.3	76.2	76.1	76.0	75.9	75.8	75.7	75.6	75.5	75.4	75.4	75.3	75.3	75.2	75.2	75.1	75.1	75.0	75.0	75.0	75.0	75.0	75.0	75.0	75.0	75.0
50¢	56.3	56.1	55.9	55.8	55.6	55.4	55.2	55.0	54.9	54.7	54.5	54.2	54.0	53.8	53.5	53.2	53.0	52.7	52.4	52.0	51.7	51.4	51.1	50.8	50.5	50.3	50.1	50.0	50.0	50.0	50.0
25¢	38.8	38.6	38.3	38.0	37.8	37.5	37.2	36.9	36.6	36.3	36.0	35.6	35.2	34.8	34.4	34.0	33.6	33.1	32.6	32.1	31.5	30.8	30.1	29.5	28.7	27.7	26.8	26.1	25.5	25.2	25.0
AT THE MONEY	26.1	25.8	25.5	25.2	24.9	24.6	24.3	23.9	23.6	23.2	22.8	22.3	21.8	21.3	20.8	20.3	19.8	19.2	18.6	17.9	17.2	16.4	15.5	14.5	13.4	11.9	10.3	8.4	6.2	3.7	0.0
OUT OF THE MONEY 25¢	17.3	17.1	16.8	16.5	16.2	15.9	15.6	15.2	14.9	14.5	14.2	13.7	13.3	12.8	12.4	11.9	11.5	10.9	10.3	9.7	9.0	8.3	7.5	6.6	5.6	4.2	2.7	1.7	1.0	0.5	0
50¢	11.6	11.4	11.2	11.0	10.8	10.5	10.2	10.0	9.7	9.4	9.1	8.7	8.4	8.0	7.7	7.3	7.0	6.6	6.2	5.7	5.2	4.6	3.9	3.3	2.6	1.6	0.7	0.4	0.1	0	0
75¢	7.5	7.3	7.1	6.9	6.7	6.4	6.2	6.0	5.8	5.6	5.3	5.0	4.7	4.4	4.1	3.8	3.6	3.3	2.9	2.5	2.2	1.8	1.5	1.2	0.9	0.4	0.1	0	0	0	0
$1.00	5.3	5.2	5.0	4.9	4.7	4.6	4.4	4.2	4.1	3.9	3.7	3.5	3.3	3.1	2.9	2.7	2.5	2.3	2.1	1.9	1.6	1.4	1.0	0.7	0.5	0.2	0	0	0	0	0
$1.25	3.1	3.0	2.9	2.8	2.7	2.6	2.5	2.4	2.2	2.1	2.0	1.8	1.7	1.6	1.5	1.4	1.2	1.0	0.8	0.6	0.5	0.4	0.3	0.2	0.1	0	0	0	0	0	0

OPTION VALUES ARE IN CENTS – to nearest tenth.

WM GRANDMILL (1985) LTD.

OPTION VALUES on SOYBEAN FUTURES – Table No: 23

WEEKS TO EXPIRATION	30	29	28	27	26	25	24	23	22	21	20	19	18	17	16	15	14	13	12	11	10	9	8	7	6	5	4	3	2	1	0
IN THE MONEY $1.25	125.0	125.0	125.0	125.0	125.0	125.0	125.0	125.0	125.0	125.0	125.0	125.0	125.0	125.0	125.0	125.0	125.0	125.0	125.0	125.0	125.0	125.0	125.0	125.0	125.0	125.0	125.0	125.0	125.0	125.0	125.0
$1.00	100.1	100.0	100.0	100.0	100.0	100.0	100.0	100.0	100.0	100.0	100.0	100.0	100.0	100.0	100.0	100.0	100.0	100.0	100.0	100.0	100.0	100.0	100.0	100.0	100.0	100.0	100.0	100.0	100.0	100.0	100.0
75¢	76.5	76.4	76.3	76.2	76.1	76.0	76.0	76.0	75.9	75.8	75.8	75.7	75.6	75.5	75.4	75.3	75.3	75.2	75.2	75.1	75.1	75.0	75.0	75.0	75.0	75.0	75.0	75.0	75.0	75.0	75.0
50¢	55.8	55.6	55.4	55.3	55.1	55.0	55.0	54.8	54.6	54.5	54.3	54.1	53.9	53.6	53.4	53.2	52.9	52.7	52.4	52.1	51.7	51.4	51.2	50.9	50.7	50.5	50.3	50.1	50.0	50.0	50.0
25¢	38.1	37.9	37.6	37.3	37.0	36.8	36.5	36.2	36.0	35.6	35.3	35.0	34.6	34.2	33.9	33.5	33.1	32.6	32.2	31.5	31.0	30.4	29.9	29.2	28.5	27.7	26.8	26.0	25.5	25.2	25.0
AT THE MONEY	25.3	25.0	24.7	24.4	24.1	23.8	23.5	23.1	22.8	22.4	22.0	21.6	21.1	20.6	20.2	19.7	19.2	18.6	18.0	17.3	16.6	15.8	15.0	14.0	13.0	11.5	10.1	8.1	6.0	3.6	0.0
OUT OF THE MONEY 25¢	16.6	16.3	16.0	15.7	15.4	15.1	14.8	14.4	14.2	13.8	13.5	13.1	12.6	12.2	11.8	11.4	10.9	10.3	9.8	9.1	8.5	7.8	7.1	6.2	5.3	4.2	2.5	1.6	0.9	0.5	0
50¢	11.0	10.9	10.6	10.3	10.1	9.9	9.6	9.3	9.1	8.8	8.6	8.2	7.9	7.6	7.3	6.9	6.5	6.1	5.8	5.2	4.7	4.2	3.7	3.0	2.4	1.6	0.7	0.3	0.1	0	0
75¢	6.9	6.7	6.5	6.3	6.1	5.9	5.7	5.5	5.3	5.1	4.9	4.6	4.3	4.0	3.8	3.5	3.3	2.9	2.6	2.2	1.9	1.6	1.4	1.1	0.7	0.4	0.1	0	0	0	0
$1.00	4.9	4.8	4.6	4.5	4.3	4.2	4.0	3.8	3.7	3.6	3.4	3.2	3.0	2.8	2.6	2.5	2.3	2.1	1.9	1.7	1.4	1.1	0.9	0.6	0.4	0.2	0.1	0	0	0	0
$1.25	2.9	2.8	2.7	2.5	2.4	2.3	2.2	2.1	2.0	1.9	1.8	1.7	1.6	1.5	1.3	1.2	1.0	0.8	0.7	0.5	0.4	0.3	0.3	0.2	0.1	0	0	0	0	0	0

OPTION VALUES ARE IN CENTS – to nearest tenth.

WM GRANDMILL (1985) LTD.

OPTION VALUES on SOYBEAN FUTURES – Table No: 26

	30	29	28	27	26	25	24	23	22	21	20	19	18	17	16	15	14	13	12	11	10	9	8	7	6	5	4	3	2	1	0
IN THE MONEY $1.25	125.0	125.0	125.0	125.0	125.0	125.0	125.0	125.0	125.0	125.0	125.0	125.0	125.0	125.0	125.0	125.0	125.0	125.0	125.0	125.0	125.0	125.0	125.0	125.0	125.0	125.0	125.0	125.0	125.0	125.0	125.0
$1.00	100.2	100.1	100.1	100.1	100.0	100.0	100.0	100.0	100.0	100.0	100.0	100.0	100.0	100.0	100.0	100.0	100.0	100.0	100.0	100.0	100.0	100.0	100.0	100.0	100.0	100.0	100.0	100.0	100.0	100.0	100.0
75¢	77.2	77.1	77.0	76.9	76.8	76.7	76.6	76.5	76.4	76.3	76.1	76.0	75.9	75.8	75.7	75.6	75.5	75.4	75.3	75.2	75.2	75.2	75.1	75.0	75.0	75.0	75.0	75.0	75.0	75.0	75.0
50¢	57.3	57.1	57.0	56.8	56.7	56.6	56.4	56.2	55.9	55.7	55.4	55.2	54.9	54.7	54.4	54.2	53.9	53.6	53.3	53.0	52.6	52.3	51.8	51.4	50.7	50.4	50.2	50.1	50.0	50.0	50.0
25¢	40.4	40.1	39.8	39.5	39.2	38.9	38.6	38.3	37.9	37.5	37.1	36.7	36.3	35.9	35.5	35.1	34.6	34.1	33.6	33.0	32.3	31.6	30.9	30.1	29.4	28.2	27.2	26.3	25.6	25.2	25.0
AT THE MONEY	27.8	27.5	27.2	26.9	26.5	26.2	25.9	25.5	25.1	24.7	24.2	23.7	23.2	22.7	22.2	21.6	21.1	20.5	19.8	19.1	18.3	17.4	16.5	15.5	14.3	12.7	11.0	8.9	6.6	4.0	0.0
OUT OF THE MONEY 25¢	18.9	18.6	18.3	18.0	17.7	17.4	17.1	16.8	16.4	16.0	15.5	15.0	14.5	14.1	13.6	13.1	12.6	12.1	11.5	10.8	10.0	9.2	8.4	7.4	6.4	5.0	3.3	1.9	0.5	0	0
50¢	12.9	12.6	12.4	12.1	11.9	11.7	11.5	11.2	10.9	10.6	10.2	9.8	9.4	9.0	8.6	8.2	7.8	7.4	7.0	6.5	5.9	5.3	4.6	3.9	3.2	2.2	1.0	0.4	0.1	0	0
75¢	8.7	8.5	8.3	8.1	7.9	7.6	7.3	7.0	6.8	6.5	6.2	5.9	5.6	5.3	5.0	4.6	4.3	3.9	3.6	3.2	2.7	2.3	1.8	1.5	1.2	0.6	0.2	0	0	0	0
$1.00	6.2	6.0	5.9	5.7	5.5	5.4	5.2	5.0	4.8	4.6	4.4	4.1	3.9	3.7	3.5	3.2	3.0	2.8	2.5	2.3	2.0	1.7	1.4	1.0	0.7	0.3	0.1	0	0	0	0
$1.25	3.8	3.6	3.5	3.4	3.2	3.1	3.0	2.9	2.8	2.7	2.5	2.3	2.1	1.9	1.8	1.7	1.6	1.4	1.2	1.0	0.7	0.5	0.4	0.3	0.2	0.1	0	0	0	0	0

WEEKS TO EXPIRATION

OPTION VALUES ARE IN CENTS – to nearest tenth.

WM GRANDMILL (1985) LTD.

OPTION VALUES on SOYBEAN FUTURES – Table No: 25

	30	29	28	27	26	25	24	23	22	21	20	19	18	17	16	15	14	13	12	11	10	9	8	7	6	5	4	3	2	1	0
IN THE MONEY $1.25	125.0	125.0	125.0	125.0	125.0	125.0	125.0	125.0	125.0	125.0	125.0	125.0	125.0	125.0	125.0	125.0	125.0	125.0	125.0	125.0	125.0	125.0	125.0	125.0	125.0	125.0	125.0	125.0	125.0	125.0	125.0
$1.00	100.2	100.2	100.1	100.1	100.1	100.1	100.0	100.0	100.0	100.0	100.0	100.0	100.0	100.0	100.0	100.0	100.0	100.0	100.0	100.0	100.0	100.0	100.0	100.0	100.0	100.0	100.0	100.0	100.0	100.0	100.0
75¢	77.0	76.9	76.8	76.7	76.6	76.5	76.4	76.3	76.2	76.1	76.0	75.9	75.8	75.7	75.6	75.5	75.4	75.3	75.2	75.2	75.2	75.1	75.1	75.0	75.0	75.0	75.0	75.0	75.0	75.0	75.0
50¢	56.9	56.7	56.5	56.3	56.1	55.9	55.7	55.4	55.2	55.0	54.8	54.6	54.3	54.1	53.8	53.6	53.3	53.0	52.7	52.4	51.9	51.5	51.2	50.9	50.6	50.4	50.2	50.0	50.0	50.0	50.0
25¢	39.7	39.4	39.1	38.8	38.5	38.2	37.9	37.6	37.3	36.9	36.5	36.1	35.7	35.3	34.9	34.5	34.1	33.6	33.1	32.5	31.9	31.3	30.6	29.9	29.0	28.0	27.0	26.2	25.5	25.2	25.0
AT THE MONEY	27.0	26.7	26.4	26.1	25.7	25.4	25.1	24.7	24.3	23.9	23.5	23.0	22.5	22.0	21.5	21.0	20.4	19.8	19.2	18.5	17.7	16.9	16.0	15.0	13.8	12.3	10.7	8.7	6.4	3.9	0.0
OUT OF THE MONEY 25¢	18.2	17.9	17.6	17.3	17.0	16.7	16.4	16.0	15.6	15.2	14.8	14.4	13.9	13.5	13.0	12.6	12.0	11.5	10.9	10.2	9.5	8.8	8.0	7.1	6.0	4.6	3.0	1.8	1.0	0.5	0.0
50¢	12.3	12.0	11.8	11.6	11.3	11.1	10.9	10.6	10.3	10.0	9.6	9.3	8.9	8.6	8.2	7.9	7.4	7.0	6.5	6.0	5.5	5.0	4.4	3.7	2.9	1.9	0.9	0.4	0.1	0	0
75¢	8.2	7.9	7.7	7.5	7.2	7.0	6.8	6.5	6.2	6.0	5.7	5.5	5.2	4.9	4.5	4.2	3.9	3.6	3.2	2.8	2.4	2.0	1.7	1.4	1.0	0.5	0.2	0	0	0	0
$1.00	5.8	5.6	5.5	5.3	5.1	5.0	4.8	4.6	4.4	4.2	4.0	3.8	3.6	3.4	3.2	3.0	2.7	2.5	2.3	2.1	1.8	1.5	1.2	0.9	0.5	0.2	0	0	0	0	0
$1.25	3.5	3.4	3.2	3.1	3.0	2.9	2.8	2.7	2.5	2.4	2.2	2.0	1.9	1.8	1.7	1.6	1.4	1.2	1.0	0.8	0.6	0.5	0.4	0.3	0.1	0	0	0	0	0	0

WEEKS TO EXPIRATION

OPTION VALUES ARE IN CENTS – to nearest tenth.

WM GRANDMILL (1985) LTD.

OPTION VALUES on SOYBEAN FUTURES – Table No:28

	30	29	28	27	26	25	24	23	22	21	20	19	18	17	16	15	14	13	12	11	10	9	8	7	6	5	4	3	2	1	0
IN THE MONEY $1.25	125.0	125.0	125.0	125.0	125.0	125.0	125.0	125.0	125.0	125.0	125.0	125.0	125.0	125.0	125.0	125.0	125.0	125.0	125.0	125.0	125.0	125.0	125.0	125.0	125.0	125.0	125.0	125.0	125.0	125.0	125.0
$1.00	100.4	100.4	100.3	100.3	100.3	100.2	100.2	100.2	100.1	100.1	100.0	100.0	100.0	100.0	100.0	100.0	100.0	100.0	100.0	100.0	100.0	100.0	100.0	100.0	100.0	100.0	100.0	100.0	100.0	100.0	100.0
75¢	77.7	77.6	77.5	77.4	77.3	77.2	77.1	77.0	76.8	76.7	76.6	76.4	76.3	76.1	76.0	75.9	75.7	75.6	75.5	75.4	75.3	75.2	75.2	75.1	75.0	75.0	75.0	75.0	75.0	75.0	75.0
50¢	58.3	58.1	57.9	57.7	57.5	57.3	57.1	56.9	56.8	56.6	56.4	56.2	56.1	55.8	55.5	55.1	54.8	54.5	54.2	53.9	53.6	53.2	52.8	52.4	51.9	51.4	51.0	50.6	50.3	50.0	50.0
25¢	41.8	41.5	41.2	40.9	40.6	40.3	40.0	39.7	39.3	38.9	38.5	38.0	37.5	37.0	36.5	36.0	35.5	35.1	34.5	33.9	33.2	32.5	31.7	30.8	29.8	28.7	27.6	26.5	25.6	25.2	25.0
AT THE MONEY	29.5	29.2	28.8	28.5	28.2	27.8	27.4	27.0	26.6	26.2	25.7	25.2	24.7	24.1	23.5	22.9	22.3	21.7	21.0	20.2	19.4	18.5	17.5	16.4	15.1	13.5	11.7	9.5	7.0	4.2	0.0
OUT OF THE MONEY 25¢	20.4	20.1	19.8	19.5	19.2	18.9	18.5	18.2	17.8	17.4	17.0	16.5	16.0	15.4	14.8	14.3	13.7	13.1	12.5	11.8	11.1	10.2	9.3	8.3	7.1	5.7	4.0	2.1	1.2	0.6	0.0
50¢	14.3	14.0	13.7	13.4	13.2	12.9	12.6	12.3	12.0	11.7	11.3	11.0	10.6	10.1	9.6	9.2	8.7	8.3	7.8	7.3	6.7	6.0	5.3	4.6	3.7	2.7	1.4	0.5	0.2	0	0
75¢	9.8	9.6	9.4	9.2	9.0	8.7	8.4	8.1	7.8	7.5	7.2	6.9	6.5	6.1	5.7	5.4	5.0	4.6	4.2	3.8	3.4	2.8	2.3	1.8	1.4	0.9	0.3	0	0	0	0
$1.00	7.1	6.9	6.7	6.5	6.4	6.2	6.0	5.8	5.6	5.4	5.1	4.9	4.6	4.2	4.0	3.8	3.5	3.3	3.0	2.7	2.4	2.1	1.7	1.3	0.9	0.5	0.1	0	0	0	0
$1.25	4.4	4.3	4.2	4.0	3.9	3.8	3.6	3.5	3.3	3.1	3.0	2.8	2.6	2.4	2.2	2.0	1.8	1.7	1.5	1.3	1.1	0.8	0.6	0.4	0.3	0.1	0	0	0	0	0

WEEKS TO EXPIRATION

OPTION VALUES ARE IN CENTS – to nearest tenth.

WM GRANDMILL (1985) LTD.

OPTION VALUES on SOYBEAN FUTURES – Table No:27

	30	29	28	27	26	25	24	23	22	21	20	19	18	17	16	15	14	13	12	11	10	9	8	7	6	5	4	3	2	1	0
IN THE MONEY $1.25	125.0	125.0	125.0	125.0	125.0	125.0	125.0	125.0	125.0	125.0	125.0	125.0	125.0	125.0	125.0	125.0	125.0	125.0	125.0	125.0	125.0	125.0	125.0	125.0	125.0	125.0	125.0	125.0	125.0	125.0	125.0
$1.00	100.3	100.3	100.3	100.3	100.2	100.2	100.2	100.1	100.1	100.0	100.0	100.0	100.0	100.0	100.0	100.0	100.0	100.0	100.0	100.0	100.0	100.0	100.0	100.0	100.0	100.0	100.0	100.0	100.0	100.0	100.0
75¢	77.7	77.6	77.5	77.4	77.3	77.2	77.1	77.0	76.8	76.7	76.6	76.5	76.4	76.2	76.1	76.0	75.9	75.8	75.7	75.6	75.5	75.4	75.3	75.2	75.2	75.1	75.0	75.0	75.0	75.0	75.0
50¢	58.3	58.1	57.9	57.7	57.5	57.3	57.2	57.0	56.8	56.6	56.4	56.2	56.0	55.7	55.4	55.2	54.9	54.5	54.2	53.9	53.6	53.3	52.9	52.5	52.1	51.6	51.2	50.8	50.5	50.3	50.0
25¢	41.2	40.9	40.6	40.3	40.0	39.7	39.3	38.9	38.6	38.2	37.8	37.4	37.0	36.5	36.0	35.5	35.1	34.6	34.0	33.4	32.8	32.2	31.4	30.5	29.6	28.5	27.3	26.4	25.6	25.2	25.0
AT THE MONEY	28.7	28.4	28.0	27.7	27.3	27.0	26.6	26.2	25.8	25.4	25.0	24.5	24.0	23.4	22.8	22.3	21.7	21.1	20.4	19.6	18.8	18.0	17.0	15.9	14.7	13.1	11.3	9.4	6.8	4.1	0.0
OUT OF THE MONEY 25¢	19.7	19.4	19.1	18.8	18.5	18.2	17.8	17.4	17.1	16.7	16.3	15.8	15.3	14.7	14.2	13.7	13.2	12.6	12.0	11.3	10.5	9.8	8.9	7.9	6.8	5.3	3.6	2.1	1.2	0.6	0.0
50¢	13.5	13.3	13.1	12.9	12.6	12.3	12.0	11.7	11.4	11.1	10.8	10.4	10.0	9.5	9.1	8.7	8.3	7.9	7.4	6.8	6.3	5.8	5.1	4.3	3.4	2.8	1.2	0.5	0.2	0	0
75¢	9.3	9.1	8.9	8.6	8.3	8.1	7.8	7.6	7.3	7.0	6.7	6.3	6.0	5.7	5.3	5.0	4.7	4.3	3.9	3.5	3.0	2.6	2.1	1.6	1.3	0.8	0.3	0	0	0	0
$1.00	6.7	6.5	6.3	6.1	5.9	5.8	5.6	5.4	5.2	5.0	4.8	4.6	4.3	4.0	3.8	3.5	3.3	3.0	2.7	2.4	2.2	1.9	1.6	1.2	0.8	0.4	0.1	0	0	0	0
$1.25	4.1	4.0	3.9	3.7	3.6	3.5	3.3	3.1	3.0	2.9	2.8	2.6	2.4	2.2	2.0	1.8	1.7	1.5	1.3	1.1	0.9	0.7	0.5	0.4	0.2	0.1	0	0	0	0	0

WEEKS TO EXPIRATION

OPTION VALUES ARE IN CENTS – to nearest tenth.

WM GRANDMILL (1985) LTD.

OPTION VALUES on SOYBEAN FUTURES – Table No:30

	30	29	28	27	26	25	24	23	22	21	20	19	18	17	16	15	14	13	12	11	10	9	8	7	6	5	4	3	2	1	0
IN THE MONEY $1.25	125.0	125.0	125.0	125.0	125.0	125.0	125.0	125.0	125.0	125.0	125.0	125.0	125.0	125.0	125.0	125.0	125.0	125.0	125.0	125.0	125.0	125.0	125.0	125.0	125.0	125.0	125.0	125.0	125.0	125.0	125.0
$1.00	100.6	100.5	100.5	100.5	100.4	100.4	100.4	100.3	100.3	100.3	100.2	100.2	100.1	100.1	100.0	100.0	100.0	100.0	100.0	100.0	100.0	100.0	100.0	100.0	100.0	100.0	100.0	100.0	100.0	100.0	100.0
75¢	78.3	78.2	78.1	77.9	77.8	77.7	77.6	77.4	77.3	77.1	77.0	76.8	76.7	76.5	76.4	76.2	76.0	75.9	75.7	75.6	75.4	75.3	75.2	75.1	75.1	75.0	75.0	75.0	75.0	75.0	75.0
50¢	59.5	59.3	59.0	58.8	58.5	58.3	58.1	57.8	57.5	57.2	56.9	56.6	56.3	55.9	55.6	55.2	54.9	54.5	54.2	53.8	53.3	52.8	52.3	51.7	51.2	50.8	50.4	50.1	50.0	50.0	50.0
25¢	43.3	43.1	42.8	42.5	42.1	41.7	41.4	41.0	40.6	40.2	39.7	39.3	38.8	38.3	37.8	37.2	36.6	36.1	35.5	34.8	34.1	33.3	32.5	31.5	30.5	29.3	28.0	26.7	25.7	25.3	25.0
AT THE MONEY	31.2	30.9	30.6	30.2	29.8	29.4	29.0	28.6	28.1	27.6	27.1	26.6	26.1	25.5	24.9	24.2	23.6	22.9	22.2	21.4	20.5	19.5	18.5	17.3	16.0	14.2	12.3	10.0	7.4	4.5	0.0
OUT OF THE MONEY 25¢	22.1	21.8	21.5	21.1	20.7	20.3	20.0	19.6	19.1	18.7	18.2	17.8	17.3	16.8	16.2	15.5	14.9	14.3	13.6	12.9	12.1	11.2	10.2	9.1	7.9	6.3	4.6	2.5	1.4	0.6	0
50¢	15.6	15.4	15.1	14.8	14.5	14.2	13.9	13.5	13.1	12.7	12.3	11.9	11.5	11.1	10.7	10.2	9.7	9.2	8.7	8.1	7.4	6.7	6.0	5.2	4.3	3.2	1.9	0.6	0.2	0	0
75¢	11.3	11.1	10.8	10.5	10.2	9.9	9.6	9.2	8.9	8.5	8.2	7.8	7.4	7.0	6.6	6.2	5.8	5.4	5.0	4.5	3.9	3.4	2.8	2.2	1.7	1.1	0.5	0.1	0	0	0
$1.00	8.1	7.9	7.7	7.5	7.2	7.0	6.8	6.6	6.3	6.1	5.8	5.6	5.3	5.0	4.7	4.4	4.1	3.8	3.5	3.2	2.8	2.4	2.1	1.7	1.2	0.6	0.2	0	0	0	0
$1.25	5.1	5.0	4.9	4.7	4.6	4.4	4.3	4.1	3.9	3.7	3.5	3.3	3.1	2.9	2.7	2.5	2.2	2.0	1.8	1.6	1.4	1.1	0.8	0.5	0.4	0.2	0	0	0	0	0

WEEKS TO EXPIRATION

WM GRANDMILL (1985) LTD.

OPTION VALUES ARE IN CENTS – to nearest tenth.

OPTION VALUES on SOYBEAN FUTURES – Table No:29

	30	29	28	27	26	25	24	23	22	21	20	19	18	17	16	15	14	13	12	11	10	9	8	7	6	5	4	3	2	1	0
IN THE MONEY $1.25	125.0	125.0	125.0	125.0	125.0	125.0	125.0	125.0	125.0	125.0	125.0	125.0	125.0	125.0	125.0	125.0	125.0	125.0	125.0	125.0	125.0	125.0	125.0	125.0	125.0	125.0	125.0	125.0	125.0	125.0	125.0
$1.00	100.5	100.5	100.5	100.4	100.4	100.4	100.3	100.3	100.2	100.2	100.2	100.1	100.1	100.0	100.0	100.0	100.0	100.0	100.0	100.0	100.0	100.0	100.0	100.0	100.0	100.0	100.0	100.0	100.0	100.0	100.0
75¢	78.0	77.9	77.8	77.7	77.6	77.4	77.3	77.2	77.1	77.0	76.8	76.7	76.5	76.3	76.1	76.0	75.9	75.7	75.6	75.5	75.4	75.3	75.2	75.1	75.1	75.0	75.0	75.0	75.0	75.0	75.0
50¢	58.9	58.7	58.5	58.3	58.1	57.9	57.6	57.3	57.1	56.8	56.5	56.2	55.9	55.5	55.2	54.9	54.6	54.2	53.9	53.5	53.0	52.6	52.1	51.6	51.1	50.6	50.3	50.1	50.0	50.0	50.0
25¢	42.7	42.4	42.1	41.7	41.4	41.0	40.7	40.4	40.0	39.6	39.1	38.6	38.2	37.7	37.2	36.6	36.1	35.5	35.0	34.5	33.7	33.0	32.2	31.3	30.2	29.0	27.8	26.5	25.7	25.2	25.0
AT THE MONEY	30.4	30.1	29.8	29.4	29.0	28.6	28.2	27.8	27.4	26.9	26.4	25.9	25.4	24.8	24.2	23.6	23.0	22.3	21.6	20.8	19.9	19.0	18.0	16.9	15.6	13.8	12.0	9.7	7.2	4.3	0.0
OUT OF THE MONEY 25¢	21.4	21.1	20.8	20.4	20.0	19.6	19.2	18.9	18.5	18.1	17.6	17.1	16.6	16.1	15.5	14.9	14.3	13.7	13.1	12.4	11.6	10.7	9.8	8.8	7.6	6.0	4.1	2.5	1.3	0.6	0
50¢	14.9	14.7	14.4	14.1	13.8	13.5	13.2	12.9	12.5	12.2	11.8	11.4	11.1	10.7	10.2	9.7	9.2	8.7	8.2	7.7	7.1	6.5	5.8	5.0	4.0	2.9	1.7	0.6	0.2	0	0
75¢	10.6	10.4	10.1	9.8	9.6	9.3	9.0	8.7	8.4	8.1	7.7	7.3	7.0	6.6	6.2	5.8	5.4	5.0	4.6	4.1	3.6	3.1	2.6	2.1	1.5	1.0	0.4	0.1	0	0	0
$1.00	7.6	7.4	7.2	7.0	6.8	6.6	6.4	6.2	6.0	5.7	5.5	5.2	5.0	4.7	4.4	4.1	3.8	3.5	3.2	2.9	2.5	2.2	1.9	1.6	1.1	0.5	0.2	0	0	0	0
$1.25	4.8	4.7	4.6	4.4	4.3	4.1	3.9	3.8	3.6	3.4	3.2	3.0	2.9	2.7	2.5	2.3	2.1	1.9	1.7	1.5	1.2	1.0	0.7	0.5	0.3	0.1	0	0	0	0	0

WEEKS TO EXPIRATION

WM GRANDMILL (1985) LTD.

OPTION VALUES ARE IN CENTS – to nearest tenth.

OPTION VALUES on SOYBEAN FUTURES – Table No: 32

OPTION VALUES ARE IN CENTS – to nearest tenth.

WEEKS TO EXPIRATION

	30	29	28	27	26	25	24	23	22	21	20	19	18	17	16	15	14	13	12	11	10	9	8	7	6	5	4	3	2	1	0
IN THE MONEY $1.25	125.0	125.0	125.0	125.0	125.0	125.0	125.0	125.0	125.0	125.0	125.0	125.0	125.0	125.0	125.0	125.0	125.0	125.0	125.0	125.0	125.0	125.0	125.0	125.0	125.0	125.0	125.0	125.0	125.0	125.0	125.0
$1.00	100.8	100.8	100.7	100.7	100.6	100.6	100.5	100.5	100.4	100.4	100.3	100.3	100.2	100.1	100.1	100.0	100.0	100.0	100.0	100.0	100.0	100.0	100.0	100.0	100.0	100.0	100.0	100.0	100.0	100.0	100.0
75¢	79.0	78.9	78.7	78.6	78.4	78.3	78.1	77.9	77.7	77.6	77.4	77.3	77.1	76.9	76.7	76.6	76.4	76.2	76.0	75.8	75.6	75.4	75.3	75.2	75.1	75.0	75.0	75.0	75.0	75.0	75.0
50¢	60.7	60.4	60.2	59.9	59.6	59.3	59.0	58.7	58.4	58.1	57.8	57.5	57.1	56.8	56.4	56.0	55.6	55.2	54.8	54.3	53.9	53.4	52.8	52.2	51.5	50.9	50.4	50.1	50.0	50.0	50.0
25¢	44.9	44.6	44.2	43.9	43.5	43.2	42.8	42.4	41.9	41.4	41.0	40.6	40.1	39.6	39.0	38.4	37.8	37.1	36.4	35.7	35.0	34.2	33.3	32.3	31.2	29.9	28.5	27.0	25.9	25.3	25.0
AT THE MONEY 25¢	32.9	32.6	32.2	31.8	31.4	31.0	30.6	30.1	29.6	29.1	28.6	28.1	27.5	26.9	26.2	25.6	24.9	24.2	23.4	22.5	21.6	20.6	19.5	18.3	16.8	15.0	13.0	10.6	7.8	4.7	0.0
OUT OF THE MONEY 25¢	23.8	23.5	23.1	22.7	22.3	21.9	21.5	21.0	20.5	20.0	19.6	19.1	18.6	18.1	17.5	16.9	16.2	15.5	14.7	13.9	13.1	12.2	11.2	10.0	8.7	7.1	5.3	2.9	1.5	0.7	0.0
50¢	17.0	16.7	16.4	16.1	15.7	15.4	15.1	14.7	14.3	13.9	13.5	13.1	12.6	12.2	11.7	11.2	10.7	10.2	9.6	8.9	8.2	7.5	6.7	5.9	4.9	3.7	2.4	0.9	0.3	0	0
75¢	12.7	12.4	12.1	11.8	11.5	11.2	10.8	10.4	10.0	9.6	9.2	8.8	8.4	8.0	7.6	7.1	6.7	6.2	5.7	5.1	4.6	4.0	3.4	2.7	2.0	1.4	0.7	0.1	0	0	0
$1.00	9.1	8.9	8.7	8.4	8.2	8.0	7.7	7.4	7.1	6.8	6.6	6.3	6.0	5.7	5.4	5.1	4.7	4.4	4.0	3.6	3.2	2.8	2.4	2.0	1.5	0.9	0.4	0	0	0	0
$1.25	5.9	5.8	5.6	5.4	5.2	5.1	4.9	4.7	4.5	4.3	4.1	3.9	3.6	3.4	3.1	2.9	2.7	2.4	2.1	1.9	1.7	1.4	1.1	0.7	0.4	0.2	0.2	0	0	0	0

WM GRANDMILL (1985) LTD.

OPTION VALUES on SOYBEAN FUTURES – Table No: 31

OPTION VALUES ARE IN CENTS – to nearest tenth.

WEEKS TO EXPIRATION

	30	29	28	27	26	25	24	23	22	21	20	19	18	17	16	15	14	13	12	11	10	9	8	7	6	5	4	3	2	1	0
IN THE MONEY $1.25	125.0	125.0	125.0	125.0	125.0	125.0	125.0	125.0	125.0	125.0	125.0	125.0	125.0	125.0	125.0	125.0	125.0	125.0	125.0	125.0	125.0	125.0	125.0	125.0	125.0	125.0	125.0	125.0	125.0	125.0	125.0
$1.00	100.8	100.7	100.7	100.7	100.6	100.6	100.5	100.5	100.4	100.3	100.3	100.2	100.2	100.1	100.0	100.0	100.0	100.0	100.0	100.0	100.0	100.0	100.0	100.0	100.0	100.0	100.0	100.0	100.0	100.0	100.0
75¢	78.7	78.5	78.4	78.3	78.1	77.9	77.8	77.6	77.5	77.4	77.2	77.0	76.9	76.7	76.5	76.4	76.2	76.0	75.8	75.7	75.5	75.4	75.3	75.2	75.1	75.0	75.0	75.0	75.0	75.0	75.0
50¢	60.1	59.8	59.5	59.2	59.0	58.8	58.5	58.2	58.0	57.7	57.4	57.1	56.8	56.4	56.0	55.6	55.2	54.9	54.5	54.0	53.6	53.1	52.6	52.0	51.4	50.8	50.4	50.1	50.0	50.0	50.0
25¢	44.1	43.8	43.5	43.2	42.9	42.5	42.1	41.7	41.3	40.9	40.5	40.0	39.5	38.9	38.3	37.8	37.2	36.6	36.0	35.3	34.6	34.8	33.0	32.0	30.8	29.6	28.2	26.8	25.8	25.3	25.0
AT THE MONEY 25¢	32.1	31.7	31.3	31.0	30.6	30.2	29.8	29.3	28.9	28.4	27.9	27.3	26.8	26.2	25.5	24.9	24.3	23.6	22.8	21.9	21.0	20.1	19.0	17.8	16.4	14.6	12.7	10.3	7.6	4.6	0.0
OUT OF THE MONEY 25¢	23.0	22.7	22.3	21.9	21.5	21.1	20.7	20.3	19.9	19.4	19.0	18.5	18.0	17.4	16.8	16.2	15.6	14.9	14.2	13.4	12.6	11.7	10.7	9.6	8.3	6.7	5.0	2.7	1.4	0.6	0
50¢	16.3	16.0	15.7	15.4	15.1	14.9	14.5	14.1	13.8	13.4	13.0	12.6	12.1	11.7	11.3	10.8	10.2	9.7	9.1	8.5	7.9	7.2	6.5	5.6	4.6	3.4	2.2	0.7	0.3	0	0
75¢	12.0	11.7	11.4	11.1	10.8	10.5	10.2	9.9	9.5	9.1	8.8	8.4	8.0	7.6	7.2	6.7	6.2	5.8	5.3	4.8	4.3	3.8	3.2	2.5	1.8	1.2	0.6	0.1	0	0	0
$1.00	8.6	8.4	8.2	8.0	7.7	7.5	7.2	6.9	6.7	6.5	6.2	5.9	5.7	5.4	5.0	4.7	4.4	4.1	3.7	3.4	3.0	2.6	2.2	1.8	1.3	0.8	0.3	0	0	0	0
$1.25	5.5	5.4	5.2	5.1	4.9	4.7	4.6	4.4	4.2	4.0	3.8	3.6	3.4	3.2	3.0	2.8	2.5	2.2	2.0	1.7	1.5	1.3	1.0	0.7	0.4	0.2	0	0	0	0	0

WM GRANDMILL (1985) LTD.

OPTION VALUES on SOYBEAN FUTURES – Table No: 34

WEEKS TO EXPIRATION	IN $1.25	IN $1.00	IN 75¢	IN 50¢	IN 25¢	AT THE MONEY	OUT 25¢	OUT 50¢	OUT 75¢	OUT $1.00	OUT $1.25
30	125.0	101.2	79.7	61.8	46.4	34.6	25.4	18.3	14.0	10.1	6.8
29	125.0	101.1	79.5	61.6	46.0	34.2	25.0	18.0	13.7	9.9	6.6
28	125.0	101.0	79.4	61.3	45.7	33.8	24.7	17.7	13.4	9.6	6.4
27	125.0	101.0	79.2	61.0	45.4	33.4	24.3	17.4	13.1	9.4	6.2
26	125.0	100.9	79.1	60.7	45.0	33.0	23.9	17.1	12.8	9.2	6.0
25	125.0	100.8	78.9	60.4	44.6	32.6	23.5	16.7	12.4	8.9	5.8
24	125.0	100.7	78.7	60.1	44.1	32.1	23.0	16.3	12.0	8.6	5.5
23	125.0	100.6	78.5	59.7	43.7	31.6	22.5	15.9	11.6	8.3	5.3
22	125.0	100.6	78.3	59.4	43.2	31.1	22.0	15.5	11.2	8.0	5.1
21	125.0	100.5	78.1	59.0	42.8	30.6	21.5	15.1	10.8	7.7	4.9
20	125.0	100.5	77.9	58.7	42.3	30.1	21.0	14.7	10.4	7.4	4.7
19	125.0	100.4	77.7	58.3	41.8	29.5	20.4	14.2	9.9	7.0	4.4
18	125.0	100.3	77.5	58.0	41.3	28.9	19.8	13.7	9.5	6.7	4.2
17	125.0	100.3	77.3	57.6	40.7	28.2	19.2	13.2	9.0	6.4	3.9
16	125.0	100.2	77.1	57.2	40.2	27.6	18.7	12.7	8.5	6.1	3.7
15	125.0	100.1	76.9	56.8	39.6	26.9	18.1	12.2	8.1	5.7	3.4
14	125.0	100.1	76.7	56.4	38.9	26.2	17.4	11.7	7.6	5.4	3.1
13	125.0	100.0	76.5	55.9	38.2	25.4	16.7	11.1	7.0	5.0	2.9
12	125.0	100.0	76.3	55.4	37.5	24.6	15.9	10.5	6.4	4.6	2.6
11	125.0	100.0	76.0	54.9	36.7	23.7	15.0	9.8	5.8	4.1	2.3
10	125.0	100.0	75.7	54.4	35.9	22.7	14.1	9.0	5.2	3.7	2.0
9	125.0	100.0	75.5	53.9	35.0	21.6	13.1	8.2	4.6	3.2	1.7
8	125.0	100.0	75.4	53.3	34.1	20.5	12.1	7.4	3.9	2.8	1.4
7	125.0	100.0	75.3	52.6	33.1	19.2	10.9	6.5	3.3	2.3	1.0
6	125.0	100.0	75.2	51.9	31.9	17.7	9.5	5.5	2.4	1.8	0.6
5	125.0	100.0	75.1	51.1	30.3	15.7	7.7	4.1	1.6	1.2	0.3
4	125.0	100.0	75.0	50.6	28.9	13.7	5.9	2.8	1.0	0.5	0.1
3	125.0	100.0	75.0	50.2	27.2	11.1	3.4	1.1	0.2	0.1	0
2	125.0	100.0	75.0	50.0	26.0	8.2	1.6	0.3	0	0	0
1	125.0	100.0	75.0	50.0	25.3	4.9	0.7	0	0	0	0
0	125.0	100.0	75.0	50.0	25.0	0.0	0	0	0	0	0

OPTION VALUES ARE IN CENTS – to nearest tenth.

WM GRANDMILL (1985) LTD.

OPTION VALUES on SOYBEAN FUTURES – Table No: 33

WEEKS TO EXPIRATION	IN $1.25	IN $1.00	IN 75¢	IN 50¢	IN 25¢	AT THE MONEY	OUT 25¢	OUT 50¢	OUT 75¢	OUT $1.00	OUT $1.25
30	125.0	101.0	79.4	61.3	45.7	33.8	24.7	17.7	13.4	9.6	6.4
29	125.0	101.0	79.2	61.0	45.3	33.4	24.3	17.3	13.0	9.4	6.2
28	125.0	100.9	79.1	60.8	45.0	33.0	23.9	17.1	12.8	9.2	6.0
27	125.0	100.9	78.9	60.4	44.6	32.6	23.5	16.7	12.4	8.9	5.8
26	125.0	100.8	78.7	60.2	44.2	32.2	23.1	16.4	12.1	8.7	5.6
25	125.0	100.7	78.6	59.9	43.9	31.8	22.7	16.1	11.8	8.4	5.4
24	125.0	100.6	78.4	59.5	43.5	31.3	22.2	15.6	11.4	8.1	5.2
23	125.0	100.6	78.2	59.3	43.1	30.9	21.8	15.4	11.1	7.9	5.0
22	125.0	100.5	78.0	58.9	42.7	30.4	21.3	14.9	10.6	7.6	4.8
21	125.0	100.5	77.8	58.6	42.2	29.9	20.8	14.6	10.3	7.3	4.6
20	125.0	100.4	77.7	58.3	41.7	29.4	20.3	14.1	9.8	7.0	4.4
19	125.0	100.3	77.5	57.9	41.2	28.8	19.8	13.7	9.4	6.7	4.2
18	125.0	100.3	77.3	57.5	40.7	28.2	19.2	13.2	9.0	6.4	3.9
17	125.0	100.2	77.1	57.1	40.1	27.5	18.6	12.6	8.5	6.0	3.6
16	125.0	100.1	76.9	56.8	39.6	26.9	18.1	12.2	8.1	5.7	3.4
15	125.0	100.1	76.7	56.4	38.9	26.2	17.4	11.7	7.6	5.4	3.1
14	125.0	100.0	76.5	55.9	38.3	25.5	16.8	11.1	7.0	5.0	2.9
13	125.0	100.0	76.3	55.5	37.7	24.8	16.1	10.7	6.6	4.7	2.7
12	125.0	100.0	76.1	55.1	37.0	24.0	15.3	10.1	6.1	4.3	2.4
11	125.0	100.0	75.9	54.6	36.2	23.1	14.4	9.3	5.5	3.8	2.0
10	125.0	100.0	75.7	54.1	35.4	22.1	13.5	8.6	4.9	3.4	1.8
9	125.0	100.0	75.5	53.6	34.6	21.1	12.6	7.9	4.3	3.0	1.6
8	125.0	100.0	75.4	53.1	33.8	20.0	11.7	7.2	3.7	2.6	1.3
7	125.0	100.0	75.3	52.5	32.7	18.7	10.4	6.2	2.9	2.1	0.9
6	125.0	100.0	75.2	51.8	31.6	17.4	9.2	5.3	2.3	1.7	0.5
5	125.0	100.0	75.1	51.2	30.4	15.8	7.8	4.2	1.6	1.1	0.3
4	125.0	100.0	75.1	50.5	28.7	13.4	5.6	2.6	0.9	0.5	0.1
3	125.0	100.0	75.0	50.2	27.1	10.8	3.1	0.9	0.2	0	0
2	125.0	100.0	75.0	50.0	25.9	8.0	1.6	0.2	0	0	0
1	125.0	100.0	75.0	50.0	25.3	4.8	0.7	0	0	0	0
0	125.0	100.0	75.0	50.0	25.0	0.0	0	0	0	0	0

OPTION VALUES ARE IN CENTS – to nearest tenth.

WM GRANDMILL (1985) LTD.

OPTION VALUES on SOYBEAN FUTURES – Table No:36

WEEKS TO EXPIRATION

	30	29	28	27	26	25	24	23	22	21	20	19	18	17	16	15	14	13	12	11	10	9	8	7	6	5	4	3	2	1	0
IN THE MONEY $1.25	125.1	125.0	125.0	125.0	125.0	125.0	125.0	125.0	125.0	125.0	125.0	125.0	125.0	125.0	125.0	125.0	125.0	125.0	125.0	125.0	125.0	125.0	125.0	125.0	125.0	125.0	125.0	125.0	125.0	125.0	125.0
$1.00	101.5	101.4	101.3	101.3	101.2	101.1	101.0	101.0	100.9	100.8	100.7	100.6	100.5	100.5	100.4	100.3	100.3	100.2	100.1	100.1	100.0	100.0	100.0	100.0	100.0	100.0	100.0	100.0	100.0	100.0	100.0
75¢	80.4	80.2	80.0	79.9	79.7	79.5	79.3	79.1	78.9	78.7	78.4	78.2	78.0	77.7	77.5	77.3	77.1	76.8	76.6	76.3	76.0	75.8	75.6	75.4	75.2	75.1	75.0	75.0	75.0	75.0	75.0
50¢	63.0	62.8	62.5	62.2	61.9	61.6	61.2	60.9	60.5	60.1	59.6	59.2	58.8	58.4	58.0	57.6	57.1	56.6	56.1	55.5	55.0	54.4	53.8	53.1	52.4	51.6	50.8	50.3	50.0	50.0	50.0
25¢	47.9	47.6	47.2	46.8	46.4	46.0	45.6	45.1	44.6	44.1	43.6	43.1	42.5	41.9	41.3	40.7	40.0	39.3	38.5	37.7	36.8	35.9	34.9	33.8	32.6	30.9	29.4	27.5	26.1	25.3	25.0
AT THE MONEY	36.3	35.9	35.4	35.0	34.6	34.2	33.7	33.2	32.7	32.1	31.5	30.9	30.3	29.6	28.9	28.2	27.5	26.7	25.8	24.8	23.8	22.7	21.5	20.1	18.6	16.5	14.3	11.6	8.6	5.2	0.0
OUT OF THE MONEY 25¢	27.1	26.7	26.2	25.8	25.4	25.0	24.6	24.1	23.6	23.0	22.4	21.8	21.2	20.5	19.9	19.3	18.6	17.8	17.0	16.1	15.1	14.1	13.0	11.7	10.3	8.4	6.4	3.9	1.8	0.8	0
50¢	19.7	19.5	19.2	18.8	18.4	18.0	17.6	17.2	16.8	16.3	15.8	15.3	14.8	14.3	13.8	13.2	12.6	12.0	11.4	10.7	9.9	9.0	8.1	7.2	6.1	4.6	3.2	1.4	0.4	0	0
75¢	15.5	15.2	14.9	14.5	14.1	13.7	13.3	12.9	12.5	12.0	11.5	11.0	10.5	10.0	9.5	9.0	8.4	7.9	7.3	6.6	5.9	5.2	4.5	3.7	2.9	1.8	1.2	0.3	0	0	0
$1.00	11.1	10.9	10.6	10.4	10.1	9.9	9.6	9.3	8.9	8.6	8.2	7.9	7.5	7.1	6.7	6.4	6.0	5.6	5.2	4.7	4.2	3.7	3.2	2.6	2.1	1.4	0.7	0.1	0	0	0
$1.25	7.6	7.4	7.2	7.0	6.8	6.6	6.3	6.1	5.8	5.5	5.2	5.0	4.8	4.5	4.2	3.9	3.6	3.3	3.0	2.7	2.3	2.0	1.7	1.3	0.8	0.4	0.2	0	0	0	0

OPTION VALUES ARE IN CENTS – to nearest tenth.

WM GRANDMILL (1985) LTD.

OPTION VALUES on SOYBEAN FUTURES – Table No:35

WEEKS TO EXPIRATION

	30	29	28	27	26	25	24	23	22	21	20	19	18	17	16	15	14	13	12	11	10	9	8	7	6	5	4	3	2	1	0
OUT OF THE MONEY $1.25	7.2	7.0	6.8	6.6	6.4	6.2	5.9	5.7	5.4	5.2	5.0	4.7	4.5	4.2	3.9	3.7	3.4	3.1	2.8	2.5	2.1	1.8	1.5	1.2	0.7	0.4	0.2	0	0	0	0
$1.00	10.6	10.4	10.1	9.9	9.6	9.4	9.1	8.8	8.5	8.2	7.8	7.5	7.1	6.7	6.4	6.1	5.7	5.3	4.9	4.4	3.9	3.5	3.0	2.5	1.9	1.2	0.6	0.1	0	0	0
75¢	14.7	14.4	14.1	13.7	13.4	13.0	12.7	12.3	11.9	11.4	11.0	10.5	10.0	9.5	9.0	8.5	8.0	7.5	6.9	6.2	5.6	5.0	4.3	3.5	2.6	1.7	1.1	0.3	0	0	0
50¢	19.0	18.7	18.4	18.0	17.7	17.3	17.0	16.6	16.2	15.7	15.3	14.8	14.3	13.8	13.2	12.7	12.1	11.6	10.9	10.2	9.4	8.7	7.9	6.9	5.8	4.4	3.0	1.2	0.4	0	0
25¢	26.2	25.8	25.4	25.0	24.7	24.2	23.8	23.3	22.8	22.3	21.7	21.1	20.5	19.9	19.3	18.7	18.0	17.3	16.5	15.5	14.6	13.6	12.6	11.5	9.8	8.0	6.2	3.7	1.7	0.8	0
AT THE MONEY	35.4	35.0	34.6	34.2	33.8	33.4	32.9	32.4	31.9	31.4	30.8	30.2	29.6	28.9	28.2	27.5	26.8	26.0	25.2	24.2	23.3	22.2	21.0	19.7	18.1	16.1	14.0	11.4	8.4	5.1	0.0
IN THE MONEY 25¢	47.1	46.8	46.4	46.0	45.7	45.3	44.9	44.4	44.0	43.5	43.0	42.5	41.9	41.3	40.8	40.2	39.5	38.8	38.0	37.1	36.3	35.5	34.6	33.5	32.2	30.6	29.2	27.4	26.1	25.3	25.0
50¢	62.4	62.2	61.9	61.6	61.3	61.0	60.7	60.3	60.0	59.6	59.2	58.8	58.4	58.0	57.6	57.2	56.8	56.3	55.8	55.2	54.7	54.2	53.6	52.9	52.1	51.3	50.6	50.3	50.0	50.0	50.0
75¢	80.0	79.9	79.7	79.5	79.4	79.2	79.0	78.8	78.6	78.4	78.2	77.9	77.7	77.5	77.3	77.1	76.9	76.7	76.4	76.1	75.9	75.7	75.5	75.3	75.2	75.1	75.0	75.0	75.0	75.0	75.0
$1.00	101.4	101.3	101.2	101.1	101.0	100.9	100.8	100.7	100.7	100.6	100.6	100.5	100.5	100.4	100.3	100.3	100.2	100.1	100.1	100.0	100.0	100.0	100.0	100.0	100.0	100.0	100.0	100.0	100.0	100.0	100.0
$1.25	125.0	125.0	125.0	125.0	125.0	125.0	125.0	125.0	125.0	125.0	125.0	125.0	125.0	125.0	125.0	125.0	125.0	125.0	125.0	125.0	125.0	125.0	125.0	125.0	125.0	125.0	125.0	125.0	125.0	125.0	125.0

OPTION VALUES ARE IN CENTS – to nearest tenth.

WM GRANDMILL (1985) LTD.

OPTION VALUES on SOYBEAN FUTURES – Table No: 38

	30	29	28	27	26	25	24	23	22	21	20	19	18	17	16	15	14	13	12	11	10	9	8	7	6	5	4	3	2	1	0
IN THE MONEY $1.25	125.4	125.3	125.2	125.2	125.1	125.1	125.0	125.0	125.0	125.0	125.0	125.0	125.0	125.0	125.0	125.0	125.0	125.0	125.0	125.0	125.0	125.0	125.0	125.0	125.0	125.0	125.0	125.0	125.0	125.0	125.0
$1.00	101.9	101.8	101.7	101.7	101.6	101.5	101.4	101.3	101.2	101.1	101.0	100.9	100.8	100.7	100.6	100.5	100.4	100.3	100.2	100.2	100.1	100.1	100.0	100.0	100.0	100.0	100.0	100.0	100.0	100.0	100.0
75¢	81.2	80.9	80.7	80.5	80.3	80.1	79.9	79.7	79.5	79.3	79.1	78.8	78.5	78.3	78.0	77.7	77.5	77.2	77.0	76.7	76.4	76.0	75.8	75.5	75.3	75.2	75.0	75.0	75.0	75.0	75.0
50¢	64.4	64.0	63.7	63.4	63.0	62.6	62.3	61.9	61.6	61.1	60.8	60.3	59.8	59.4	58.8	58.3	57.7	57.4	56.9	56.3	55.6	55.0	54.3	53.6	52.8	52.0	51.0	50.4	50.1	50.0	50.0
25¢	49.5	49.0	48.6	48.3	47.8	47.4	46.9	46.5	46.0	45.5	45.0	44.4	43.8	43.2	42.6	41.8	41.1	40.5	39.7	38.8	37.8	36.8	35.7	34.6	33.3	32.0	29.9	27.9	26.3	25.4	25.0
AT THE MONEY	38.0	37.5	37.1	36.7	36.2	35.7	35.2	34.7	34.2	33.6	33.0	32.4	31.7	31.0	30.3	29.5	28.7	27.9	27.0	26.0	24.9	23.8	22.5	21.1	19.5	17.8	15.1	12.2	9.0	5.4	0.0
OUT OF THE MONEY 25¢	28.8	28.3	27.9	27.5	27.0	26.5	26.0	25.5	25.0	24.5	23.9	23.3	22.6	21.9	21.2	20.4	19.7	19.0	18.2	17.3	16.2	15.1	13.9	12.6	11.2	9.6	7.1	4.5	1.9	0.8	0.0
50¢	21.3	20.8	20.4	20.1	19.7	19.3	18.9	18.5	18.0	17.5	17.1	16.5	16.0	15.5	14.8	14.2	13.6	13.0	12.3	11.6	10.8	9.9	8.8	7.9	6.7	5.6	3.7	1.8	0.4	0	0
75¢	17.1	16.6	16.2	15.9	15.4	15.0	14.6	14.2	13.7	13.2	12.8	12.2	11.7	11.2	10.5	9.9	9.3	8.8	8.2	7.5	6.7	5.9	5.1	4.3	3.4	2.5	1.4	0.5	0	0	0
$1.00	12.3	11.8	11.6	11.3	11.1	10.7	10.5	10.1	9.9	9.5	9.2	8.8	8.3	8.0	7.5	7.0	6.6	6.2	5.8	5.3	4.7	4.2	3.6	3.0	2.4	1.8	0.9	0.2	0	0	0
$1.25	8.5	8.2	8.0	7.8	7.6	7.3	7.1	6.8	6.6	6.3	6.0	5.7	5.3	5.1	4.8	4.4	4.1	3.8	3.5	3.1	2.8	2.3	1.9	1.6	1.1	0.6	0.3	0	0	0	0

WEEKS TO EXPIRATION

OPTION VALUES ARE IN CENTS – to nearest tenth.

WM GRANDMILL (1985) LTD.

OPTION VALUES on SOYBEAN FUTURES – Table No: 37

	30	29	28	27	26	25	24	23	22	21	20	19	18	17	16	15	14	13	12	11	10	9	8	7	6	5	4	3	2	1	0
IN THE MONEY $1.25	125.2	125.2	125.1	125.1	125.0	125.0	125.0	125.0	125.0	125.0	125.0	125.0	125.0	125.0	125.0	125.0	125.0	125.0	125.0	125.0	125.0	125.0	125.0	125.0	125.0	125.0	125.0	125.0	125.0	125.0	125.0
$1.00	101.7	101.6	101.5	101.4	101.3	101.2	101.1	101.0	100.9	100.8	100.7	100.6	100.5	100.4	100.3	100.2	100.1	100.0	100.0	100.0	100.0	100.0	100.0	100.0	100.0	100.0	100.0	100.0	100.0	100.0	100.0
75¢	80.7	80.7	80.5	80.3	80.2	80.0	79.8	79.6	79.4	79.2	79.0	78.8	78.5	78.3	78.0	77.7	77.5	77.3	77.0	76.8	76.5	76.2	75.9	75.7	75.5	75.3	75.1	75.0	75.0	75.0	75.0
50¢	63.7	63.4	63.0	62.7	62.4	62.1	61.7	61.4	61.0	60.7	60.2	59.8	59.4	58.9	58.4	57.9	57.5	57.0	56.5	55.9	55.3	54.7	54.1	53.4	52.6	51.5	50.8	50.3	50.0	50.0	50.0
25¢	48.6	48.2	47.8	47.5	47.1	46.7	46.2	45.8	45.3	44.9	44.4	43.8	43.2	42.6	41.9	41.2	40.6	39.9	39.1	38.2	37.3	36.3	35.4	34.2	33.0	31.3	29.6	27.7	26.2	25.3	25.0
AT THE MONEY	37.1	36.7	36.2	35.8	35.4	34.9	34.4	33.9	33.4	32.9	32.3	31.7	31.0	30.3	29.6	28.8	28.1	27.3	26.4	25.4	24.4	23.2	22.0	20.6	19.0	16.9	14.7	11.9	8.8	5.3	0.0
OUT OF THE MONEY 25¢	27.9	27.5	27.0	26.6	26.2	25.7	25.2	24.8	24.3	23.8	23.2	22.6	21.9	21.2	20.5	19.8	19.1	18.4	17.6	16.7	15.7	14.5	13.5	12.2	10.7	8.8	6.8	4.2	1.8	0.8	0.0
50¢	20.4	20.1	19.7	19.4	19.0	18.6	18.2	17.8	17.4	17.0	16.5	16.0	15.5	14.9	14.3	13.7	13.1	12.4	11.8	11.1	10.3	9.4	8.6	7.5	6.5	5.0	3.4	1.6	0.4	0	0
75¢	16.2	15.9	15.5	15.1	14.7	14.3	13.9	13.5	13.1	12.7	12.2	11.7	11.2	10.6	10.0	9.4	8.9	8.3	7.7	7.0	6.3	5.6	4.9	4.0	3.2	2.0	1.3	0.8	0.2	0	0
$1.00	11.6	11.3	11.1	10.8	10.6	10.3	10.0	9.7	9.4	9.1	8.7	8.3	7.9	7.5	7.1	6.7	6.3	5.9	5.5	5.0	4.5	3.9	3.4	2.8	2.2	1.5	0.8	0.2	0	0	0
$1.25	8.0	7.8	7.6	7.4	7.2	6.9	6.7	6.4	6.2	5.9	5.6	5.3	5.1	4.8	4.5	4.2	3.9	3.6	3.2	2.9	2.5	2.1	1.8	1.5	1.0	0.5	0.2	0	0	0	0

WEEKS TO EXPIRATION

OPTION VALUES ARE IN CENTS – to nearest tenth.

WM GRANDMILL (1985) LTD.

OPTION VALUES on SOYBEAN FUTURES — Table No: 40

OPTION VALUES ARE IN CENTS – to nearest tenth.

	WEEKS TO EXPIRATION																														
	30	29	28	27	26	25	24	23	22	21	20	19	18	17	16	15	14	13	12	11	10	9	8	7	6	5	4	3	2	1	0
IN THE MONEY $1.25	125.7	125.6	125.5	125.5	125.4	125.3	125.2	125.1	125.1	125.0	125.0	125.0	125.0	125.0	125.0	125.0	125.0	125.0	125.0	125.0	125.0	125.0	125.0	125.0	125.0	125.0	125.0	125.0	125.0	125.0	125.0
IN THE MONEY $1.00	102.2	102.1	102.0	101.9	101.9	101.8	101.7	101.6	101.5	101.4	101.3	101.2	101.0	100.9	100.8	100.7	100.6	100.5	100.4	100.3	100.2	100.1	100.0	100.0	100.0	100.0	100.0	100.0	100.0	100.0	100.0
IN THE MONEY 75¢	82.0	81.8	81.6	81.3	81.2	81.1	80.9	80.7	80.5	80.3	80.0	79.8	79.6	79.4	79.1	78.8	78.5	78.2	77.9	77.6	77.3	77.0	76.7	76.3	76.0	75.7	75.4	75.2	75.0	75.0	75.0
IN THE MONEY 50¢	65.5	65.2	64.9	64.5	64.3	64.2	63.7	63.4	63.0	62.6	62.2	61.7	61.3	60.8	60.3	59.7	59.2	58.7	58.1	57.6	57.0	56.3	55.5	54.8	54.1	53.2	52.1	51.1	50.4	50.1	50.0
IN THE MONEY 25¢	50.9	50.5	50.1	49.7	49.3	48.8	48.4	47.9	47.4	46.8	46.3	45.7	45.0	44.4	43.8	43.1	42.3	41.5	40.7	39.8	38.8	37.7	36.5	35.4	33.9	32.2	30.3	28.2	26.4	25.4	25.0
AT THE MONEY	39.6	39.2	38.8	38.3	37.8	37.3	36.8	36.3	35.7	35.1	34.5	33.8	33.1	32.4	31.6	30.8	30.0	29.1	28.2	27.1	26.0	24.8	23.5	22.0	20.3	18.0	15.7	12.7	9.4	5.7	0.0
OUT OF THE MONEY 25¢	30.3	29.9	29.5	29.1	28.6	28.1	27.6	27.1	26.5	25.9	25.3	24.7	24.0	23.3	22.5	21.7	20.9	20.0	19.2	18.3	17.3	16.1	14.8	13.5	11.9	9.8	7.7	5.0	2.1	0.9	0
OUT OF THE MONEY 50¢	22.7	22.3	21.9	21.5	21.1	20.6	20.2	19.7	19.3	18.8	18.3	17.7	17.1	16.5	15.9	15.3	14.6	13.9	13.2	12.4	11.6	10.7	9.6	8.6	7.3	5.8	4.1	2.2	0.5	0.5	0
OUT OF THE MONEY 75¢	18.4	18.0	17.6	17.2	16.8	16.4	16.0	15.5	15.0	14.5	14.0	13.4	12.8	12.2	11.6	11.0	10.4	9.7	9.0	8.2	7.5	6.6	5.7	4.9	3.8	2.6	1.6	0.6	0	0	0
OUT OF THE MONEY $1.00	13.4	13.1	12.8	12.4	12.1	11.7	11.4	11.1	10.7	10.4	10.0	9.6	9.2	8.8	8.3	7.8	7.3	6.8	6.4	5.9	5.3	4.7	4.0	3.4	2.7	1.9	1.1	0.3	0.3	0	0
OUT OF THE MONEY $1.25	9.3	9.1	8.9	8.6	8.4	8.1	7.9	7.6	7.3	7.0	6.7	6.4	6.0	5.7	5.3	5.0	4.7	4.3	3.9	3.5	3.1	2.7	2.2	1.8	1.4	0.7	0.3	0	0	0	0

WM GRANDMILL (1985) LTD.

OPTION VALUES on SOYBEAN FUTURES — Table No: 39

OPTION VALUES ARE IN CENTS – to nearest tenth.

	WEEKS TO EXPIRATION																														
	30	29	28	27	26	25	24	23	22	21	20	19	18	17	16	15	14	13	12	11	10	9	8	7	6	5	4	3	2	1	0
IN THE MONEY $1.25	125.5	125.4	125.5	125.3	125.4	125.3	125.2	125.1	125.1	125.0	125.0	125.0	125.0	125.0	125.0	125.0	125.0	125.0	125.0	125.0	125.0	125.0	125.0	125.0	125.0	125.0	125.0	125.0	125.0	125.0	125.0
IN THE MONEY $1.00	102.0	101.9	101.9	101.8	101.8	101.7	101.6	101.6	101.5	101.4	101.2	101.1	101.0	100.9	100.8	100.7	100.6	100.5	100.4	100.3	100.2	100.1	100.0	100.0	100.0	100.0	100.0	100.0	100.0	100.0	100.0
IN THE MONEY 75¢	81.6	81.4	81.2	80.9	80.7	80.5	80.3	80.0	79.8	79.6	79.4	79.1	78.8	78.5	78.2	77.9	77.7	77.4	77.1	76.8	76.5	76.2	75.9	75.6	75.4	75.2	75.0	75.0	75.0	75.0	75.0
IN THE MONEY 50¢	64.9	64.6	64.3	64.0	63.7	63.3	62.9	62.5	62.1	61.7	61.3	60.8	60.3	59.8	59.3	58.8	58.3	57.7	57.2	56.6	55.9	55.2	54.6	53.9	53.0	52.0	51.0	50.4	50.1	50.0	50.0
IN THE MONEY 25¢	50.2	49.8	49.4	49.0	48.6	48.1	47.7	47.2	46.7	46.2	45.7	45.0	44.4	43.8	43.1	42.4	41.7	41.0	40.2	39.3	38.3	37.2	36.2	35.0	33.7	32.0	30.0	28.0	26.4	25.4	25.0
AT THE MONEY	38.8	38.4	38.0	37.5	37.0	36.5	36.0	35.5	34.9	34.4	33.8	33.1	32.4	31.7	30.9	30.1	29.4	28.5	27.6	26.6	25.5	24.3	23.0	21.6	19.9	17.8	15.3	12.4	9.2	5.5	0.0
OUT OF THE MONEY 25¢	29.6	29.2	28.8	28.3	27.8	27.3	26.8	26.3	25.7	25.2	24.6	24.0	23.3	22.6	21.8	21.1	20.3	19.5	18.7	17.8	16.8	15.6	14.4	13.1	11.6	9.6	7.3	4.7	2.0	0.8	0
OUT OF THE MONEY 50¢	22.0	21.6	21.2	20.8	20.4	20.0	19.6	19.2	18.7	18.2	17.7	17.1	16.5	16.0	15.4	14.8	14.1	13.4	12.7	11.9	11.1	10.2	9.3	8.2	7.1	5.6	3.8	2.0	0.5	0	0
OUT OF THE MONEY 75¢	17.7	17.3	17.0	16.6	16.2	15.7	15.3	14.8	14.4	13.9	13.4	12.8	12.2	11.7	11.1	10.4	9.8	9.1	8.5	7.8	7.0	6.2	5.5	4.6	3.6	2.5	1.4	1.0	0.5	0	0
OUT OF THE MONEY $1.00	12.8	12.5	12.2	11.9	11.6	11.3	11.0	10.6	10.3	10.0	9.6	9.2	8.8	8.4	7.9	7.4	7.0	6.5	6.1	5.6	5.0	4.4	3.8	3.2	2.5	1.8	1.0	0.5	0	0	0
OUT OF THE MONEY $1.25	8.9	8.7	8.5	8.2	8.0	7.7	7.5	7.2	6.9	6.7	6.4	6.0	5.7	5.4	5.0	4.7	4.4	4.0	3.7	3.3	2.9	2.5	2.0	1.7	1.2	0.6	0.3	0	0	0	0

WM GRANDMILL (1985) LTD.

OPTION VALUES on SOYBEAN FUTURES – Table No: 42

	WEEKS TO EXPIRATION	30	29	28	27	26	25	24	23	22	21	20	19	18	17	16	15	14	13	12	11	10	9	8	7	6	5	4	3	2	1	0
IN THE MONEY	$1.25	126.4	126.2	126.0	126.0	125.8	125.7	125.5	125.4	125.3	125.2	125.1	125.1	125.0	125.0	125.0	125.0	125.0	125.0	125.0	125.0	125.0	125.0	125.0	125.0	125.0	125.0	125.0	125.0	125.0	125.0	125.0
	$1.00	103.0	102.7	102.5	102.3	102.2	102.0	101.9	101.8	101.7	101.6	101.4	101.3	101.2	101.0	100.8	100.7	100.6	100.5	100.4	100.3	100.2	100.1	100.0	100.0	100.0	100.0	100.0	100.0	100.0	100.0	100.0
	75¢	82.9	82.6	82.4	82.1	81.9	81.6	81.4	81.1	80.8	80.5	80.3	80.0	79.6	79.3	79.0	78.7	78.4	78.0	77.7	77.3	77.0	76.6	76.2	75.9	75.5	75.3	75.1	75.0	75.0	75.0	75.0
	50¢	66.9	66.5	66.1	65.8	65.4	65.0	64.6	64.2	63.8	63.3	62.8	62.3	61.7	61.2	60.7	60.1	59.5	58.9	58.3	57.6	56.9	56.2	55.3	54.6	53.7	52.5	51.3	50.5	50.1	50.0	50.0
	25¢	52.5	52.1	51.6	51.2	50.7	50.3	49.8	49.3	48.7	48.2	47.7	47.0	46.3	45.6	44.9	44.1	43.4	42.6	41.7	40.7	39.7	38.6	37.4	36.2	34.7	32.8	30.8	28.6	26.6	25.4	25.0
AT THE MONEY		41.4	40.9	40.4	39.9	39.4	38.9	38.4	37.8	37.2	36.6	36.0	35.3	34.5	33.7	32.9	32.1	31.3	30.4	29.4	28.3	27.1	25.9	24.5	23.0	21.2	18.8	16.3	13.3	9.8	5.9	0.0
OUT OF THE MONEY	25¢	32.1	31.6	31.1	30.6	30.1	29.6	29.1	28.6	28.0	27.4	26.7	26.0	25.3	24.6	23.8	23.0	22.2	21.3	20.3	19.3	18.2	17.2	15.8	14.4	12.7	10.5	8.2	5.5	2.3	0.9	0.0
	50¢	24.3	23.9	23.4	23.0	22.5	22.1	21.6	21.1	20.5	20.0	19.6	19.0	18.3	17.6	17.0	16.3	15.6	14.9	14.1	13.2	12.3	11.4	10.4	9.3	8.0	6.3	4.5	2.5	0.6	0.0	0
	75¢	20.0	19.6	19.1	18.7	18.2	17.8	17.3	16.8	16.3	15.8	15.3	14.7	14.0	13.3	12.7	12.0	11.3	10.6	9.8	9.0	8.2	7.3	6.2	5.5	4.4	3.0	1.8	0.8	0.0	0	0
	$1.00	14.6	14.3	13.9	13.6	13.2	12.9	12.5	12.1	11.7	11.3	10.9	10.5	10.0	9.5	9.1	8.6	8.1	7.6	7.0	6.4	5.8	5.2	4.5	3.8	3.1	2.2	1.3	0.4	0.0	0	0
	$1.25	10.3	10.0	9.7	9.4	9.2	8.9	8.7	8.4	8.1	7.8	7.5	7.1	6.7	6.3	5.9	5.5	5.2	4.8	4.4	4.0	3.5	3.0	2.5	2.0	1.6	0.9	0.4	0.1	0.0	0	0

OPTION VALUES ARE IN CENTS – to nearest tenth.

WM GRANDMILL (1985) LTD.

OPTION VALUES on SOYBEAN FUTURES – Table No: 41

	WEEKS TO EXPIRATION	30	29	28	27	26	25	24	23	22	21	20	19	18	17	16	15	14	13	12	11	10	9	8	7	6	5	4	3	2	1	0
IN THE MONEY	$1.25	126.0	125.9	125.7	125.6	125.5	125.4	125.3	125.2	125.1	125.0	125.0	125.0	125.0	125.0	125.0	125.0	125.0	125.0	125.0	125.0	125.0	125.0	125.0	125.0	125.0	125.0	125.0	125.0	125.0	125.0	125.0
	$1.00	102.6	102.4	102.2	102.1	102.0	101.9	101.8	101.7	101.6	101.4	101.3	101.2	101.0	100.9	100.7	100.6	100.5	100.4	100.3	100.2	100.1	100.0	100.0	100.0	100.0	100.0	100.0	100.0	100.0	100.0	100.0
	75¢	82.4	82.2	82.0	81.7	81.5	81.2	80.9	80.7	80.4	80.2	79.9	79.6	79.3	79.0	78.7	78.4	78.1	77.8	77.5	77.2	76.8	76.5	76.1	75.8	75.5	75.2	75.1	75.0	75.0	75.0	75.0
	50¢	66.2	65.9	65.5	65.1	64.7	64.4	64.0	63.6	63.2	62.8	62.3	61.8	61.3	60.8	60.2	59.6	59.0	58.5	57.9	57.3	56.6	55.8	55.1	54.3	53.4	52.3	51.2	50.5	50.1	50.0	50.0
	25¢	51.7	51.3	50.9	50.4	50.0	49.5	49.1	48.6	48.1	47.5	46.9	46.3	45.7	45.0	44.2	43.5	42.8	42.0	41.2	40.3	39.3	38.1	37.0	35.7	34.3	32.4	30.6	28.5	26.5	25.4	25.0
AT THE MONEY		40.5	40.1	39.6	39.1	38.6	38.1	37.6	37.1	36.5	35.9	35.2	34.5	33.8	33.0	32.2	31.4	30.6	29.8	28.8	27.7	26.6	25.3	24.0	22.5	20.7	18.4	16.0	13.0	9.6	5.8	0.0
OUT OF THE MONEY	25¢	31.2	30.8	30.3	29.8	29.4	28.9	28.4	27.9	27.3	26.7	26.0	25.3	24.6	23.9	23.1	22.3	21.5	20.7	19.8	18.8	17.8	16.6	15.3	13.9	12.3	10.1	8.0	5.3	2.2	0.9	0.0
	50¢	23.5	23.1	22.7	22.2	21.8	21.3	20.9	20.4	19.9	19.4	18.9	18.3	17.7	17.1	16.4	15.7	15.1	14.4	13.6	12.8	11.9	11.0	10.1	8.8	7.6	6.0	4.4	2.4	0.6	0.0	0
	75¢	19.2	18.8	18.4	17.9	17.5	17.1	16.7	16.2	15.7	15.2	14.6	14.0	13.4	12.8	12.1	11.4	10.8	10.1	9.4	8.6	7.8	6.9	6.1	5.1	4.0	2.8	1.7	0.7	0.0	0	0
	$1.00	14.0	13.7	13.3	13.0	12.6	12.3	11.9	11.6	11.2	10.9	10.5	10.0	9.6	9.2	8.7	8.2	7.7	7.2	6.7	6.1	5.5	4.9	4.3	3.6	2.9	2.0	1.2	0.4	0.0	0	0
	$1.25	9.7	9.5	9.3	9.0	8.8	8.5	8.3	8.0	7.7	7.4	7.1	6.7	6.4	6.0	5.6	5.2	4.9	4.6	4.2	3.8	3.3	2.9	2.4	1.9	1.5	0.8	0.4	0.1	0.0	0	0

OPTION VALUES ARE IN CENTS – to nearest tenth.

WM GRANDMILL (1985) LTD.

OPTION VALUES on SOYBEAN FUTURES – Table No: 44

OPTION VALUES ARE IN CENTS – to nearest tenth.

		30	29	28	27	26	25	24	23	22	21	20	19	18	17	16	15	14	13	12	11	10	9	8	7	6	5	4	3	2	1	0
IN THE MONEY	$1.25	127.4	127.0	126.8	126.5	126.3	126.0	125.8	125.6	125.5	125.4	125.2	125.1	125.0	125.0	125.0	125.0	125.0	125.0	125.0	125.0	125.0	125.0	125.0	125.0	125.0	125.0	125.0	125.0	125.0	125.0	125.0
	$1.00	103.9	103.6	103.3	103.0	102.8	102.5	102.3	102.1	101.9	101.7	101.6	101.4	101.2	101.1	100.9	100.8	100.6	100.5	100.4	100.3	100.2	100.1	100.0	100.0	100.0	100.0	100.0	100.0	100.0	100.0	100.0
	75¢	83.7	83.4	83.2	82.9	82.7	82.4	82.1	81.8	81.5	81.2	80.9	80.5	80.2	79.9	79.6	79.2	78.8	78.5	78.1	77.7	77.3	76.9	76.5	76.1	75.7	75.4	75.1	75.0	75.0	75.0	75.0
	50¢	68.3	67.9	67.5	67.1	66.7	66.2	65.8	65.3	64.8	64.4	63.9	63.4	62.8	62.2	61.6	61.0	60.3	59.7	59.0	58.3	57.6	56.8	55.9	55.0	54.1	52.9	51.6	50.6	50.1	50.0	50.0
	25¢	54.0	53.5	53.1	52.6	52.2	51.7	51.2	50.6	50.1	49.5	48.9	48.3	47.6	46.8	46.1	45.3	44.5	43.7	42.7	41.7	40.7	39.6	38.3	36.9	35.4	33.4	31.4	28.7	26.8	25.5	25.0
AT THE MONEY	25¢	43.0	42.5	42.0	41.5	41.0	40.5	39.9	39.3	38.7	38.1	37.4	36.7	35.9	35.1	34.3	33.4	32.5	31.6	30.6	29.4	28.2	26.9	25.5	23.9	22.0	19.6	17.0	13.5	10.2	6.2	0.0
OUT OF THE MONEY	25¢	33.7	33.2	32.7	32.2	31.7	31.2	30.6	30.0	29.5	28.9	28.2	27.5	26.7	25.9	25.1	24.3	23.4	22.5	21.5	20.3	19.2	18.1	16.8	15.2	13.5	11.3	8.9	5.7	2.6	1.0	0.0
	50¢	25.8	25.3	24.9	24.4	24.0	23.5	23.0	22.4	21.9	21.3	20.7	20.1	19.5	18.8	18.1	17.3	16.6	15.9	15.1	14.1	13.2	12.2	11.1	10.0	8.6	6.8	5.1	2.7	0.9	0.1	0
	75¢	21.5	21.0	20.6	20.1	19.7	19.2	18.7	18.1	17.6	17.1	16.5	15.9	15.2	14.5	13.8	13.0	12.3	11.6	10.8	9.9	9.0	8.1	7.0	6.0	4.9	3.5	2.1	0.9	0.1	0	0
	$1.00	15.8	15.4	15.0	14.6	14.3	13.9	13.5	13.1	12.7	12.3	11.8	11.3	10.9	10.4	9.9	9.4	8.8	8.3	7.7	7.0	6.4	5.7	5.0	4.2	3.4	2.4	1.6	0.5	0.1	0	0
	$1.25	11.2	10.9	10.6	10.3	10.0	9.7	9.4	9.1	8.8	8.5	8.2	7.8	7.4	7.0	6.6	6.2	5.7	5.3	4.9	4.4	3.9	3.4	2.9	2.4	1.8	1.1	0.5	0.1	0	0	0

WEEKS TO EXPIRATION

OPTION VALUES on SOYBEAN FUTURES – Table No: 43

OPTION VALUES ARE IN CENTS – to nearest tenth.

		30	29	28	27	26	25	24	23	22	21	20	19	18	17	16	15	14	13	12	11	10	9	8	7	6	5	4	3	2	1	0
IN THE MONEY	$1.25	126.9	126.6	126.4	126.2	126.0	125.8	125.6	125.5	125.4	125.3	125.2	125.1	125.0	125.0	125.0	125.0	125.0	125.0	125.0	125.0	125.0	125.0	125.0	125.0	125.0	125.0	125.0	125.0	125.0	125.0	125.0
	$1.00	103.4	103.1	102.8	102.6	102.4	102.2	102.1	101.9	101.7	101.6	101.5	101.3	101.1	101.0	101.0	100.8	100.7	100.6	100.5	100.3	100.2	100.2	100.1	100.0	100.0	100.0	100.0	100.0	100.0	100.0	100.0
	75¢	83.3	83.0	82.8	82.5	82.3	82.0	81.8	81.5	81.2	80.9	80.5	80.2	79.9	79.6	79.3	79.0	78.6	78.3	77.9	77.5	77.2	76.8	76.4	76.0	75.6	75.3	75.1	75.0	75.0	75.0	75.0
	50¢	67.6	67.2	66.8	66.4	66.0	65.6	65.2	64.8	64.4	63.9	63.4	62.9	62.3	61.7	61.1	60.6	60.0	59.4	58.7	58.0	57.3	56.5	55.7	54.8	53.9	52.7	51.6	50.6	50.1	50.0	50.0
	25¢	53.2	52.8	52.3	51.9	51.4	51.0	50.5	50.0	49.5	48.9	48.3	47.6	46.9	46.2	45.5	44.8	44.0	43.2	42.3	41.3	40.3	39.1	37.9	36.5	35.0	33.1	30.9	28.7	26.7	25.4	25.0
AT THE MONEY	25¢	42.2	41.7	41.2	40.7	40.2	39.7	39.2	38.6	38.0	37.4	36.7	36.0	35.2	34.4	33.6	32.8	31.9	31.0	30.0	28.9	27.7	26.4	25.0	23.4	21.6	19.2	16.7	13.5	10.0	6.0	0.0
OUT OF THE MONEY	25¢	32.9	32.4	31.9	31.4	30.9	30.4	29.9	29.4	28.8	28.2	27.5	26.8	26.0	25.2	24.5	23.7	22.8	21.9	20.9	19.9	18.8	17.6	16.3	14.7	13.1	10.9	8.9	5.7	2.5	0.9	0.0
	50¢	25.0	24.6	24.1	23.7	23.2	22.8	22.3	21.8	21.3	20.7	20.1	19.5	18.9	18.2	17.5	16.9	16.2	15.5	14.7	13.8	12.8	11.8	10.7	9.5	8.2	6.6	5.1	2.7	0.6	0.1	0
	75¢	20.7	20.3	19.8	19.4	18.9	18.5	18.0	17.5	17.1	16.5	15.9	15.3	14.6	13.9	13.2	12.6	11.9	11.2	10.4	9.5	8.6	7.7	6.8	5.7	4.6	3.4	2.1	0.9	0.1	0	0
	$1.00	15.2	14.8	14.5	14.1	13.8	13.4	13.1	12.6	12.3	11.8	11.4	11.0	10.5	10.0	9.5	9.0	8.5	8.0	7.4	6.7	6.1	5.5	4.8	4.0	3.2	2.3	1.6	0.5	0.1	0	0
	$1.25	10.7	10.4	10.2	9.9	9.6	9.3	9.1	8.8	8.5	8.2	7.8	7.5	7.1	6.7	6.3	5.9	5.5	5.1	4.7	4.2	3.7	3.2	2.6	2.0	1.5	1.0	0.5	0.1	0	0	0

WEEKS TO EXPIRATION

OPTION VALUES on SOYBEAN FUTURES – Table No:46

OPTION VALUES ARE IN CENTS – to nearest tenth.

		WEEKS TO EXPIRATION																														
		30	29	28	27	26	25	24	23	22	21	20	19	18	17	16	15	14	13	12	11	10	9	8	7	6	5	4	3	2	1	0
IN THE MONEY	$1.25	128.2	128.0	127.7	127.4	127.1	126.8	126.5	126.2	126.0	125.7	125.5	125.4	125.2	125.1	125.0	125.0	125.0	125.0	125.0	125.0	125.0	125.0	125.0	125.0	125.0	125.0	125.0	125.0	125.0	125.0	125.0
	$1.00	104.8	104.5	104.2	103.9	103.6	103.3	103.0	102.7	102.5	102.2	102.0	101.9	101.7	101.6	101.4	101.2	101.0	100.8	100.7	100.5	100.4	100.3	100.1	100.0	100.0	100.0	100.0	100.0	100.0	100.0	100.0
	75¢	84.5	84.3	84.0	83.8	83.5	83.2	82.9	82.6	82.3	82.0	81.6	81.2	80.8	80.4	80.1	79.7	79.4	79.0	78.6	78.2	77.8	77.3	76.8	76.3	75.9	75.4	75.2	75.0	75.0	75.0	75.0
	50¢	69.6	69.2	68.8	68.4	67.9	67.5	67.0	66.5	66.0	65.5	65.0	64.4	63.8	63.2	62.5	61.9	61.3	60.6	59.8	59.0	58.3	57.5	56.6	55.5	54.5	53.3	51.7	50.7	50.2	50.0	50.0
	25¢	55.5	55.0	54.6	54.1	53.6	53.1	52.6	52.1	51.5	50.9	50.2	49.5	48.8	48.1	47.3	46.5	45.7	44.8	43.9	42.9	41.8	40.6	39.2	37.7	36.1	34.0	31.8	29.4	27.0	25.5	25.0
AT THE MONEY	25¢	44.7	44.2	43.7	43.2	42.6	42.1	41.5	40.9	40.3	39.6	38.9	38.1	37.3	36.5	35.6	34.7	33.8	32.8	31.8	30.6	29.4	28.0	26.5	24.8	22.9	20.4	17.6	14.3	10.6	6.4	0.0
OUT OF THE MONEY	25¢	35.3	34.8	34.4	33.9	33.3	32.8	32.2	31.6	31.0	30.3	29.6	28.9	28.1	27.3	26.4	25.5	24.6	23.7	22.7	21.5	20.3	19.1	17.7	16.1	14.3	12.0	9.4	6.4	2.9	1.0	0
	50¢	27.3	26.8	26.4	25.9	25.4	24.9	24.4	23.9	23.3	22.7	22.0	21.3	20.6	19.9	19.2	18.5	17.7	16.9	16.0	15.1	14.1	13.0	11.8	10.6	9.2	7.4	5.4	3.2	0.8	0.1	0
	75¢	23.1	22.6	22.1	21.6	21.1	20.6	20.1	19.6	19.0	18.4	17.8	17.1	16.5	15.8	15.0	14.2	13.4	12.6	11.7	10.8	9.9	8.9	7.7	6.6	5.4	3.9	2.4	1.2	0.1	0	0
	$1.00	17.2	16.8	16.4	16.0	15.5	15.1	14.7	14.3	13.8	13.3	12.8	12.3	11.7	11.2	10.7	10.1	9.6	9.0	8.4	7.7	7.0	6.3	5.5	4.7	3.8	2.7	1.8	0.7	0	0	0
	$1.25	12.2	11.9	11.6	11.3	11.0	10.7	10.3	10.0	9.6	9.3	8.9	8.5	8.1	7.7	7.3	6.8	6.4	5.9	5.4	4.9	4.4	3.9	3.2	2.7	2.0	1.4	0.6	0.2	0	0	0

WM GRANDMILL (1985) LTD.

OPTION VALUES on SOYBEAN FUTURES – Table No:45

OPTION VALUES ARE IN CENTS – to nearest tenth.

		WEEKS TO EXPIRATION																														
		30	29	28	27	26	25	24	23	22	21	20	19	18	17	16	15	14	13	12	11	10	9	8	7	6	5	4	3	2	1	0
IN THE MONEY	$1.25	127.9	127.6	127.3	126.9	126.7	126.4	126.1	125.9	125.7	125.5	125.4	125.2	125.1	125.0	125.0	125.0	125.0	125.0	125.0	125.0	125.0	125.0	125.0	125.0	125.0	125.0	125.0	125.0	125.0	125.0	125.0
	$1.00	104.4	104.1	103.8	103.5	103.2	102.9	102.6	102.4	102.2	102.0	101.9	101.7	101.6	101.4	101.3	101.1	100.9	100.7	100.6	100.5	100.3	100.2	100.1	100.0	100.0	100.0	100.0	100.0	100.0	100.0	100.0
	75¢	84.1	83.9	83.6	83.3	83.1	82.8	82.5	82.2	81.9	81.6	81.3	80.9	80.5	80.2	79.9	79.5	79.1	78.7	78.3	77.9	77.5	77.1	76.7	76.2	75.8	75.4	75.1	75.0	75.0	75.0	75.0
	50¢	69.0	68.5	68.1	67.6	67.2	66.8	66.4	65.9	65.4	65.0	64.5	63.9	63.3	62.7	62.1	61.5	60.9	60.2	59.5	58.7	57.9	57.1	56.2	55.3	54.3	53.1	51.7	50.7	50.2	50.0	50.0
	25¢	54.8	54.3	53.9	53.3	52.9	52.4	51.9	51.3	50.8	50.2	49.6	48.9	48.2	47.5	46.7	45.9	45.1	44.2	43.3	42.3	41.2	40.1	38.8	37.3	35.7	33.8	31.5	29.2	26.9	25.5	25.0
AT THE MONEY	25¢	43.9	43.4	42.9	42.3	41.8	41.3	40.7	40.1	39.5	38.9	38.2	37.4	36.6	35.8	35.0	34.1	33.2	32.2	31.2	30.0	28.8	27.5	26.0	24.4	22.5	20.0	17.3	14.1	10.4	6.3	0.0
OUT OF THE MONEY	25¢	34.6	34.1	33.6	33.0	32.5	32.0	31.4	30.8	30.3	29.7	29.0	28.2	27.4	26.6	25.8	25.0	24.1	23.1	22.0	20.9	19.8	18.6	17.3	15.7	13.9	12.0	9.1	6.2	2.8	1.0	0
	50¢	26.6	26.1	25.7	25.2	24.7	24.2	23.7	23.1	22.6	22.0	21.4	20.7	20.1	19.5	18.8	18.0	17.2	16.4	15.6	14.7	13.7	12.6	11.6	10.3	8.8	7.2	5.2	3.1	0.8	0.1	0
	75¢	22.2	21.8	21.4	20.8	20.4	19.9	19.4	18.8	18.3	17.8	17.2	16.5	15.8	15.1	14.4	13.6	12.9	12.1	11.3	10.4	9.4	8.4	7.4	6.3	5.1	3.6	2.2	1.1	0.1	0	0
	$1.00	16.5	16.1	15.8	15.2	14.9	14.5	14.1	13.7	13.2	12.8	12.4	11.8	11.3	10.8	10.3	9.8	9.3	8.7	8.1	7.4	6.7	6.0	5.3	4.5	3.6	2.6	1.7	0.6	0	0	0
	$1.25	11.8	11.5	11.2	10.8	10.5	10.2	9.8	9.5	9.2	8.9	8.6	8.2	7.8	7.4	7.0	6.5	6.1	5.6	5.1	4.7	4.2	3.7	3.1	2.5	1.9	1.3	0.5	0.2	0	0	0

WM GRANDMILL (1985) LTD.

OPTION VALUES on SOYBEAN FUTURES – Table No: 48

	30	29	28	27	26	25	24	23	22	21	20	19	18	17	16	15	14	13	12	11	10	9	8	7	6	5	4	3	2	1	0
IN THE MONEY																															
$1.25	129.4	129.1	128.6	128.3	128.0	127.7	127.4	127.0	126.7	126.3	126.0	125.7	125.5	125.3	125.2	125.1	125.0	125.0	125.0	125.0	125.0	125.0	125.0	125.0	125.0	125.0	125.0	125.0	125.0	125.0	125.0
$1.00	105.9	105.6	105.2	104.9	104.6	104.2	103.9	103.5	103.2	102.8	102.5	102.2	101.9	101.7	101.5	101.3	101.1	100.9	100.8	100.7	100.5	100.4	100.3	100.2	100.1	100.0	100.0	100.0	100.0	100.0	100.0
75¢	85.5	85.2	84.9	84.6	84.3	83.9	83.6	83.4	83.1	82.7	82.4	82.0	81.6	81.1	80.7	80.3	79.9	79.5	79.1	78.6	78.1	77.6	77.1	76.6	76.0	75.5	75.2	75.0	75.0	75.0	75.0
50¢	70.9	70.5	70.1	69.7	69.2	68.8	68.3	67.8	67.3	66.7	66.1	65.5	64.9	64.3	63.6	62.9	62.2	61.5	60.7	59.9	59.0	58.1	57.1	56.1	55.0	53.6	52.3	50.9	50.2	50.0	50.0
25¢	57.0	56.5	56.0	55.5	55.0	54.5	54.0	53.5	52.9	52.2	51.6	50.9	50.2	49.4	48.6	47.7	46.8	45.9	44.9	43.9	42.8	41.6	40.1	38.6	36.8	34.6	32.3	29.8	27.2	25.6	25.0
AT THE MONEY	46.4	45.9	45.3	44.8	44.2	43.7	43.1	42.5	41.8	41.1	40.4	39.6	38.8	37.9	37.0	36.1	35.1	34.1	33.0	31.8	30.5	29.0	27.5	25.8	23.8	21.1	18.3	14.9	11.0	6.6	0.0
OUT OF THE MONEY																															
25¢	37.0	36.5	35.9	35.4	34.9	34.4	33.8	33.2	32.5	31.8	31.1	30.3	29.5	28.7	27.8	26.9	25.9	24.9	23.8	22.7	21.4	20.0	18.6	17.0	15.1	12.6	10.0	7.0	3.3	1.1	0
50¢	28.8	28.3	27.8	27.3	26.8	26.3	25.8	25.3	24.7	24.0	23.4	22.7	22.0	21.2	20.4	19.6	18.8	18.0	17.1	16.1	15.0	13.9	12.6	11.3	9.9	7.9	5.9	3.6	1.0	0.1	0
75¢	24.6	24.1	23.6	23.1	22.6	22.1	21.5	21.0	20.4	19.7	19.1	18.4	17.7	17.0	16.2	15.3	14.5	13.7	12.8	11.8	10.7	9.6	8.4	7.2	5.9	4.3	2.7	1.3	0.2	0	0
$1.00	18.6	18.2	17.7	17.3	16.8	16.4	15.9	15.4	14.9	14.4	13.9	13.3	12.8	12.2	11.6	11.0	10.4	9.8	9.1	8.4	7.6	6.8	6.0	5.1	4.2	3.0	2.0	0.9	0.1	0	0
$1.25	13.4	13.1	12.7	12.4	12.0	11.6	11.3	10.9	10.5	10.1	9.7	9.3	8.9	8.4	8.0	7.5	7.0	6.5	6.0	5.4	4.8	4.2	3.6	3.0	2.3	1.6	0.7	0.2	0	0	0
WEEKS TO EXPIRATION																															

OPTION VALUES ARE IN CENTS – to nearest tenth.

WM GRANDMILL (1985) LTD.

OPTION VALUES on SOYBEAN FUTURES – Table No: 47

	30	29	28	27	26	25	24	23	22	21	20	19	18	17	16	15	14	13	12	11	10	9	8	7	6	5	4	3	2	1	0
IN THE MONEY																															
$1.25	128.7	128.4	128.1	127.9	127.6	127.4	127.0	126.9	126.6	126.3	126.0	125.7	125.5	125.4	125.2	125.0	125.0	125.0	125.0	125.0	125.0	125.0	125.0	125.0	125.0	125.0	125.0	125.0	125.0	125.0	125.0
$1.00	105.3	105.0	104.7	104.4	104.1	103.8	103.5	103.1	102.8	102.5	102.2	101.9	101.7	101.5	101.3	101.0	100.8	100.6	100.4	100.3	100.1	100.0	100.0	100.0	100.0	100.0	100.0	100.0	100.0	100.0	100.0
75¢	85.0	84.8	84.5	84.2	83.9	83.6	83.3	83.0	82.7	82.3	82.0	81.6	81.2	80.8	80.4	80.0	79.6	79.2	78.8	78.3	77.8	77.4	76.9	76.4	75.9	75.5	75.2	75.0	75.0	75.0	75.0
50¢	70.2	69.9	69.5	69.1	68.6	68.1	67.6	67.1	66.6	66.0	65.5	64.9	64.4	63.8	63.1	62.4	61.7	61.0	60.3	59.5	58.6	57.7	56.8	55.8	54.7	53.4	52.1	50.8	50.2	50.0	50.0
25¢	56.2	55.8	55.3	54.9	54.4	53.9	53.3	52.8	52.2	51.5	50.9	50.2	49.5	48.7	47.9	47.1	46.3	45.4	44.4	43.3	42.2	40.9	39.6	38.1	36.3	34.3	32.2	29.6	27.1	25.5	25.0
AT THE MONEY	45.5	45.0	44.5	44.0	43.5	42.9	42.3	41.7	41.0	40.3	39.6	38.8	38.0	37.2	36.3	35.4	34.5	33.5	32.4	31.2	29.9	28.5	26.9	25.3	23.3	20.7	18.0	14.6	10.8	6.5	0.0
OUT OF THE MONEY																															
25¢	36.1	35.6	35.1	34.7	34.2	33.6	33.0	32.4	31.7	31.0	30.3	29.6	28.8	28.0	27.1	26.2	25.3	24.3	23.2	22.0	20.8	19.5	18.1	16.6	14.6	12.3	9.8	6.7	3.1	1.1	0
50¢	28.0	27.6	27.1	26.7	26.2	25.7	25.1	24.6	24.0	23.3	22.7	22.0	21.3	20.5	19.7	19.0	18.2	17.4	16.5	15.6	14.6	13.4	12.2	11.0	9.4	7.6	5.8	3.4	0.9	0.1	0
75¢	23.8	23.4	22.9	22.4	21.9	21.4	20.8	20.3	19.7	19.0	18.4	17.7	17.1	16.3	15.5	14.7	13.9	13.1	12.2	11.3	10.3	9.2	8.1	6.9	5.6	4.1	2.6	1.3	0.2	0	0
$1.00	17.8	17.4	17.0	16.6	16.2	15.8	15.3	14.8	14.3	13.8	13.3	12.8	12.3	11.7	11.1	10.6	10.0	9.4	8.8	8.1	7.3	6.5	5.7	4.8	3.9	2.9	1.9	0.8	0	0	0
$1.25	12.9	12.6	12.2	11.9	11.5	11.2	10.8	10.4	10.1	9.7	9.3	8.9	8.5	8.1	7.6	7.2	6.7	6.2	5.7	5.1	4.6	4.0	3.4	2.9	2.1	1.5	0.7	0.2	0	0	0
WEEKS TO EXPIRATION																															

OPTION VALUES ARE IN CENTS – to nearest tenth.

WM GRANDMILL (1985) LTD.

OPTION VALUES on SOYBEAN FUTURES – Table No:50

	30	29	28	27	26	25	24	23	22	21	20	19	18	17	16	15	14	13	12	11	10	9	8	7	6	5	4	3	2	1	0
IN THE MONEY $1.25	130.6	130.2	129.9	129.4	129.1	128.8	128.5	128.2	127.9	127.5	127.1	126.7	126.3	125.9	125.6	125.2	125.1	125.0	125.0	125.0	125.0	125.0	125.0	125.0	125.0	125.0	125.0	125.0	125.0	125.0	125.0
$1.00	106.9	106.6	106.4	106.3	105.9	105.5	105.2	104.8	104.4	104.0	103.6	103.2	102.8	102.4	102.1	101.9	101.7	101.5	101.3	101.1	100.8	100.6	100.5	100.3	100.1	100.0	100.0	100.0	100.0	100.0	100.0
75¢	86.6	86.3	86.0	86.0	85.6	85.2	84.9	84.5	84.2	83.8	83.5	83.1	82.7	82.3	81.8	81.4	80.9	80.4	80.0	79.5	79.0	78.5	77.9	77.4	76.9	76.3	75.7	75.3	75.0	75.0	75.0
50¢	72.3	71.9	71.6	71.4	70.9	70.5	70.0	69.5	69.0	68.4	67.9	67.3	66.7	66.0	65.3	64.6	63.9	63.1	62.3	61.5	60.6	59.7	58.7	57.7	56.6	55.4	54.0	52.6	51.0	50.3	50.0
25¢	58.5	58.1	57.8	57.6	57.0	56.5	55.9	55.4	54.8	54.2	53.6	52.9	52.2	51.4	50.6	49.8	48.9	48.0	47.0	46.0	44.9	43.7	42.4	41.0	39.4	37.5	35.3	33.0	30.1	27.4	25.0
AT THE MONEY	48.1	47.6	47.2	47.0	46.4	45.8	45.2	44.6	44.0	43.3	42.6	41.8	41.0	40.2	39.3	38.4	37.4	36.4	35.3	34.2	32.9	31.6	30.1	28.5	26.7	24.6	21.9	19.0	15.4	11.4	0.0
OUT OF THE MONEY 25¢	38.7	38.2	37.8	37.6	37.0	36.4	35.8	35.3	34.7	34.0	33.3	32.5	31.7	30.9	30.1	29.2	28.2	27.2	26.1	25.0	23.8	22.5	21.0	19.5	17.9	15.9	13.4	10.7	7.4	3.7	0
50¢	30.4	29.9	29.5	29.4	28.8	28.3	27.7	27.2	26.6	26.0	25.4	24.7	24.0	23.2	22.4	21.6	20.7	19.8	18.9	18.0	17.0	15.9	14.7	12.0	10.5	8.5	6.5	3.9	1.2	0.2	0
75¢	26.3	25.8	25.4	25.2	24.6	24.1	23.5	23.0	22.4	21.7	21.1	20.4	19.7	18.9	18.1	17.3	16.5	15.6	14.6	13.7	12.7	11.6	10.4	9.1	7.9	6.4	4.8	3.2	1.5	0.3	0
$1.00	19.9	19.5	19.2	19.0	18.5	18.1	17.6	17.1	16.6	16.0	15.4	14.9	14.4	13.8	13.1	12.5	11.8	11.2	10.6	9.9	9.1	8.3	7.4	6.5	5.6	4.6	3.4	2.2	1.0	0.1	0
$1.25	14.4	14.1	13.8	13.8	13.4	13.0	12.7	12.3	11.9	11.4	11.0	10.5	10.1	9.6	9.1	8.7	8.2	7.7	7.1	6.5	5.9	5.3	4.7	4.0	3.3	2.6	1.7	1.0	0.3	0	0

WEEKS TO EXPIRATION

OPTION VALUES ARE IN CENTS – to nearest tenth.

WM GRANDMILL (1985) LTD.

OPTION VALUES on SOYBEAN FUTURES – Table No:49

	30	29	28	27	26	25	24	23	22	21	20	19	18	17	16	15	14	13	12	11	10	9	8	7	6	5	4	3	2	1	0
IN THE MONEY $1.25	130.0	129.6	129.2	128.8	128.5	128.2	127.8	127.5	127.0	126.7	126.3	126.0	125.7	125.5	125.3	125.1	125.0	125.0	125.0	125.0	125.0	125.0	125.0	125.0	125.0	125.0	125.0	125.0	125.0	125.0	125.0
$1.00	106.4	106.0	105.7	105.4	105.1	104.7	104.4	104.0	103.6	103.2	102.8	102.5	102.2	102.0	101.8	101.6	101.4	101.2	101.0	100.8	100.6	100.4	100.3	100.1	100.0	100.0	100.0	100.0	100.0	100.0	100.0
75¢	86.0	85.7	85.4	85.1	84.8	84.4	84.1	83.8	83.4	83.1	82.7	82.3	81.9	81.4	80.9	80.5	80.1	79.6	79.3	78.8	78.3	77.7	77.2	76.7	76.1	75.6	75.2	75.0	75.0	75.0	75.0
50¢	71.6	71.2	70.7	70.3	69.9	69.4	68.9	68.4	67.8	67.3	66.7	66.0	65.3	64.6	64.0	63.4	62.6	61.9	61.1	60.2	59.4	58.5	57.5	56.5	55.2	53.8	52.4	51.0	50.2	50.0	50.0
25¢	57.8	57.3	56.7	56.3	55.8	55.3	54.7	54.1	53.5	52.9	52.2	51.5	50.7	49.9	49.1	48.3	47.4	46.4	45.4	44.3	43.2	41.8	40.6	39.0	37.1	34.9	32.6	30.0	27.3	25.6	25.0
AT THE MONEY	47.2	46.7	46.1	45.6	45.0	44.5	43.9	43.2	42.5	41.8	41.1	40.3	39.4	38.5	37.6	36.7	35.7	34.7	33.6	32.3	31.0	29.6	28.0	26.3	24.2	21.5	18.6	15.2	11.2	6.8	0.0
OUT OF THE MONEY 25¢	37.8	37.3	36.7	36.3	35.6	35.1	34.5	33.9	33.2	32.5	31.8	31.0	30.1	29.3	28.4	27.5	26.5	25.5	24.4	23.2	21.9	20.5	19.1	17.5	15.5	13.0	10.3	7.2	3.5	1.2	0
50¢	29.5	29.1	28.5	28.1	27.6	27.1	26.5	25.9	25.3	24.7	24.0	23.3	22.5	21.7	20.9	20.1	19.3	18.4	17.4	16.4	15.5	14.4	13.1	11.7	10.2	8.1	6.1	3.8	1.1	0.2	0
75¢	25.4	24.9	24.4	23.9	23.4	22.9	22.3	21.6	21.0	20.4	19.7	19.0	18.2	17.4	16.7	15.9	15.0	14.1	13.1	12.1	11.2	10.1	8.9	7.6	6.2	4.4	2.9	1.4	0.2	0	0
$1.00	19.2	18.8	18.3	17.9	17.5	17.0	16.6	16.0	15.4	14.9	14.4	13.8	13.2	12.5	11.9	11.3	10.7	10.1	9.4	8.6	7.9	7.1	6.3	5.4	4.4	3.2	2.1	0.9	0.1	0	0
$1.25	13.8	13.5	13.2	12.9	12.6	12.2	11.8	11.4	10.9	10.5	10.1	9.6	9.2	8.7	8.3	7.8	7.3	6.8	6.2	5.6	5.1	4.5	3.9	3.2	2.5	1.7	0.8	0.3	0	0	0

WEEKS TO EXPIRATION

OPTION VALUES ARE IN CENTS – to nearest tenth.

WM GRANDMILL (1985) LTD.

OPTION VALUES on SOYBEAN FUTURES – Table No: 52

OPTION VALUES ARE IN CENTS – to nearest tenth.

WEEKS TO EXPIRATION

	30	29	28	27	26	25	24	23	22	21	20	19	18	17	16	15	14	13	12	11	10	9	8	7	6	5	4	3	2	1	0
IN THE MONEY $1.25	127.0	126.5	126.1	125.8	125.5	125.3	125.1	125.0	125.0	125.0	125.0	125.0	125.0	125.0	125.0	125.0	125.0	125.0	125.0	125.0	125.0	125.0	125.0	125.0	125.0	125.0	125.0	125.0	125.0	125.0	125.0
IN THE MONEY $1.00	108.0	107.5	107.1	106.7	106.4	106.0	105.7	105.3	104.9	104.5	104.0	103.5	103.0	102.6	102.3	102.1	101.8	101.6	101.3	101.1	100.8	100.6	100.4	100.2	100.2	100.0	100.0	100.0	100.0	100.0	100.0
IN THE MONEY 75¢	87.6	87.3	86.9	86.6	86.2	85.8	85.4	85.0	84.6	84.2	83.8	83.4	83.0	82.5	82.0	81.5	81.0	80.5	80.0	79.5	78.9	78.3	77.7	77.1	76.5	75.8	75.3	75.1	75.0	75.0	75.0
IN THE MONEY 50¢	73.8	73.3	72.8	72.3	71.8	71.3	70.8	70.2	69.7	69.1	68.4	67.7	67.0	66.3	65.6	64.8	64.1	63.3	62.4	61.5	60.5	59.4	58.3	57.2	55.9	54.4	52.9	51.2	50.3	50.0	50.0
IN THE MONEY 25¢	60.1	59.5	59.0	58.5	57.9	57.4	56.8	56.2	55.6	54.9	54.2	53.4	52.6	51.8	51.0	50.1	49.2	48.2	47.1	45.9	44.7	43.3	41.8	40.2	38.3	35.9	33.4	30.6	27.6	25.7	25.0
AT THE MONEY	49.8	49.2	48.6	48.0	47.4	46.8	46.2	45.5	44.8	44.1	43.3	42.4	41.5	40.6	39.7	38.7	37.7	36.6	35.4	34.1	32.7	31.2	29.5	27.6	25.5	22.7	19.6	16.0	11.8	7.1	0.0
OUT OF THE MONEY 25¢	40.3	39.7	39.2	38.6	38.0	37.4	36.8	36.1	35.4	34.7	33.9	33.1	32.2	31.3	30.4	29.5	28.5	27.4	26.2	24.9	23.6	22.1	20.4	18.7	16.8	14.1	11.3	8.0	4.1	1.3	0
OUT OF THE MONEY 50¢	32.0	31.4	30.8	30.3	29.7	29.2	28.6	28.0	27.4	26.7	26.0	25.2	24.4	23.6	22.8	21.9	21.0	20.0	19.0	17.9	16.8	15.6	14.2	12.7	11.1	9.0	6.8	4.4	1.5	0.2	0
OUT OF THE MONEY 75¢	27.9	27.3	26.8	26.2	25.6	25.0	24.4	23.8	23.2	22.5	21.7	20.9	20.1	19.3	18.5	17.7	16.8	15.8	14.7	13.6	12.5	11.3	9.9	8.5	7.0	5.2	3.5	1.7	0.4	0	0
OUT OF THE MONEY $1.00	21.3	20.8	20.3	19.8	19.3	18.9	18.4	17.9	17.3	16.7	16.1	15.3	14.6	14.0	13.4	12.7	12.0	11.3	10.6	9.8	8.9	8.0	7.0	6.0	5.0	3.7	2.4	1.2	0.2	0.1	0
OUT OF THE MONEY $1.25	15.4	15.1	14.7	14.4	14.0	13.6	13.2	12.8	12.4	11.9	11.4	10.9	10.3	9.8	9.3	8.8	8.3	7.8	7.2	6.5	5.8	5.1	4.4	3.7	2.9	1.9	1.1	0.4	0	0	0

WM GRANDMILL (1985) LTD.

OPTION VALUES on SOYBEAN FUTURES – Table No: 51

OPTION VALUES ARE IN CENTS – to nearest tenth.

WEEKS TO EXPIRATION

	30	29	28	27	26	25	24	23	22	21	20	19	18	17	16	15	14	13	12	11	10	9	8	7	6	5	4	3	2	1	0
IN THE MONEY $1.25	131.8	131.4	131.0	130.6	130.1	129.7	129.2	128.7	128.3	127.9	127.5	127.1	126.7	126.2	125.9	125.6	125.4	125.2	125.0	125.0	125.0	125.0	125.0	125.0	125.0	125.0	125.0	125.0	125.0	125.0	125.0
IN THE MONEY $1.00	108.0	107.6	107.2	106.9	106.5	106.1	105.7	105.3	104.9	104.5	104.0	103.6	103.2	102.7	102.4	102.1	101.9	101.7	101.4	101.2	101.0	100.7	100.5	100.4	100.2	100.2	100.0	100.0	100.0	100.0	100.0
IN THE MONEY 75¢	87.6	87.3	86.9	86.6	86.2	85.8	85.4	85.0	84.6	84.2	83.8	83.5	83.1	82.6	82.2	81.7	81.2	80.7	80.2	79.7	79.2	78.7	78.1	77.6	77.0	76.4	75.7	75.3	75.0	75.0	75.0
IN THE MONEY 50¢	73.2	72.6	72.1	71.6	71.1	70.6	70.1	69.6	69.1	68.5	67.9	67.3	66.6	65.9	65.1	64.4	63.6	62.8	61.9	61.0	60.1	59.1	58.1	57.0	55.7	54.2	52.7	51.1	50.3	50.0	50.0
IN THE MONEY 25¢	59.4	58.8	58.3	57.9	57.3	56.7	56.2	55.5	54.9	54.2	53.4	52.7	51.8	51.0	50.1	49.2	48.2	47.1	45.9	44.7	43.3	41.8	40.2	38.3	36.0	33.4	30.6	27.6	25.7	25.6	25.0
AT THE MONEY	49.0	48.4	47.8	47.2	46.6	46.0	45.4	44.7	44.0	43.3	42.6	41.8	40.9	40.0	39.0	38.0	37.0	35.9	34.8	33.5	32.1	30.6	29.0	27.2	25.1	22.3	19.3	15.7	11.6	7.0	0.0
OUT OF THE MONEY 25¢	39.6	39.0	38.4	37.8	37.2	36.6	36.0	35.3	34.7	34.0	33.3	32.5	31.6	30.7	29.8	28.8	27.8	26.7	25.6	24.4	23.0	21.5	20.0	18.3	16.4	13.7	11.0	7.7	3.9	1.2	0.0
OUT OF THE MONEY 50¢	31.2	30.6	30.1	29.5	29.0	28.5	28.0	27.3	26.7	26.0	25.4	24.7	24.0	23.1	22.2	21.3	20.4	19.5	18.5	17.4	16.3	15.1	13.9	12.4	10.9	9.4	7.7	5.9	4.8	3.5	0
OUT OF THE MONEY 75¢	27.2	26.6	26.0	25.5	24.9	24.3	23.7	23.1	22.4	21.7	21.0	20.4	19.6	18.8	17.9	17.1	16.2	15.2	14.2	13.1	12.0	10.8	9.6	8.3	6.8	5.0	3.3	1.6	0.3	0	0
OUT OF THE MONEY $1.00	20.7	20.2	19.7	19.2	18.7	18.2	17.7	17.2	16.7	16.1	15.5	14.9	14.3	13.7	13.0	12.3	11.6	10.9	10.2	9.4	8.6	7.7	6.8	5.9	5.0	4.1	3.3	2.3	1.4	0.7	0
OUT OF THE MONEY $1.25	15.0	14.6	14.2	13.9	13.5	13.2	12.8	12.3	11.9	11.4	11.0	10.5	10.0	9.5	9.0	8.5	8.0	7.4	6.8	6.1	5.5	4.9	4.3	3.5	2.8	1.8	1.0	0.3	0	0	0

WM GRANDMILL (1985) LTD.

OPTION VALUES on SOYBEAN FUTURES – Table No: 54

OPTION VALUES ARE IN CENTS – to nearest tenth.

WEEKS TO EXPIRATION	30	29	28	27	26	25	24	23	22	21	20	19	18	17	16	15	14	13	12	11	10	9	8	7	6	5	4	3	2	1	0
IN THE MONEY $1.25	132.9	132.5	132.1	131.7	131.3	130.8	130.3	129.8	129.3	128.8	128.3	127.8	127.3	126.8	126.3	125.9	125.5	125.3	125.1	125.0	125.0	125.0	125.0	125.0	125.0	125.0	125.0	125.0	125.0	125.0	125.0
IN THE MONEY $1.00	109.1	108.7	108.3	107.9	107.5	107.1	106.7	106.3	105.8	105.4	104.9	104.4	103.8	103.3	102.8	102.4	102.0	101.8	101.6	101.3	101.0	100.7	100.5	100.3	100.1	100.1	100.0	100.0	100.0	100.0	100.0
IN THE MONEY 75¢	88.7	88.3	87.9	87.5	87.2	86.8	86.4	86.0	85.5	85.1	84.6	84.1	83.6	83.2	82.7	82.2	81.6	81.1	80.5	79.9	79.3	78.7	78.0	77.4	76.7	76.1	75.4	75.1	75.0	75.0	75.0
IN THE MONEY 50¢	75.2	74.8	74.3	73.8	73.2	72.6	72.1	71.5	70.9	70.3	69.7	69.0	68.2	67.5	66.7	65.9	65.0	64.2	63.3	62.3	61.3	60.2	59.0	57.8	56.5	55.4	53.2	51.4	50.4	50.0	50.0
IN THE MONEY 25¢	61.8	61.2	60.6	60.0	59.4	58.8	58.2	57.6	56.9	56.3	55.6	54.8	54.1	53.3	52.4	51.3	50.3	49.3	48.2	46.9	45.6	44.2	42.7	41.0	39.0	36.5	33.9	30.9	27.9	25.7	25.0
AT THE MONEY	51.5	50.9	50.3	49.7	49.1	48.4	47.8	47.1	46.3	45.5	44.8	43.9	42.9	42.0	41.0	40.0	38.9	37.8	36.6	35.2	33.8	32.2	30.5	28.6	26.4	23.4	20.3	16.5	12.2	7.4	0.0
OUT OF THE MONEY 25¢	42.0	41.4	40.8	40.2	39.6	39.0	38.4	37.7	36.9	36.2	35.4	34.7	33.6	32.7	31.7	30.7	29.7	28.6	27.4	26.1	24.7	23.1	21.4	19.6	17.6	14.7	11.9	8.4	4.5	1.4	0.0
OUT OF THE MONEY 50¢	33.5	33.0	32.4	31.9	31.3	30.6	30.1	29.4	28.7	28.1	27.4	26.6	25.7	24.9	24.0	23.1	22.1	21.1	20.0	18.9	17.7	16.4	15.0	13.5	11.8	9.5	7.3	4.6	1.8	0.2	0.0
OUT OF THE MONEY 75¢	29.5	29.0	28.4	27.8	27.2	26.6	26.0	25.3	24.6	23.9	23.1	22.3	21.4	20.6	19.7	18.8	17.8	16.8	15.7	14.6	13.4	12.1	10.7	9.2	7.7	5.7	3.8	1.8	0.5	0.0	0.0
OUT OF THE MONEY $1.00	22.9	22.4	21.8	21.3	20.7	20.2	19.7	19.1	18.5	17.9	17.3	16.6	16.0	15.1	14.4	13.7	12.9	12.1	11.3	10.5	9.6	8.6	7.6	6.6	5.5	4.1	2.7	1.4	0.2	0.0	0.0
OUT OF THE MONEY $1.25	16.5	16.1	15.7	15.3	15.0	14.6	14.2	13.8	13.3	12.9	12.4	11.8	11.2	10.7	10.1	9.5	8.9	8.4	7.8	7.1	6.4	5.5	4.8	4.0	3.2	2.3	1.4	0.4	0.0	0.0	0.0

WM GRANDMILL (1985) LTD.

OPTION VALUES on SOYBEAN FUTURES – Table No: 53

OPTION VALUES ARE IN CENTS – to nearest tenth.

WEEKS TO EXPIRATION	30	29	28	27	26	25	24	23	22	21	20	19	18	17	16	15	14	13	12	11	10	9	8	7	6	5	4	3	2	1	0
IN THE MONEY $1.25	132.4	132.0	131.5	131.1	130.7	130.2	129.8	129.3	128.8	128.4	127.9	127.5	126.9	126.4	126.0	125.7	125.4	125.2	125.1	125.0	125.0	125.0	125.0	125.0	125.0	125.0	125.0	125.0	125.0	125.0	125.0
IN THE MONEY $1.00	108.5	108.1	107.7	107.3	107.0	106.6	106.2	105.8	105.4	105.0	104.5	104.0	103.4	102.9	102.5	102.2	101.9	101.7	101.5	101.2	100.9	100.7	100.5	100.3	100.1	100.1	100.0	100.0	100.0	100.0	100.0
IN THE MONEY 75¢	88.1	87.8	87.4	87.0	86.7	86.3	85.9	85.5	85.1	84.7	84.2	83.8	83.3	82.8	82.3	81.8	81.3	80.8	80.3	79.7	79.1	78.5	77.9	77.3	76.7	75.9	75.4	75.1	75.0	75.0	75.0
IN THE MONEY 50¢	74.5	74.0	73.5	73.0	72.4	71.9	71.4	70.8	70.3	69.7	69.1	68.4	67.6	66.8	66.0	65.3	64.5	63.7	62.9	61.8	60.9	59.8	58.7	57.5	56.2	54.6	53.1	51.3	50.3	50.0	50.0
IN THE MONEY 25¢	60.9	60.3	59.7	59.2	58.6	58.1	57.6	57.0	56.4	55.7	54.9	54.1	53.3	52.4	51.5	50.6	49.7	48.7	47.6	46.4	45.1	43.8	42.3	40.6	38.7	36.2	33.8	30.7	27.8	25.7	25.0
AT THE MONEY	50.6	50.0	49.4	48.8	48.2	47.6	47.0	46.3	45.5	44.9	44.1	43.2	42.3	41.3	40.3	39.3	38.3	37.2	36.0	34.6	33.2	31.7	30.0	28.1	25.9	23.0	20.0	16.2	12.0	7.2	0.0
OUT OF THE MONEY 25¢	41.1	40.5	39.9	39.4	38.8	38.2	37.6	36.9	36.2	35.5	34.7	33.9	33.0	32.0	31.0	30.0	29.0	27.9	26.7	25.4	24.1	22.6	20.9	19.1	17.2	14.4	11.5	8.1	4.3	1.3	0.0
OUT OF THE MONEY 50¢	32.7	32.2	31.6	31.0	30.4	29.9	29.3	28.7	28.1	27.5	26.9	26.2	25.4	24.6	23.8	22.9	22.0	21.0	20.0	18.9	17.7	16.4	15.0	13.5	11.8	9.3	7.2	4.5	1.7	0.2	0.0
OUT OF THE MONEY 75¢	28.7	28.1	27.5	27.0	26.4	25.8	25.2	24.5	23.9	23.2	22.4	21.6	20.8	19.9	19.0	18.1	17.2	16.3	15.3	14.2	13.0	11.7	10.4	8.9	7.4	5.5	3.7	1.7	0.4	0.0	0.0
OUT OF THE MONEY $1.00	22.0	21.5	21.0	20.5	20.0	19.5	19.1	18.6	18.0	17.4	16.7	16.0	15.2	14.5	13.8	13.1	12.4	11.7	11.0	10.2	9.3	8.3	7.4	6.3	5.2	3.8	2.6	1.3	0.2	0.0	0.0
OUT OF THE MONEY $1.25	15.9	15.6	15.2	14.8	14.5	14.1	13.7	13.3	12.9	12.4	11.9	11.4	10.8	10.2	9.6	9.1	8.6	8.1	7.5	6.8	6.1	5.3	4.7	3.9	3.0	2.0	1.3	0.4	0.0	0.0	0.0

WM GRANDMILL (1985) LTD.

OPTION VALUES on SOYBEAN FUTURES – Table No: 55

	30	29	28	27	26	25	24	23	22	21	20	19	18	17	16	15	14	13	12	11	10	9	8	7	6	5	4	3	2	1	0
IN THE MONEY $1.25	134.1	133.5	133.1	132.7	132.3	131.9	131.4	130.8	130.4	129.9	129.3	128.7	128.2	127.7	127.1	126.6	126.1	125.7	125.4	125.2	125.0	125.0	125.0	125.0	125.0	125.0	125.0	125.0	125.0	125.0	125.0
$1.00	110.4	109.7	109.3	108.9	108.5	108.1	107.6	107.2	106.7	106.3	105.8	105.3	104.8	104.2	103.6	103.1	102.6	102.2	101.9	101.7	101.4	101.1	100.8	100.6	100.4	100.2	100.1	100.1	100.0	100.0	100.0
75¢	89.3	88.9	88.5	88.1	87.7	87.3	86.7	86.4	86.0	85.5	85.0	84.5	84.0	83.5	83.0	82.5	82.0	81.4	80.8	80.2	79.6	78.9	78.3	77.6	76.9	76.0	75.4	75.1	75.0	75.0	75.0
50¢	75.9	75.4	74.9	74.4	73.9	73.3	72.7	72.1	71.5	70.8	70.2	69.5	68.7	67.9	67.1	66.3	65.5	64.6	63.7	62.7	61.6	60.5	59.4	58.1	56.8	55.0	53.4	51.5	50.4	50.0	50.0
25¢	62.6	62.0	61.4	60.8	60.2	59.5	58.9	58.3	57.6	56.9	56.2	55.4	54.5	53.6	52.7	51.8	50.8	49.8	48.7	47.5	46.1	44.7	43.2	41.4	39.5	36.9	34.2	31.2	28.0	25.8	25.0
AT THE MONEY 25¢	52.3	51.7	51.1	50.5	49.9	49.2	48.5	47.8	47.1	46.3	45.5	44.6	43.6	42.6	41.6	40.6	39.6	38.4	37.2	35.8	34.3	32.7	31.0	29.1	26.8	23.8	20.6	16.8	12.4	7.5	0.0
OUT OF THE MONEY 25¢	42.8	42.2	41.6	41.0	40.4	39.7	39.1	38.4	37.7	36.9	36.1	35.2	34.3	33.3	32.3	31.3	30.3	29.2	28.0	26.6	25.1	23.6	21.9	20.0	18.0	15.3	12.2	8.7	4.7	1.4	0
50¢	34.2	33.7	33.1	32.6	32.0	31.4	30.7	30.1	29.4	28.7	28.0	27.2	26.3	25.4	24.5	23.6	22.6	21.6	20.5	19.3	18.1	16.8	15.5	13.9	12.1	9.9	7.5	4.9	2.0	0.2	0
75¢	30.2	29.7	29.1	28.6	28.0	27.3	26.7	26.0	25.3	24.6	23.8	22.9	22.0	21.1	20.2	19.3	18.3	17.3	16.3	15.1	13.8	12.5	11.2	9.6	8.0	5.9	4.0	2.0	0.5	0	0
$1.00	23.6	23.1	22.5	22.0	21.4	20.8	20.2	19.7	19.1	18.4	17.8	17.1	16.3	15.5	14.7	14.0	13.3	12.5	11.7	10.8	9.9	8.8	8.0	6.8	5.7	4.2	2.8	1.5	0.3	0	0
$1.25	17.1	16.7	16.3	15.9	15.5	15.1	14.6	14.2	13.8	13.3	12.8	12.2	11.6	11.0	10.4	9.8	9.3	8.7	8.1	7.4	6.6	5.8	5.1	4.3	3.4	2.3	1.5	0.5	0	0	0

WEEKS TO EXPIRATION

OPTION VALUES ARE IN CENTS – to nearest tenth.

WM GRANDMILL (1985) LTD.

OPTION VALUES on SOYBEAN FUTURES – Table No: 56

	30	29	28	27	26	25	24	23	22	21	20	19	18	17	16	15	14	13	12	11	10	9	8	7	6	5	4	3	2	1	0
IN THE MONEY $1.25	134.1	133.6	133.3	132.8	132.4	132.0	131.4	130.9	130.4	129.9	129.3	128.7	128.1	127.6	127.0	126.4	125.9	125.6	125.3	125.1	125.0	125.0	125.0	125.0	125.0	125.0	125.0	125.0	125.0	125.0	125.0
$1.00	110.4	109.9	109.5	109.0	108.6	108.1	107.6	107.2	106.8	106.3	105.8	105.3	104.6	104.1	103.5	102.9	102.5	102.2	101.8	101.5	101.2	100.9	100.6	100.4	100.2	100.0	100.0	100.0	100.0	100.0	100.0
75¢	89.9	89.5	89.1	88.6	88.2	87.8	87.3	86.9	86.5	86.0	85.5	84.9	84.4	83.9	83.4	82.8	82.3	81.7	81.1	80.4	79.8	79.2	78.4	77.7	77.0	76.1	75.5	75.1	75.0	75.0	75.0
50¢	76.6	76.1	75.6	75.0	74.6	74.0	73.4	72.8	72.2	71.5	70.8	70.0	69.2	68.5	67.7	66.8	66.0	65.1	64.1	63.1	62.0	60.8	59.6	58.3	57.0	55.2	53.6	51.6	50.4	50.0	50.0
25¢	63.4	62.8	62.2	61.6	61.0	60.3	59.6	59.0	58.3	57.6	56.8	56.0	55.1	54.3	53.4	52.4	51.4	50.4	49.3	48.1	46.7	45.2	43.5	41.8	39.8	37.1	34.6	31.4	28.1	25.8	25.0
AT THE MONEY 25¢	53.1	52.5	51.9	51.3	50.7	50.0	49.3	48.6	47.9	47.1	46.2	45.3	44.3	43.4	42.4	41.3	40.2	39.0	37.8	36.4	34.9	33.3	31.4	29.5	27.2	24.2	21.0	17.0	12.5	7.6	0.0
OUT OF THE MONEY 25¢	43.5	43.0	42.4	41.8	41.2	40.5	39.8	39.2	38.5	37.7	36.8	35.9	34.9	34.0	33.0	32.0	30.9	29.8	28.6	27.2	25.7	24.2	22.3	20.4	18.3	15.5	12.6	8.9	4.8	1.4	0
50¢	35.0	34.4	33.9	33.3	32.8	32.2	31.5	30.8	30.1	29.4	28.6	27.8	26.9	26.1	25.2	24.2	23.2	22.2	21.1	19.9	18.7	17.2	15.7	14.2	12.4	10.2	7.9	5.1	2.0	0.3	0
75¢	31.0	30.4	29.9	29.3	28.7	28.1	27.4	26.8	26.1	25.3	24.4	23.6	22.7	21.8	20.9	19.9	18.9	17.9	16.8	15.6	14.4	12.9	11.4	9.9	8.3	6.2	4.3	2.1	0.6	0	0
$1.00	24.3	23.8	23.3	22.7	22.2	21.6	20.9	20.3	19.7	19.1	18.4	17.6	16.8	16.1	15.3	14.5	13.8	13.0	12.1	11.2	10.3	9.3	8.2	7.0	5.9	4.4	3.0	1.6	0.3	0	0
$1.25	17.7	17.3	16.9	16.4	16.0	15.6	15.1	14.7	14.3	13.8	13.3	12.7	12.1	11.5	10.9	10.2	9.6	9.0	8.4	7.7	6.9	6.1	5.2	4.4	3.5	2.5	1.6	0.5	0.0	0	0

WEEKS TO EXPIRATION

OPTION VALUES ARE IN CENTS – to nearest tenth.

WM GRANDMILL (1985) LTD.

OPTION VALUES on SOYBEAN FUTURES – Table No:58

OPTION VALUES ARE IN CENTS – to nearest tenth.

	Strike	30	29	28	27	26	25	24	23	22	21	20	19	18	17	16	15	14	13	12	11	10	9	8	7	6	5	4	3	2	1	0
IN THE MONEY	$1.25	135.3	134.9	134.4	134.0	133.5	133.3	132.6	132.1	131.5	130.9	130.3	129.7	129.0	128.3	127.7	127.1	126.5	126.0	125.6	125.3	125.1	125.0	125.0	125.0	125.0	125.0	125.0	125.0	125.0	125.0	125.0
	$1.00	111.9	111.3	110.8	110.3	109.8	109.3	108.8	108.3	107.7	107.2	106.6	106.1	105.6	105.1	104.5	103.8	103.2	102.7	102.3	101.9	101.6	101.3	101.0	100.7	100.5	100.3	100.0	100.0	100.0	100.0	100.0
	75¢	91.2	90.7	90.2	89.6	89.3	88.8	88.4	87.9	87.4	86.9	86.3	85.8	85.2	84.6	84.0	83.5	82.9	82.3	81.7	81.0	80.3	79.6	78.8	78.0	77.3	76.4	75.6	75.2	75.0	75.0	75.0
	50¢	78.2	77.6	77.1	76.5	75.9	75.3	74.8	74.2	73.5	72.8	72.0	71.3	70.5	69.7	68.8	67.9	67.0	66.0	65.0	63.9	62.8	61.6	60.3	58.9	57.5	55.7	53.9	51.9	50.5	50.0	50.0
	25¢	65.2	64.5	63.9	63.2	62.6	61.9	61.2	60.5	59.9	59.0	58.2	57.4	56.5	55.6	54.6	53.6	52.6	51.5	50.3	49.1	47.7	46.1	44.4	42.8	40.6	37.9	35.0	31.8	28.4	25.9	25.0
AT THE MONEY	25¢	54.9	54.2	53.6	52.9	52.3	51.6	50.9	50.2	49.4	48.6	47.7	46.8	45.8	44.8	43.7	42.6	41.5	40.3	39.0	37.5	36.0	34.3	32.4	30.5	28.1	25.0	21.6	17.6	12.9	7.8	0.0
OUT OF THE MONEY	25¢	45.3	44.6	44.0	43.4	42.8	42.1	41.4	40.7	39.9	39.1	38.3	37.4	36.4	35.4	34.4	33.3	32.2	31.0	29.7	28.3	26.8	25.1	23.3	21.4	19.1	16.3	13.1	9.4	5.2	1.5	0
	50¢	36.8	36.1	35.5	34.8	34.2	33.6	33.0	32.3	31.6	30.8	30.0	29.2	28.3	27.4	26.4	25.4	24.4	23.3	22.1	20.9	19.6	18.1	16.5	15.0	13.1	10.9	8.2	5.4	2.3	0.3	0
	75¢	32.8	32.1	31.5	30.8	30.2	29.6	29.0	28.3	27.5	26.7	25.9	25.0	24.1	23.2	22.1	21.1	20.1	19.0	17.8	16.6	15.3	13.8	12.2	10.7	8.9	6.8	4.6	2.4	0.7	0	0
	$1.00	26.0	25.3	24.8	24.2	23.6	23.0	22.4	21.7	21.0	20.3	19.6	18.9	18.1	17.3	16.4	15.5	14.6	13.7	12.8	11.8	10.9	9.9	8.8	7.6	6.3	4.8	3.2	1.8	0.4	0	0
	$1.25	19.0	18.5	18.0	17.6	17.1	16.6	16.2	15.7	15.2	14.7	14.1	13.6	13.0	12.3	11.6	11.0	10.3	9.6	8.9	8.2	7.4	6.6	5.7	4.8	3.9	2.8	1.7	0.6	0	0	0

WM GRANDMILL (1985) LTD.

OPTION VALUES on SOYBEAN FUTURES – Table No:57

OPTION VALUES ARE IN CENTS – to nearest tenth.

	Strike	30	29	28	27	26	25	24	23	22	21	20	19	18	17	16	15	14	13	12	11	10	9	8	7	6	5	4	3	2	1	0
IN THE MONEY	$1.25	134.8	134.3	133.8	133.4	133.0	132.5	132.0	131.5	130.9	130.4	129.8	129.2	128.5	127.9	127.3	126.7	126.2	125.8	125.4	125.1	125.0	125.0	125.0	125.0	125.0	125.0	125.0	125.0	125.0	125.0	125.0
	$1.00	111.2	110.6	110.1	109.6	109.1	108.7	108.2	107.7	107.2	106.7	106.2	105.7	105.1	104.5	103.8	103.2	102.7	102.3	101.9	101.6	101.3	101.0	100.7	100.5	100.2	100.0	100.0	100.0	100.0	100.0	100.0
	75¢	90.6	90.1	89.6	89.2	88.7	88.3	87.8	87.4	86.9	86.4	85.9	85.4	84.8	84.2	83.7	83.1	82.6	82.0	81.3	80.6	80.0	79.4	78.6	77.9	77.1	76.3	75.6	75.1	75.0	75.0	75.0
	50¢	77.5	76.9	76.3	75.7	75.2	74.7	74.1	73.5	72.8	72.1	71.4	70.7	69.9	69.1	68.3	67.5	66.6	65.6	64.6	63.5	62.4	61.3	60.0	58.7	57.2	55.4	53.7	51.7	50.4	50.0	50.0
	25¢	64.3	63.7	63.0	62.4	61.8	61.1	60.4	59.7	59.0	58.3	57.5	56.7	55.8	54.9	54.0	53.1	52.1	51.0	49.8	48.5	47.1	45.7	44.0	42.3	40.2	37.5	34.7	31.5	28.2	25.8	25.0
AT THE MONEY	25¢	54.0	53.4	52.7	52.1	51.5	50.8	50.1	49.4	48.6	47.8	47.0	46.1	45.1	44.1	43.1	41.9	40.9	39.7	38.4	36.9	35.4	33.8	31.9	30.0	27.6	24.6	21.3	17.3	12.7	7.7	0.0
OUT OF THE MONEY	25¢	44.4	43.8	43.2	42.6	42.0	41.3	40.6	39.9	39.2	38.4	37.6	36.7	35.7	34.7	33.7	32.7	31.6	30.4	29.1	27.7	26.2	24.7	22.8	20.9	18.7	15.9	12.8	9.1	5.0	1.5	0
	50¢	35.9	35.3	34.6	34.0	33.5	32.9	32.2	31.5	30.8	30.1	29.3	28.5	27.6	26.7	25.8	24.8	23.8	22.7	21.5	20.3	19.0	17.6	16.2	14.7	12.7	10.5	8.0	5.2	2.2	0.3	0
	75¢	31.9	31.3	30.6	30.0	29.5	28.9	28.2	27.5	26.8	26.0	25.2	24.3	23.4	22.5	21.5	20.5	19.6	18.4	17.2	16.0	14.7	13.4	11.9	10.4	8.5	6.4	4.4	2.2	0.6	0	0
	$1.00	25.2	24.6	24.0	23.4	22.9	22.3	21.6	21.0	20.4	19.8	19.1	18.3	17.5	16.7	15.9	15.1	14.3	13.4	12.4	11.5	10.6	9.6	8.5	7.4	6.1	4.6	3.1	1.7	0.3	0	0
	$1.25	18.4	17.9	17.4	17.0	16.5	16.1	15.6	15.2	14.7	14.2	13.7	13.2	12.6	11.9	11.3	10.6	10.0	9.3	8.6	7.9	7.2	6.4	5.3	4.5	3.7	2.6	1.6	0.5	0	0	0

WM GRANDMILL (1985) LTD.

OPTION VALUES on SOYBEAN FUTURES – Table No. 60

OPTION VALUES ARE IN CENTS – to nearest tenth.

	30	29	28	27	26	25	24	23	22	21	20	19	18	17	16	15	14	13	12	11	10	9	8	7	6	5	4	3	2	1	0
IN THE MONEY $1.25	136.7	136.2	135.7	135.2	134.7	134.2	133.6	133.1	132.6	132.0	131.4	130.7	130.0	129.2	128.5	127.8	127.2	126.5	125.9	125.5	125.2	125.2	125.0	125.0	125.0	125.0	125.0	125.0	125.0	125.0	125.0
IN THE MONEY $1.00	113.2	112.7	112.1	111.6	111.1	110.5	110.0	109.4	108.8	108.2	107.6	107.0	106.4	105.7	105.0	104.3	103.6	103.0	102.5	102.0	101.7	101.3	100.9	100.6	100.3	100.0	100.0	100.0	100.0	100.0	100.0
IN THE MONEY 75¢	92.5	92.0	91.5	91.0	90.5	90.0	89.4	88.9	88.4	87.8	87.3	86.7	86.1	85.4	84.8	84.2	83.6	82.9	82.2	81.5	80.7	80.0	79.2	78.4	77.5	76.6	75.7	75.2	75.0	75.0	75.0
IN THE MONEY 50¢	79.8	79.2	78.6	78.0	77.4	76.7	76.1	75.4	74.8	74.1	73.3	72.6	71.8	71.0	70.1	69.2	68.4	67.5	66.5	65.5	64.4	63.2	62.0	60.7	59.3	57.7	55.8	54.1	52.0	50.5	50.0
IN THE MONEY 25¢	66.9	66.2	65.6	64.9	64.2	63.5	62.8	62.0	61.2	60.4	59.5	58.6	57.7	56.7	55.8	54.8	53.7	52.6	51.4	50.1	48.6	47.1	45.3	43.5	41.3	38.5	35.5	32.2	28.6	26.0	25.0
AT THE MONEY	56.6	55.9	55.3	54.6	53.9	53.2	52.5	51.7	50.9	50.1	49.2	48.2	47.2	46.1	45.0	43.9	42.8	41.5	40.2	38.7	37.1	35.4	33.4	31.4	28.9	25.7	22.3	18.1	13.3	8.1	0.0
OUT OF THE MONEY 25¢	47.0	46.3	45.7	45.0	44.3	43.6	42.9	42.2	41.4	40.6	39.7	38.8	37.8	36.7	35.7	34.6	33.4	32.2	30.9	29.5	27.9	26.2	24.3	22.3	19.9	17.0	13.7	9.8	5.5	1.6	0
OUT OF THE MONEY 50¢	38.3	37.7	37.1	36.5	35.8	35.1	34.4	33.7	33.0	32.2	31.3	30.4	29.5	28.5	27.6	26.6	25.6	24.4	23.2	21.9	20.5	19.0	17.3	15.7	13.8	11.3	8.7	5.8	2.5	0.3	0
OUT OF THE MONEY 75¢	34.4	33.7	33.1	32.5	31.8	31.1	30.4	29.7	29.0	28.2	27.3	26.4	25.4	24.3	23.3	22.3	21.3	20.1	18.9	17.6	16.2	14.7	13.0	11.4	9.5	7.2	5.0	2.6	0.8	0	0
OUT OF THE MONEY $1.00	27.6	26.9	26.3	25.7	25.1	24.4	23.8	23.1	22.4	21.6	20.8	20.0	19.2	18.3	17.5	16.6	15.6	14.6	13.7	12.7	11.6	10.6	9.4	8.2	6.7	5.1	3.5	1.9	0.4	0	0
OUT OF THE MONEY $1.25	20.3	19.8	19.3	18.8	18.3	17.8	17.2	16.7	16.2	15.6	15.1	14.5	13.9	13.2	12.5	11.8	11.1	10.3	9.6	8.8	8.0	7.1	6.2	5.2	4.2	3.0	1.8	0.7	0	0	0

WEEKS TO EXPIRATION

WM GRANDMILL (1985) LTD.

OPTION VALUES on SOYBEAN FUTURES – Table No:59

OPTION VALUES ARE IN CENTS – to nearest tenth.

	30	29	28	27	26	25	24	23	22	21	20	19	18	17	16	15	14	13	12	11	10	9	8	7	6	5	4	3	2	1	0
IN THE MONEY $1.25	136.0	135.5	135.0	134.5	134.1	133.6	133.1	132.6	132.0	131.4	130.8	130.1	129.4	128.7	128.1	127.5	126.7	126.2	125.8	125.4	125.1	125.0	125.0	125.0	125.0	125.0	125.0	125.0	125.0	125.0	125.0
IN THE MONEY $1.00	112.5	112.0	111.4	110.9	110.4	109.8	109.3	108.8	108.2	107.6	107.1	106.5	105.9	105.3	104.6	104.0	103.3	102.7	102.2	101.8	101.5	101.1	100.8	100.5	100.3	100.0	100.0	100.0	100.0	100.0	100.0
IN THE MONEY 75¢	91.8	91.3	90.8	90.3	89.9	89.4	88.9	88.4	87.8	87.3	86.8	86.2	85.6	85.0	84.4	83.8	83.2	82.6	81.9	81.2	80.5	79.8	79.0	78.2	77.4	76.5	75.7	75.2	75.0	75.0	75.0
IN THE MONEY 50¢	79.0	78.4	77.8	77.2	76.6	76.0	75.4	74.8	74.1	73.4	72.6	71.8	71.0	70.1	69.2	68.4	67.5	66.5	65.5	64.4	63.2	62.0	60.7	59.3	57.7	55.8	54.1	52.1	50.9	50.5	50.0
IN THE MONEY 25¢	66.0	65.3	64.7	64.0	63.4	62.7	62.0	61.2	60.4	59.6	58.8	58.0	57.1	56.1	55.1	54.1	53.1	52.1	50.9	49.6	48.2	46.6	44.9	43.1	40.9	38.1	34.8	30.9	28.5	25.9	25.0
AT THE MONEY	55.7	55.0	54.4	53.7	53.1	52.4	51.7	50.9	50.1	49.3	48.4	47.5	46.5	45.4	44.3	43.2	42.1	40.9	39.6	38.1	36.6	34.8	32.9	30.9	28.5	25.3	22.0	17.9	13.1	8.0	0.0
OUT OF THE MONEY 25¢	46.1	45.4	44.8	44.1	43.5	42.9	42.2	41.4	40.6	39.8	39.0	38.1	37.1	36.0	34.9	33.9	32.8	31.6	30.3	28.9	27.4	25.6	23.8	21.8	19.5	16.6	13.5	9.7	5.3	1.6	0
OUT OF THE MONEY 50¢	37.5	36.9	36.3	35.6	35.0	34.3	33.7	33.0	32.2	31.4	30.6	29.8	28.8	28.0	26.9	25.9	24.9	23.9	22.7	21.4	20.0	18.6	17.0	15.4	13.4	11.0	8.6	5.7	2.4	0.3	0
OUT OF THE MONEY 75¢	33.5	32.9	32.3	31.6	31.0	30.3	29.7	29.0	28.2	27.4	26.6	25.7	24.7	23.7	22.7	21.6	20.7	19.6	18.4	17.1	15.7	14.3	12.7	11.1	9.1	6.9	4.9	2.5	0.8	0	0
OUT OF THE MONEY $1.00	26.7	26.1	25.5	24.9	24.3	23.7	23.1	22.4	21.6	20.9	20.1	19.4	18.6	17.7	16.8	16.0	15.2	14.3	13.3	12.3	11.3	10.2	9.1	7.9	6.5	4.9	3.4	1.9	0.4	0	0
OUT OF THE MONEY $1.25	19.6	19.1	18.6	18.1	17.7	17.2	16.7	16.2	15.6	15.1	14.6	14.0	13.4	12.7	12.0	11.4	10.7	10.0	9.3	8.6	7.8	6.9	5.9	5.0	4.0	2.9	1.8	0.6	0.1	0	0

WEEKS TO EXPIRATION

WM GRANDMILL (1985) LTD.

OPTION VALUES on SOYBEAN FUTURES – Table No: 62

		30	29	28	27	26	25	24	23	22	21	20	19	18	17	16	15	14	13	12	11	10	9	8	7	6	5	4	3	2	1	0
														WEEKS TO EXPIRATION																		
IN THE MONEY	$1.25	138.1	137.5	137.0	136.4	135.8	135.3	134.8	134.2	133.6	133.1	132.5	131.9	131.2	130.8	130.1	129.4	128.9	128.2	127.6	126.9	126.5	125.9	125.4	125.1	125.0	125.0	125.0	125.0	125.0	125.0	125.0
	$1.00	114.5	114.0	113.5	112.9	112.3	111.8	111.2	110.5	109.9	109.3	108.7	108.1	107.7	107.1	106.5	105.9	105.4	104.8	104.1	103.4	103.0	102.4	101.9	101.5	101.1	100.7	100.4	100.1	100.0	100.0	100.0
	75¢	93.8	93.3	92.8	92.2	91.6	91.1	90.6	90.0	89.4	88.7	88.0	87.4	86.8	86.2	85.6	84.9	84.2	83.7	82.9	82.1	81.3	80.5	79.7	78.8	77.8	76.8	75.8	75.2	75.0	75.0	75.0
	50¢	81.3	80.7	80.1	79.4	78.8	78.2	77.5	76.8	76.1	75.4	74.7	73.9	73.1	72.7	71.8	70.9	70.0	69.1	68.1	66.9	65.7	64.5	63.1	61.7	60.2	58.5	56.6	54.6	52.5	50.6	50.0
	25¢	68.8	68.0	67.3	66.5	65.8	65.1	64.3	63.6	62.7	61.8	60.8	59.8	58.9	58.0	57.0	55.9	54.9	53.8	52.5	51.1	49.6	48.0	46.2	44.3	42.1	39.2	36.2	32.7	28.9	26.0	25.0
AT THE MONEY	25¢	58.3	57.6	56.9	56.2	55.5	54.8	54.0	53.2	52.4	51.5	50.5	49.5	48.5	47.5	46.4	45.2	44.0	42.8	41.4	39.8	38.2	36.4	34.4	32.3	29.8	26.5	23.0	18.7	13.7	8.3	0.0
OUT OF THE MONEY	25¢	48.7	48.0	47.4	46.6	45.9	45.2	44.4	43.7	42.9	42.0	41.0	40.0	39.1	38.1	37.0	35.8	34.7	33.5	32.1	30.5	28.9	27.2	25.2	23.2	20.7	17.7	14.4	10.4	5.9	1.7	0
	50¢	40.0	39.3	38.5	37.7	36.9	36.2	35.9	35.1	34.2	33.5	32.6	31.7	30.7	29.8	28.8	27.7	26.7	25.6	24.3	22.9	21.4	19.8	18.2	16.4	14.5	11.8	9.3	6.2	2.8	0.4	0
	75¢	36.1	35.4	34.7	34.0	33.3	32.6	31.9	31.1	30.3	29.5	28.6	27.6	26.7	25.7	24.6	23.5	22.4	21.2	20.0	18.6	17.1	15.6	13.9	12.1	10.2	7.7	5.5	2.9	1.0	0	0
	$1.00	29.2	28.5	27.9	27.2	26.5	25.9	25.2	24.4	23.7	22.9	22.0	21.1	20.2	19.4	18.5	17.6	16.7	15.7	14.6	13.5	12.4	11.2	10.0	8.7	7.2	5.5	3.8	2.1	0.5	0	0
	$1.25	21.6	21.1	20.6	20.0	19.4	18.9	18.4	17.8	17.2	16.5	15.8	15.2	14.6	14.0	13.4	12.7	11.9	11.1	10.3	9.4	8.6	7.7	6.7	5.6	4.6	3.2	2.0	0.9	0.1	0	0

OPTION VALUES ARE IN CENTS – to nearest tenth.

WM GRANDMILL (1985) LTD.

OPTION VALUES on SOYBEAN FUTURES – Table No: 61

		30	29	28	27	26	25	24	23	22	21	20	19	18	17	16	15	14	13	12	11	10	9	8	7	6	5	4	3	2	1	0
														WEEKS TO EXPIRATION																		
IN THE MONEY	$1.25	137.3	136.8	136.3	135.7	135.2	134.7	134.2	133.6	133.1	132.5	131.9	131.2	130.5	129.7	128.9	128.2	127.6	126.9	126.2	125.7	125.3	125.1	125.0	125.0	125.0	125.0	125.0	125.0	125.0	125.0	125.0
	$1.00	113.8	113.3	112.8	112.2	111.7	111.2	110.5	109.9	109.3	108.7	108.1	107.4	106.8	106.1	105.4	104.8	104.1	103.4	102.7	102.2	101.8	101.4	101.0	100.7	100.4	100.1	100.0	100.0	100.0	100.0	100.0
	75¢	93.1	92.6	92.1	91.5	91.0	90.5	90.0	89.4	88.9	88.3	87.7	87.1	86.5	85.8	85.1	84.5	83.9	83.3	82.6	81.8	81.0	80.2	79.4	78.6	77.7	76.7	75.8	75.2	75.0	75.0	75.0
	50¢	80.5	79.9	79.3	78.7	78.1	77.5	76.8	76.1	75.4	74.7	73.9	73.1	72.2	71.3	70.4	69.5	68.6	67.6	66.5	65.3	64.1	62.8	61.4	60.0	58.3	56.3	54.4	52.3	50.6	50.0	50.0
	25¢	67.7	67.0	66.3	65.7	65.0	64.3	63.6	62.8	62.0	61.1	60.2	59.3	58.4	57.4	56.4	55.4	54.3	53.2	52.0	50.7	49.2	47.6	45.8	44.0	41.7	38.8	35.8	32.4	28.7	26.0	25.0
AT THE MONEY	25¢	57.4	56.7	56.0	55.4	54.7	54.0	53.3	52.5	51.7	50.8	49.9	48.9	47.9	46.8	45.7	44.6	43.4	42.2	40.8	39.3	37.7	35.9	33.9	31.9	29.4	26.1	22.6	18.4	13.5	8.2	0.0
OUT OF THE MONEY	25¢	47.8	47.1	46.4	45.8	45.1	44.4	43.7	43.0	42.2	41.3	40.4	39.5	38.5	37.4	36.3	35.2	34.1	32.9	31.5	30.0	28.4	26.7	24.8	22.8	20.3	17.3	14.0	10.1	5.7	1.6	0
	50¢	39.1	38.4	37.8	37.2	36.6	35.9	35.2	34.4	33.7	32.9	32.0	31.1	30.2	29.2	28.2	27.2	26.1	25.0	23.8	22.4	21.0	19.5	17.8	16.0	14.1	11.6	8.9	6.0	2.7	0.3	0
	75¢	35.2	34.5	33.8	33.2	32.6	31.9	31.2	30.4	29.7	28.9	28.0	27.1	26.1	25.0	24.0	22.9	21.8	20.6	19.4	18.1	16.8	15.2	13.5	11.9	9.8	7.5	5.2	2.8	0.9	0	0
	$1.00	28.3	27.7	27.0	26.4	25.8	25.2	24.5	23.8	23.1	22.3	21.5	20.6	19.8	18.9	18.0	17.1	16.1	15.2	14.2	13.1	12.0	10.9	9.7	8.5	7.0	5.3	3.7	2.0	0.5	0	0
	$1.25	20.9	20.4	19.9	19.3	18.8	18.3	17.8	17.2	16.7	16.1	15.5	14.9	14.3	13.6	12.9	12.2	11.5	10.7	9.9	9.1	8.3	7.4	6.4	5.4	4.4	3.1	1.9	0.8	0.1	0	0

OPTION VALUES ARE IN CENTS – to nearest tenth.

WM GRANDMILL (1985) LTD.

OPTION VALUES on SOYBEAN FUTURES – Table No:64

	30	29	28	27	26	25	24	23	22	21	20	19	18	17	16	15	14	13	12	11	10	9	8	7	6	5	4	3	2	1	0
IN THE MONEY																															
25¢	70.5	69.8	69.0	68.2	67.5	66.7	65.9	65.1	64.2	63.3	62.4	61.4	60.3	59.3	58.2	57.1	56.0	54.9	53.6	52.2	50.6	48.9	47.1	45.2	43.0	39.9	36.6	33.1	29.2	26.1	25.0
50¢	82.8	82.1	81.5	80.9	80.2	79.6	78.9	78.2	77.4	76.6	75.7	74.9	74.1	73.1	72.0	71.0	70.0	69.1	67.9	66.7	65.3	63.9	62.4	60.9	59.1	57.0	54.9	52.7	50.7	50.0	50.0
75¢	95.3	94.6	94.0	93.5	92.9	92.3	91.7	91.1	90.5	89.8	89.2	88.5	87.8	87.1	86.3	85.6	84.9	84.2	83.5	82.7	81.8	80.9	80.0	79.1	78.1	77.0	76.0	75.3	75.0	75.0	75.0
$1.00	116.0	115.3	114.7	114.1	113.6	113.0	112.4	111.8	111.1	110.4	109.6	108.9	108.2	107.4	106.6	105.9	105.2	104.4	103.6	102.8	102.2	101.8	101.3	100.9	100.5	100.2	100.0	100.0	100.0	100.0	100.0
$1.25	139.6	138.9	138.3	137.7	137.1	136.5	135.9	135.3	134.7	134.1	133.4	132.7	132.0	131.2	130.3	129.4	128.6	127.6	126.8	126.0	125.6	125.3	125.0	125.0	125.0	125.0	125.0	125.0	125.0	125.0	125.0
AT THE MONEY	59.9	59.2	58.5	57.8	57.1	56.4	55.6	54.8	53.9	53.0	52.1	51.1	50.0	48.9	47.7	46.5	45.3	44.0	42.6	41.0	39.3	37.5	35.4	33.3	30.7	27.3	23.6	19.2	14.1	8.6	0.0
OUT OF THE MONEY																															
25¢	50.3	49.6	48.9	48.2	47.5	46.8	46.0	45.2	44.3	43.5	42.6	41.6	40.5	39.5	38.3	37.1	35.9	34.7	33.3	31.7	30.0	28.2	26.2	24.2	21.6	18.4	14.9	10.9	6.2	1.8	
50¢	41.5	40.8	40.2	39.5	38.8	38.1	37.4	36.6	35.8	34.9	34.0	33.1	32.1	31.1	30.0	28.9	27.8	26.7	25.4	24.0	22.4	20.8	19.0	17.2	15.2	12.4	9.7	6.6	3.1	0.4	0
75¢	37.6	36.9	36.3	35.6	34.9	34.2	33.4	32.6	31.8	30.9	30.0	29.1	28.1	27.0	25.9	24.7	23.6	22.4	21.1	19.7	18.2	16.6	14.8	12.9	10.9	8.3	5.9	3.3	1.1	0	0
$1.00	30.7	30.0	29.4	28.7	28.0	27.3	26.6	25.9	25.1	24.3	23.4	22.5	21.6	20.6	19.6	18.6	17.6	16.7	15.5	14.4	13.1	11.8	10.6	9.3	7.7	5.9	4.1	2.3	0.6	0	
$1.25	23.0	22.4	21.8	21.3	20.7	20.1	19.5	18.9	18.3	17.7	17.0	16.3	15.6	14.9	14.1	13.4	12.7	11.9	11.0	10.1	9.1	8.2	7.2	6.1	4.9	3.6	2.2	1.0	0.2	0	

WEEKS TO EXPIRATION

OPTION VALUES ARE IN CENTS – to nearest tenth.

WM GRANDMILL (1985) LTD.

OPTION VALUES on SOYBEAN FUTURES – Table No:63

	30	29	28	27	26	25	24	23	22	21	20	19	18	17	16	15	14	13	12	11	10	9	8	7	6	5	4	3	2	1	0
IN THE MONEY																															
25¢	69.7	68.9	68.1	67.4	66.6	65.9	65.1	64.3	63.5	62.6	61.7	60.7	59.6	58.6	57.6	56.6	55.5	54.3	53.0	51.6	50.2	48.6	46.8	44.8	42.5	39.6	36.3	32.9	29.1	26.1	25.0
50¢	82.0	81.4	80.8	80.2	79.5	78.9	78.2	77.5	76.7	75.9	75.1	74.3	73.4	72.4	71.5	70.6	69.6	68.5	67.5	66.1	64.9	63.7	62.1	60.6	58.6	56.8	54.7	52.6	50.6	50.0	50.0
75¢	94.5	93.9	93.4	92.9	92.3	91.7	91.1	90.6	90.0	89.3	88.7	88.0	87.3	86.7	86.0	85.3	84.6	83.9	83.2	82.4	81.6	80.7	79.8	79.0	77.9	76.9	75.9	75.3	75.0	75.0	75.0
$1.00	115.2	114.6	114.1	113.6	113.0	112.4	111.8	111.2	110.5	109.7	109.1	108.4	107.6	107.0	106.3	105.6	104.8	104.1	103.3	102.6	102.0	101.6	101.2	100.8	100.5	100.1	100.0	100.0	100.0	100.0	100.0
$1.25	138.8	138.2	137.6	137.1	136.5	135.9	135.2	134.8	134.2	133.5	132.9	132.2	131.4	130.7	129.9	129.1	128.3	127.6	126.8	126.0	125.5	125.2	125.0	125.0	125.0	125.0	125.0	125.0	125.0	125.0	125.0
AT THE MONEY	59.1	58.4	57.7	57.0	56.3	55.6	54.8	54.0	53.2	52.3	51.4	50.4	49.3	48.2	47.1	45.9	44.7	43.4	42.0	40.4	38.8	37.0	34.9	32.8	30.2	26.9	23.3	18.9	13.9	8.4	0.0
OUT OF THE MONEY																															
25¢	49.5	48.8	48.1	47.4	46.7	46.0	45.2	44.4	43.6	42.8	41.9	40.9	39.8	38.8	37.7	36.5	35.3	34.1	32.7	31.1	29.7	27.9	25.8	23.6	21.1	18.1	14.6	10.6	6.1	1.7	
50¢	40.7	40.1	39.4	38.7	38.0	37.4	36.7	35.9	35.1	34.2	33.4	32.5	31.5	30.4	29.4	28.4	27.3	26.1	24.8	23.4	22.0	20.4	18.7	16.9	14.8	12.2	9.4	6.4	3.0	0.4	0
75¢	36.8	36.2	35.5	34.8	34.1	33.4	32.7	31.9	31.1	30.2	29.3	28.4	27.4	26.4	25.3	24.2	23.1	21.8	20.5	19.1	17.7	16.2	14.4	12.6	10.5	8.1	5.6	3.1	1.0	0	0
$1.00	29.9	29.3	28.6	28.0	27.3	26.6	25.9	25.2	24.4	23.6	22.8	21.9	20.9	20.0	19.1	18.2	17.2	16.1	15.0	13.9	12.8	11.6	10.3	9.0	7.5	5.7	3.9	2.2	0.6	0	
$1.25	22.3	21.7	21.2	20.6	20.0	19.5	18.9	18.4	17.8	17.1	16.5	15.8	15.1	14.5	13.8	13.1	12.3	11.5	10.7	9.8	8.9	8.0	6.9	5.9	4.7	3.1	2.1	0.9	0.1	0	

WEEKS TO EXPIRATION

OPTION VALUES ARE IN CENTS – to nearest tenth.

WM GRANDMILL (1985) LTD.

OPTION VALUES on SOYBEAN FUTURES – Table No: 66

WEEKS TO EXPIRATION

	30	29	28	27	26	25	24	23	22	21	20	19	18	17	16	15	14	13	12	11	10	9	8	7	6	5	4	3	2	1	0
OUT OF THE MONEY $1.25	24.4	23.8	23.2	22.6	22.0	21.4	20.7	20.0	19.3	18.6	17.9	17.2	16.5	15.7	15.0	14.3	13.5	12.6	11.7	10.7	9.7	8.7	7.7	6.6	5.2	3.9	2.5	1.2	0.2	0	0
OUT $1.00	32.2	31.6	30.9	30.2	29.5	28.8	28.0	27.2	26.4	25.6	24.7	23.8	22.8	21.8	20.8	19.8	18.7	17.6	16.5	15.2	13.9	12.5	11.2	9.9	8.2	6.3	4.4	2.5	0.7	0	0
OUT 75¢	39.1	38.5	37.8	37.1	36.4	35.7	34.9	34.1	33.2	32.3	31.4	30.4	29.4	28.3	27.2	26.0	24.8	23.5	22.1	20.6	19.1	17.4	15.6	13.7	11.5	8.9	6.2	3.6	1.2	0	0
OUT 50¢	43.1	42.4	41.7	41.0	40.3	39.6	38.8	38.0	37.2	36.3	35.4	34.4	33.4	32.4	31.3	30.2	29.0	27.7	26.4	24.9	23.4	21.7	19.8	18.0	15.8	13.1	10.3	7.0	3.3	0.4	0
OUT 25¢	51.9	51.2	50.5	49.8	49.1	48.3	47.5	46.7	45.8	44.9	43.9	42.9	41.9	40.8	39.6	38.4	37.2	35.8	34.4	32.8	31.1	29.2	27.2	25.0	22.4	19.1	15.6	11.5	6.6	1.8	0
AT THE MONEY 25¢	61.5	60.8	60.1	59.4	58.7	57.9	57.1	56.3	55.4	54.5	53.5	52.5	51.4	50.3	49.1	47.9	46.6	45.2	43.8	42.1	40.4	38.5	36.4	34.2	31.5	28.0	24.3	19.8	14.5	8.8	0.0
IN THE MONEY 25¢	72.3	71.5	70.8	70.0	69.2	68.3	67.5	66.6	65.7	64.8	63.8	62.8	61.7	60.6	59.4	58.3	57.2	55.9	54.6	53.1	51.6	49.9	48.0	46.0	43.6	40.6	37.2	33.6	29.5	26.2	25.0
IN 50¢	84.3	83.6	82.9	82.3	81.7	81.0	80.2	79.5	78.7	77.9	77.0	76.1	75.1	74.2	73.2	72.2	71.1	70.0	68.8	67.5	66.1	64.6	63.1	61.6	59.6	57.5	55.2	53.0	50.8	50.0	50.0
IN 75¢	96.7	96.1	95.4	94.8	94.2	93.6	92.9	92.2	91.5	90.8	90.1	89.4	88.7	87.9	87.2	86.5	85.7	84.9	84.1	83.2	82.3	81.4	80.4	79.5	78.4	77.3	76.2	75.4	75.0	75.0	75.0
IN $1.00	117.5	116.8	116.1	115.4	114.8	114.3	113.6	113.0	112.4	111.7	111.0	110.2	109.4	108.6	107.8	107.1	106.4	105.6	104.8	104.0	103.2	102.5	101.9	101.4	101.0	100.6	100.2	100.0	100.0	100.0	100.0
IN $1.25	134.3	133.6	132.9	132.1	131.3	130.4	129.5	128.6	127.7	126.8	126.0	125.5	125.1	125.0	125.0	125.0	125.0	125.0	125.0	125.0	125.0	125.0	125.0	125.0	125.0	125.0	125.0	125.0	125.0	125.0	125.0

OPTION VALUES ARE IN CENTS – to nearest tenth.

WM GRANDMILL (1985) LTD.

OPTION VALUES on SOYBEAN FUTURES – Table No: 65

WEEKS TO EXPIRATION

	30	29	28	27	26	25	24	23	22	21	20	19	18	17	16	15	14	13	12	11	10	9	8	7	6	5	4	3	2	1	0
OUT OF THE MONEY $1.25	23.7	23.1	22.4	21.9	21.4	20.8	20.1	19.5	18.8	18.2	17.5	16.8	16.0	15.3	14.6	13.9	13.1	12.3	11.4	10.4	9.4	8.5	7.4	6.3	5.1	3.7	2.4	1.1	0.2	0	0
OUT $1.00	31.5	30.8	30.1	29.5	28.8	28.1	27.4	26.6	25.8	25.0	24.1	23.2	22.2	21.2	20.2	19.2	18.2	17.1	16.0	14.8	13.6	12.3	10.9	9.5	8.0	6.1	4.3	2.4	0.7	0	0
OUT 75¢	38.4	37.7	37.0	36.4	35.7	35.0	34.2	33.4	32.6	31.7	30.7	29.8	28.8	27.7	26.6	25.4	24.2	23.0	21.6	20.2	18.7	17.0	15.2	13.3	11.2	8.5	6.7	3.4	1.2	0	0
OUT 50¢	42.3	41.6	40.9	40.3	39.6	38.9	38.1	37.4	36.6	35.7	34.7	33.8	32.8	31.7	30.6	29.5	28.4	27.2	25.9	24.5	23.0	21.3	19.5	17.6	15.5	12.7	10.1	6.7	3.2	0.4	0
OUT 25¢	51.1	50.4	49.7	49.0	48.3	47.6	46.8	46.0	45.1	44.2	43.3	42.3	41.2	40.1	39.0	37.8	36.6	35.2	33.8	32.3	30.6	28.7	26.7	24.6	22.0	18.7	15.3	11.2	6.4	1.8	0
AT THE MONEY 25¢	60.7	60.0	59.3	58.6	57.9	57.2	56.4	55.6	54.7	53.8	52.8	51.8	50.7	49.6	48.4	47.2	46.0	44.6	43.2	41.6	39.9	38.0	35.9	33.7	31.1	27.6	24.0	19.5	14.3	8.7	0.0
IN THE MONEY 25¢	71.4	70.7	69.9	69.1	68.3	67.5	66.7	65.9	65.0	64.1	63.1	62.1	61.0	59.9	58.8	57.7	56.6	55.4	54.1	52.7	51.2	49.5	47.6	45.6	43.2	40.2	37.0	33.3	29.4	26.2	25.0
IN 50¢	83.5	82.9	82.2	81.6	81.0	80.3	79.6	78.9	78.1	77.3	76.4	75.5	74.6	73.6	72.6	71.6	70.6	69.5	68.4	67.1	65.8	64.4	62.8	61.2	59.4	57.2	55.1	52.8	50.7	50.0	50.0
IN 75¢	96.0	95.4	94.7	94.1	93.5	92.9	92.3	91.7	91.0	90.4	89.7	89.0	88.2	87.5	86.8	86.1	85.3	84.5	83.7	82.9	82.1	81.2	80.2	79.3	78.3	77.1	76.1	75.3	75.0	75.0	75.0
IN $1.00	116.7	116.1	115.4	114.8	114.1	113.6	113.0	112.4	111.7	111.0	110.2	109.4	108.6	107.8	107.1	106.4	105.6	104.8	104.0	103.2	102.5	101.9	101.4	101.0	100.6	100.2	100.0	100.0	100.0	100.0	100.0
IN $1.25	140.3	139.7	139.1	138.4	137.8	137.2	136.5	135.9	135.2	134.6	133.9	133.2	132.4	131.6	130.8	130.0	129.2	128.4	127.5	126.6	125.8	125.0	125.0	125.0	125.0	125.0	125.0	125.0	125.0	125.0	125.0

OPTION VALUES ARE IN CENTS – to nearest tenth.

WM GRANDMILL (1985) LTD.

OPTION VALUES on SOYBEAN FUTURES – Table No:68

WEEKS TO EXPIRATION

Position	30	29	28	27	26	25	24	23	22	21	20	19	18	17	16	15	14	13	12	11	10	9	8	7	6	5	4	3	2	1	0
IN THE MONEY $1.25	142.7	142.0	141.3	140.6	139.9	139.2	138.5	137.8	137.1	136.3	135.5	134.7	133.9	133.0	132.2	131.4	130.5	129.5	128.5	127.5	126.5	125.7	125.2	125.0	125.0	125.0	125.0	125.0	125.0	125.0	125.0
IN THE MONEY $1.00	119.2	118.5	117.8	117.1	116.3	115.6	114.9	114.3	113.6	112.8	112.0	111.1	110.2	109.3	108.4	107.6	106.8	105.9	105.1	104.1	103.1	102.3	101.7	101.2	100.7	100.3	100.0	100.0	100.0	100.0	100.0
IN THE MONEY 75¢	98.2	97.6	97.0	96.3	95.6	94.9	94.2	93.6	92.9	92.1	91.3	90.5	89.7	88.8	88.0	87.3	86.5	85.6	84.7	83.8	82.9	82.0	80.9	79.9	78.8	77.5	76.4	75.4	75.0	75.0	75.0
IN THE MONEY 50¢	86.5	85.6	84.7	83.8	82.9	82.0	80.9	79.9	78.8	77.5	76.4	75.4	74.3	73.2	72.2	71.0	69.7	68.4	67.0	65.5	63.9	62.2	60.2	57.9	55.7	53.2	50.9	50.1	50.0	50.0	50.0
IN THE MONEY 25¢	74.2	73.4	72.6	71.8	71.0	70.1	69.3	68.3	67.4	66.4	65.4	64.3	63.1	61.9	60.7	59.5	58.3	57.0	55.7	54.2	52.6	50.9	48.9	46.8	44.2	41.2	37.9	33.9	29.8	26.3	25.0
AT THE MONEY	63.2	62.5	61.8	61.1	60.3	59.5	58.7	57.9	57.0	56.1	55.1	54.0	52.8	51.6	50.4	49.2	47.9	46.5	45.0	43.3	41.5	39.6	37.4	35.1	32.4	28.8	25.0	20.3	14.9	9.0	0.0
OUT OF THE MONEY 25¢	53.6	52.9	52.2	51.5	50.7	49.9	49.1	48.3	47.4	46.5	45.5	44.4	43.3	42.1	40.9	39.7	38.5	37.1	35.6	34.0	32.3	30.3	28.2	25.9	23.1	19.8	16.3	11.9	7.0	1.9	0
OUT OF THE MONEY 50¢	44.8	44.1	43.4	42.7	41.9	41.1	40.4	39.6	38.7	37.8	36.8	35.8	34.7	33.6	32.5	31.4	30.2	28.9	27.6	26.0	24.4	22.7	20.7	18.7	16.5	13.5	10.9	7.3	3.6	0.4	0
OUT OF THE MONEY 75¢	40.8	40.1	39.4	38.7	38.0	37.0	36.6	35.8	34.7	33.9	32.9	31.8	30.7	29.6	28.5	27.3	26.1	24.7	23.3	21.7	20.1	18.4	16.5	14.5	12.1	9.4	6.6	3.8	0.9	0	0
OUT OF THE MONEY $1.00	33.8	33.2	32.5	31.8	31.1	30.3	29.6	28.8	28.0	27.1	26.2	25.1	24.1	23.0	21.9	20.8	19.8	18.6	17.4	16.0	14.6	13.3	11.8	10.4	8.7	6.8	4.8	2.7	0.9	0	0
OUT OF THE MONEY $1.25	25.9	25.3	24.7	24.0	23.3	22.6	22.0	21.4	20.7	19.9	19.1	18.3	17.5	16.6	15.8	15.1	14.3	13.4	12.4	11.4	10.3	9.3	8.2	7.0	5.7	4.2	3.8	1.4	0.2	0	0

OPTION VALUES ARE IN CENTS – to nearest tenth.

WM GRANDMILL (1985) LTD.

OPTION VALUES on SOYBEAN FUTURES – Table No:67

WEEKS TO EXPIRATION

Position	30	29	28	27	26	25	24	23	22	21	20	19	18	17	16	15	14	13	12	11	10	9	8	7	6	5	4	3	2	1	0
IN THE MONEY $1.25	141.9	141.2	140.6	139.9	139.2	138.5	137.8	137.1	136.4	135.6	134.9	134.2	133.4	132.6	131.7	130.8	130.0	129.1	128.1	127.1	126.3	125.6	125.1	125.0	125.0	125.0	125.0	125.0	125.0	125.0	125.0
IN THE MONEY $1.00	118.4	117.7	117.0	116.3	115.6	114.9	114.3	113.6	112.9	112.1	111.2	110.5	109.6	108.8	107.9	107.1	106.3	105.6	104.7	103.6	102.8	102.1	101.6	101.1	100.7	100.3	100.0	100.0	100.0	100.0	100.0
IN THE MONEY 75¢	97.5	96.9	96.3	95.6	94.9	94.2	93.6	92.9	92.2	91.4	90.7	90.0	89.2	88.3	87.5	86.8	86.1	85.3	84.4	83.6	82.7	81.7	80.7	79.7	78.7	77.6	76.3	75.4	75.0	75.0	75.0
IN THE MONEY 50¢	85.2	84.5	83.8	83.1	82.4	81.7	81.0	80.2	79.4	78.6	77.7	76.7	75.7	74.8	73.8	72.7	71.6	70.5	69.3	68.4	66.7	65.1	63.6	61.9	60.0	57.7	55.4	53.1	50.8	50.0	50.0
IN THE MONEY 25¢	73.3	72.5	71.8	71.0	70.1	69.2	68.4	67.5	66.5	65.6	64.6	63.4	62.4	61.2	60.0	58.9	57.7	56.6	55.2	53.7	52.2	50.4	48.5	46.5	44.0	40.8	37.5	33.8	29.6	26.3	25.0
AT THE MONEY	62.4	61.7	61.0	60.3	59.5	58.7	57.9	57.1	56.2	55.3	54.3	53.2	52.1	50.9	49.7	48.5	47.2	45.9	44.4	42.7	41.0	39.1	36.9	34.7	32.0	28.4	24.6	20.0	14.7	8.9	0.0
OUT OF THE MONEY 25¢	52.8	52.1	51.4	50.7	49.9	49.1	48.3	47.5	46.6	45.7	44.7	43.6	42.5	41.4	40.3	39.1	37.8	36.4	35.0	33.4	31.7	29.8	27.7	25.5	22.6	19.4	15.9	11.7	6.8	1.9	0
OUT OF THE MONEY 50¢	44.0	43.3	42.6	41.9	41.2	40.4	39.6	38.8	37.9	37.1	36.1	35.1	34.0	33.0	31.9	30.7	29.5	28.3	27.0	25.6	24.0	22.2	20.3	18.5	16.0	13.3	10.5	7.2	3.4	0.4	0
OUT OF THE MONEY 75¢	40.0	39.3	38.7	38.0	37.0	36.5	35.7	34.9	34.0	33.1	32.1	31.1	30.0	28.9	27.8	26.7	25.5	24.2	22.8	21.3	19.7	17.9	16.1	14.2	11.8	9.1	6.4	3.7	1.3	0	0
OUT OF THE MONEY $1.00	33.1	32.4	31.8	31.1	30.3	29.6	28.8	28.0	27.2	26.3	25.4	24.4	23.4	22.4	21.3	20.2	19.2	18.1	16.9	15.7	14.4	13.0	11.5	10.1	8.4	6.5	4.6	2.6	0.8	0	0
OUT OF THE MONEY $1.25	25.2	24.6	24.0	23.4	22.7	22.0	21.4	20.7	20.0	19.2	18.5	17.8	17.0	16.2	15.5	14.7	13.9	13.1	12.1	11.1	10.1	9.0	7.9	6.8	5.5	4.0	2.6	1.3	0.2	0	0

OPTION VALUES ARE IN CENTS – to nearest tenth.

WM GRANDMILL (1985) LTD.

OPTION VALUES on SOYBEAN FUTURES – Table No:70

Position		30	29	28	27	26	25	24	23	22	21	20	19	18	17	16	15	14	13	12	11	10	9	8	7	6	5	4	3	2	1	0
IN THE MONEY	$1.25	144.4	143.7	143.0	142.2	141.4	140.6	139.9	139.1	138.3	137.4	136.6	135.7	134.9	134.1	133.1	132.2	131.3	130.3	129.3	128.1	127.1	126.1	125.4	125.1	125.0	125.0	125.0	125.0	125.0	125.0	125.0
	$1.00	120.9	120.2	119.5	118.7	117.9	117.1	116.3	115.5	114.7	113.9	113.1	112.2	111.3	110.4	109.3	108.4	107.5	106.6	105.7	104.7	103.6	102.6	101.9	101.5	100.9	100.4	100.0	100.0	100.0	100.0	100.0
	75¢	99.9	99.2	98.5	97.8	97.1	96.3	95.6	94.8	94.0	93.2	92.4	91.5	90.7	89.9	88.9	88.0	87.2	86.3	85.5	84.4	83.5	82.5	81.4	80.3	79.2	77.7	76.6	75.5	75.0	75.0	75.0
	50¢	87.7	87.0	86.3	85.4	84.7	83.9	83.1	82.4	81.6	80.8	80.0	79.1	78.1	77.0	75.9	74.9	73.8	72.7	71.5	70.3	69.0	67.5	66.0	64.6	62.9	60.9	58.4	56.0	53.5	51.0	50.1
	25¢	76.0	75.3	74.5	73.6	72.7	71.9	71.0	70.0	69.0	67.9	66.8	65.7	64.5	63.3	62.0	60.7	59.4	58.2	56.8	55.2	53.6	51.9	49.8	47.7	45.2	41.9	38.4	34.5	30.0	26.4	25.0
AT THE MONEY		64.9	64.2	63.5	62.7	61.9	61.1	60.3	59.4	58.5	57.5	56.5	55.4	54.2	53.0	51.7	50.4	49.1	47.7	46.2	44.4	42.6	40.7	38.4	36.1	33.3	29.6	25.6	20.8	15.3	9.3	0.0
OUT OF THE MONEY	25¢	55.3	54.6	53.9	53.1	52.3	51.5	50.7	49.8	48.9	47.9	46.9	45.8	44.6	43.5	42.2	40.9	39.6	38.3	36.8	35.0	33.3	31.4	29.2	26.9	24.2	20.5	16.9	12.4	7.3	2.0	0
	50¢	46.5	45.8	45.1	44.3	43.5	42.7	41.9	41.0	40.2	39.2	38.2	37.2	36.1	34.9	33.7	32.5	31.3	30.0	28.6	27.0	25.4	23.7	21.6	19.6	17.2	14.3	11.2	7.7	3.8	0.5	0
	75¢	42.5	41.8	41.1	40.3	39.5	38.7	38.0	37.1	36.3	35.3	34.3	33.2	32.0	30.9	29.7	28.5	27.2	25.9	24.4	22.8	21.1	19.4	17.3	15.3	12.9	10.0	7.1	4.1	1.4	0	0
	$1.00	35.5	34.8	34.1	33.4	32.6	31.8	31.1	30.2	29.4	28.4	27.5	26.4	25.3	24.3	23.1	21.9	20.7	19.6	18.4	16.9	15.5	14.1	12.5	11.0	9.3	7.1	5.1	2.9	1.0	0	0
	$1.25	27.5	26.8	26.2	25.5	24.8	24.0	23.3	22.5	21.8	21.0	20.2	19.3	18.5	17.7	16.7	15.8	15.0	14.1	13.3	12.1	11.0	9.8	8.7	7.5	6.1	4.5	2.9	1.5	0.3	0	0

WEEKS TO EXPIRATION

OPTION VALUES ARE IN CENTS – to nearest tenth.

WM GRANDMILL (1985) LTD.

OPTION VALUES on SOYBEAN FUTURES – Table No: 69

Position		30	29	28	27	26	25	24	23	22	21	20	19	18	17	16	15	14	13	12	11	10	9	8	7	6	5	4	3	2	1	0
IN THE MONEY	$1.25	143.5	143.7	143.0	142.1	141.4	140.6	139.9	139.2	138.4	137.6	136.9	136.1	135.2	134.3	133.4	132.7	131.8	130.8	129.8	128.8	127.8	126.8	125.9	125.3	125.1	125.0	125.0	125.0	125.0	125.0	125.0
	$1.00	120.0	119.3	118.6	117.9	117.1	116.3	115.6	114.8	114.1	113.4	112.6	111.7	110.7	109.8	108.9	108.0	107.1	106.3	105.4	104.4	103.3	102.5	101.8	101.3	100.8	100.4	100.0	100.0	100.0	100.0	100.0
	75¢	99.0	98.3	97.7	97.1	96.3	95.6	94.9	94.1	93.4	92.7	91.9	91.0	90.1	89.3	88.5	87.6	86.8	86.0	85.1	84.1	83.2	82.2	81.1	80.1	79.1	77.6	76.5	75.4	75.0	75.0	75.0
	50¢	86.8	86.1	85.4	84.7	83.9	83.1	82.4	81.6	80.8	80.0	79.1	78.1	77.0	75.9	74.9	73.8	72.7	71.5	70.3	69.0	67.5	65.9	64.2	62.5	60.5	58.2	55.8	53.4	51.0	50.1	50.0
	25¢	75.1	74.3	73.5	72.7	71.9	71.0	70.1	69.1	68.1	67.1	66.1	65.0	63.8	62.6	61.4	60.1	58.9	57.6	56.3	54.8	53.1	51.2	49.1	47.1	44.8	41.5	38.1	34.2	29.9	26.4	25.0
AT THE MONEY		64.0	63.3	62.6	61.9	61.1	60.3	59.5	58.6	57.7	56.8	55.8	54.7	53.5	52.3	51.1	49.8	48.5	47.1	45.6	43.9	42.1	40.1	37.6	35.6	32.8	29.2	25.3	20.6	15.1	9.2	0.0
OUT OF THE MONEY	25¢	54.4	53.7	53.0	52.3	51.5	50.7	49.9	49.0	48.1	47.2	46.2	45.1	43.9	42.8	41.6	40.3	39.0	37.7	36.3	34.6	32.8	30.8	28.6	26.4	23.5	20.1	16.6	12.2	7.1	2.0	0
	50¢	45.6	44.9	44.2	43.5	42.7	41.9	41.1	40.3	39.4	38.5	37.5	36.5	35.4	34.2	33.1	32.0	30.7	29.4	28.1	26.6	24.9	23.1	21.0	19.2	16.7	14.0	11.0	7.5	3.7	0.5	0
	75¢	41.6	40.9	40.2	39.5	38.7	38.0	37.2	36.4	35.5	34.6	33.6	32.5	31.4	30.2	29.1	27.9	26.6	25.3	23.9	22.3	20.6	18.8	16.7	14.9	12.5	9.7	6.9	4.0	1.4	0	0
	$1.00	34.6	33.9	33.3	32.6	31.8	31.1	30.3	29.5	28.7	27.8	26.8	25.8	24.7	23.6	22.5	21.4	20.2	19.1	17.9	16.6	15.1	13.5	11.9	10.6	9.0	6.9	4.9	2.8	0.9	0	0
	$1.25	26.7	26.0	25.4	24.7	24.0	23.3	22.6	21.9	21.2	20.5	19.7	18.8	17.9	17.1	16.3	15.4	14.7	13.8	12.8	11.8	10.7	9.5	8.3	7.1	5.9	4.3	2.9	1.5	0.3	0	0

WEEKS TO EXPIRATION

OPTION VALUES ARE IN CENTS – to nearest tenth.

WM GRANDMILL (1985) LTD.

OPTION VALUES on SOYBEAN FUTURES — Table No:72

	30	29	28	27	26	25	24	23	22	21	20	19	18	17	16	15	14	13	12	11	10	9	8	7	6	5	4	3	2	1	0
IN THE MONEY $1.25	146.2	145.4	144.6	143.8	143.0	142.2	141.3	140.5	139.7	138.8	137.9	136.9	135.9	135.0	134.1	133.2	132.2	131.3	130.1	129.8	127.7	126.6	125.7	125.2	125.0	125.0	125.0	125.0	125.0	125.0	125.0
$1.00	122.8	121.9	121.1	120.3	119.5	118.7	117.8	116.9	116.1	115.2	114.3	113.4	112.4	111.4	110.4	109.4	108.4	107.5	106.5	105.4	104.3	103.2	102.2	101.7	101.1	100.5	100.1	100.0	100.0	100.0	100.0
75¢	101.7	100.9	100.1	99.3	98.5	97.8	97.0	96.2	95.4	94.5	93.6	92.7	91.7	90.8	89.9	89.0	88.0	87.1	86.2	85.1	84.1	83.0	81.9	80.7	79.5	78.0	76.7	75.6	75.0	75.0	75.0
50¢	89.5	88.7	87.9	87.1	86.3	85.5	84.5	83.7	82.9	82.0	81.0	80.0	78.9	77.8	76.6	75.5	74.3	73.2	71.7	70.7	68.8	67.2	65.4	63.7	61.5	58.8	56.5	53.8	51.1	50.1	50.0
25¢	78.0	77.1	76.3	75.4	74.5	73.6	72.6	71.6	70.6	69.6	68.4	67.1	65.9	64.7	63.4	62.1	60.8	59.4	57.9	56.3	54.6	52.8	50.7	48.6	45.9	42.6	39.0	34.8	30.3	26.5	25.0
AT THE MONEY	66.7	65.9	65.1	64.3	63.5	62.7	61.8	60.9	60.0	59.0	58.0	56.8	55.6	54.4	53.1	51.8	50.4	49.0	47.4	45.6	43.8	41.7	39.4	37.0	34.1	30.3	26.3	21.4	15.7	9.5	0.0
OUT OF THE MONEY 25¢	57.1	56.3	55.5	54.7	53.9	53.1	52.2	51.3	50.4	49.4	48.3	47.2	46.0	44.8	43.5	42.3	40.9	39.6	38.0	36.2	34.4	32.4	30.1	27.6	24.9	21.2	17.5	12.9	7.7	2.1	0.0
50¢	48.1	47.4	46.6	45.9	45.1	44.3	43.4	42.5	41.6	40.6	39.6	38.5	37.4	36.2	35.0	33.8	32.5	31.2	29.7	28.1	26.4	24.6	22.5	20.4	17.9	14.8	11.7	8.1	4.1	0.5	0
75¢	44.2	43.4	42.6	41.9	41.1	40.3	39.4	38.6	37.7	36.7	35.7	34.6	33.4	32.3	31.0	29.8	28.5	27.1	25.6	23.9	22.2	20.3	18.2	16.2	13.6	10.5	7.6	4.5	1.6	0	0
$1.00	37.2	36.4	35.6	34.8	34.1	33.4	32.5	31.7	30.8	29.9	28.9	27.8	26.6	25.5	24.3	23.1	21.9	20.7	19.3	17.9	16.4	14.8	13.2	11.6	9.8	7.5	5.4	3.1	1.1	0	0
$1.25	29.1	28.4	27.6	26.9	26.2	25.5	24.7	23.9	23.1	22.3	21.5	20.5	19.5	18.6	17.7	16.8	15.8	15.0	14.0	12.9	11.7	10.4	9.2	8.0	6.5	4.8	3.2	1.6	0.3	0	0

OPTION VALUES ARE IN CENTS - to nearest tenth.

WM GRANDMILL (1985) LTD.

OPTION VALUES on SOYBEAN FUTURES — Table No:71

	30	29	28	27	26	25	24	23	22	21	20	19	18	17	16	15	14	13	12	11	10	9	8	7	6	5	4	3	2	1	0
IN THE MONEY $1.25	146.2	145.4	144.6	143.8	143.0	142.2	141.4	140.6	139.8	139.0	138.1	137.2	136.3	135.3	134.5	132.7	131.7	130.7	129.7	128.5	127.5	126.4	125.7	125.1	125.0	125.0	125.0	125.0	125.0	125.0	125.0
$1.00	121.9	121.1	120.3	119.5	118.7	117.9	117.1	116.2	115.4	114.5	113.7	112.8	111.9	110.9	109.9	108.9	108.0	107.0	106.1	105.1	104.0	102.9	102.2	101.6	101.0	100.5	100.1	100.0	100.0	100.0	100.0
75¢	100.9	100.1	99.3	98.5	97.8	97.1	96.3	95.5	94.7	93.8	93.0	92.1	91.2	90.3	89.4	88.5	87.6	86.7	85.8	84.8	83.8	82.8	81.6	80.5	79.2	78.0	76.7	75.5	75.0	75.0	75.0
50¢	88.7	87.9	87.1	86.3	85.5	84.7	83.9	83.0	82.2	81.3	80.4	79.3	78.3	77.2	76.0	74.9	73.9	72.6	71.3	69.9	68.4	66.8	65.0	63.3	61.2	58.7	56.3	53.6	51.1	50.1	50.0
25¢	77.1	76.3	75.4	74.5	73.6	72.7	71.8	70.9	69.9	68.8	67.7	66.4	65.2	64.0	62.7	61.4	60.1	58.7	57.4	55.8	54.1	52.3	50.3	48.2	45.6	42.3	38.8	34.6	30.1	26.4	25.0
AT THE MONEY	65.9	65.1	64.3	63.5	62.7	61.9	61.1	60.2	59.3	58.3	57.3	56.1	54.9	53.7	52.4	51.1	49.8	48.3	46.8	45.0	43.2	41.2	38.9	36.6	33.7	30.0	26.0	21.1	15.5	19.4	0.0
OUT OF THE MONEY 25¢	56.3	55.5	54.7	53.9	53.1	52.3	51.5	50.6	49.7	48.7	47.6	46.5	45.3	44.1	42.9	41.6	40.3	39.9	37.4	35.6	33.9	31.9	29.7	27.4	24.6	20.9	17.3	12.2	7.5	2.1	0.0
50¢	47.4	46.6	45.9	45.1	44.3	43.5	42.7	41.8	40.9	40.0	39.0	37.8	36.7	35.6	34.3	33.1	31.8	30.5	29.1	27.6	25.9	24.1	22.1	20.0	17.6	14.7	11.6	7.9	3.9	0.5	0
75¢	43.4	42.6	41.9	41.1	40.3	39.5	38.7	37.9	37.0	36.1	35.1	33.9	32.8	31.6	30.3	29.1	27.9	26.5	25.0	23.4	21.6	19.8	17.8	15.8	13.3	10.4	7.5	4.3	1.5	0.5	0
$1.00	36.4	35.6	34.9	34.1	33.4	32.6	31.8	31.0	30.1	29.2	28.2	27.1	26.0	24.9	23.7	22.5	21.4	20.2	18.9	17.5	16.0	14.5	12.9	11.3	9.5	7.4	5.3	3.0	1.0	0	0
$1.25	28.4	27.6	26.9	26.2	25.5	24.8	24.0	23.2	22.4	21.6	20.8	19.9	19.0	18.1	17.2	16.3	15.4	14.5	13.6	12.6	11.4	10.2	8.9	7.8	6.3	4.7	3.1	1.6	0.3	0	0

OPTION VALUES ARE IN CENTS - to nearest tenth.

WM GRANDMILL (1985) LTD.

OPTION VALUES on SOYBEAN FUTURES – Table No:74

	Strike	30	29	28	27	26	25	24	23	22	21	20	19	18	17	16	15	14	13	12	11	10	9	8	7	6	5	4	3	2	1	0
IN THE MONEY	$1.25	148.0	147.1	146.2	145.4	144.6	143.8	142.9	142.0	141.1	140.2	139.2	138.1	137.1	136.0	135.0	134.1	133.1	132.0	130.9	129.7	128.4	127.2	126.0	125.4	125.0	125.0	125.0	125.0	125.0	125.0	125.0
	$1.00	124.6	123.7	122.8	121.9	121.1	120.3	119.4	118.5	117.6	116.6	115.6	114.5	113.6	112.5	111.4	110.4	109.3	108.3	107.2	106.1	105.0	103.7	102.5	101.9	101.3	100.6	100.1	100.1	100.0	100.0	100.0
	75¢	103.3	102.5	101.7	100.9	100.1	99.3	98.4	97.6	96.8	95.9	94.9	93.8	92.9	91.8	90.8	89.9	88.9	87.9	86.9	85.8	84.7	83.6	82.4	81.2	79.9	78.3	76.9	75.7	75.1	75.0	75.0
	50¢	91.1	90.3	89.5	88.7	87.9	87.1	86.2	85.3	84.4	83.4	82.4	81.3	80.2	79.0	77.8	76.6	75.4	74.2	72.8	71.3	69.7	68.0	66.1	64.2	62.2	59.4	56.8	54.0	51.3	50.1	50.0
	25¢	79.8	78.9	78.0	77.1	76.3	75.4	74.4	73.4	72.4	71.3	70.1	68.8	67.4	66.0	64.7	63.4	62.0	60.5	59.0	57.4	55.7	53.8	51.6	49.5	46.8	43.2	39.6	35.3	30.6	26.6	25.0
AT THE MONEY	25¢	68.3	67.5	66.7	65.9	65.1	64.3	63.4	62.5	61.6	60.6	59.5	58.3	57.0	55.7	54.4	53.1	51.7	50.2	48.6	46.8	44.9	42.8	40.4	38.0	35.0	31.1	26.9	21.9	16.1	9.8	0.0
OUT OF THE MONEY	25¢	58.7	57.9	57.1	56.3	55.5	54.7	53.8	52.9	52.0	51.0	49.9	48.7	47.4	46.1	44.8	43.5	42.2	40.7	39.2	37.4	35.5	33.5	31.1	28.8	25.8	22.0	18.1	13.4	8.0	2.3	0
	50¢	49.7	48.9	48.1	47.4	46.6	45.9	45.0	44.1	43.2	42.2	41.1	40.0	38.7	37.5	36.3	35.0	33.7	32.3	30.8	29.2	27.5	25.6	23.4	21.3	18.8	15.5	12.2	8.5	4.4	0.6	0
	75¢	45.8	45.0	44.2	43.4	42.6	41.9	41.0	40.1	39.2	38.3	37.2	36.1	34.8	33.5	32.3	31.0	29.7	28.3	26.8	25.0	23.3	21.3	19.1	17.1	14.5	11.2	8.1	4.8	1.7	0	0
	$1.00	38.7	37.9	37.2	36.4	35.6	34.9	34.0	33.2	32.3	31.4	30.3	29.2	28.0	26.7	25.5	24.3	23.1	21.7	20.3	18.9	17.4	15.7	13.9	12.3	10.4	8.0	5.7	3.4	1.2	0	0
	$1.25	30.5	29.8	29.1	28.4	27.6	26.9	26.1	25.3	24.5	23.6	22.6	21.6	20.7	19.6	18.6	17.7	16.7	15.7	14.7	13.6	12.5	11.1	9.7	8.5	7.0	5.1	3.4	1.7	0.4	0	0

WEEKS TO EXPIRATION

OPTION VALUES ARE IN CENTS – to nearest tenth.

WM GRANDMILL (1985) LTD.

OPTION VALUES on SOYBEAN FUTURES – Table No:73

	Strike	30	29	28	27	26	25	24	23	22	21	20	19	18	17	16	15	14	13	12	11	10	9	8	7	6	5	4	3	2	1	0
IN THE MONEY	$1.25	147.1	146.2	145.4	144.6	143.8	143.0	142.1	141.2	140.4	139.5	138.5	137.4	136.4	135.5	134.6	133.6	132.7	131.6	130.5	129.3	128.0	126.9	125.8	125.3	125.0	125.0	125.0	125.0	125.0	125.0	125.0
	$1.00	123.7	122.8	121.9	121.1	120.3	119.5	118.6	117.7	116.8	115.9	114.9	113.9	112.9	112.0	111.0	109.9	108.9	107.8	106.8	105.8	104.6	103.4	102.3	101.8	101.2	100.5	100.1	100.1	100.0	100.0	100.0
	75¢	102.5	101.7	100.9	100.1	99.3	98.5	97.7	96.9	96.1	95.2	94.2	93.2	92.2	91.3	90.4	89.4	88.5	87.5	86.5	85.5	84.3	83.3	82.1	80.9	79.7	78.1	76.8	75.6	75.0	75.0	75.0
	50¢	90.3	89.5	88.7	87.9	87.1	86.3	85.4	84.5	83.6	82.7	81.7	80.6	79.5	78.4	77.3	76.0	74.9	73.7	72.3	70.8	69.2	67.6	65.8	63.9	61.8	59.1	56.6	53.9	51.2	50.1	50.0
	25¢	78.9	78.0	77.1	76.3	75.4	74.5	73.5	72.5	71.5	70.4	69.2	67.9	66.6	65.4	64.1	62.7	61.4	59.9	58.5	56.8	55.1	53.2	51.2	49.0	46.4	43.0	39.3	35.0	30.5	26.5	25.0
AT THE MONEY	25¢	67.5	66.7	65.9	65.1	64.3	63.5	62.6	61.7	60.8	59.8	58.7	57.5	56.3	55.1	53.8	52.4	51.1	49.6	48.0	46.2	44.3	42.2	39.9	37.5	34.6	30.7	26.6	21.6	15.9	9.6	0.0
OUT OF THE MONEY	25¢	57.9	57.1	56.3	55.5	54.7	53.9	53.0	52.1	51.2	50.2	49.1	47.9	46.7	45.5	44.2	42.9	41.6	40.2	38.6	36.8	34.9	32.9	30.6	28.3	25.4	21.6	17.8	13.1	7.9	2.2	0
	50¢	48.9	48.1	47.4	46.6	45.9	45.1	44.2	43.3	42.4	41.4	40.4	39.2	38.0	36.9	35.7	34.2	33.1	31.8	30.3	28.6	26.9	25.0	23.0	20.8	18.4	15.2	11.9	8.2	4.3	0.6	0
	75¢	45.0	44.2	43.4	42.6	41.9	41.1	40.2	39.3	38.5	37.5	36.5	35.3	34.1	32.9	31.7	30.3	29.1	27.7	26.2	24.4	22.7	20.7	18.7	16.6	14.1	10.9	7.8	4.6	1.6	0	0
	$1.00	37.9	37.2	36.4	35.6	34.9	34.1	33.3	32.4	31.5	30.6	29.5	28.4	27.3	26.1	25.0	23.7	22.5	21.2	19.9	18.4	16.8	15.2	13.6	11.8	10.1	7.7	5.6	3.2	1.2	0	0
	$1.25	29.8	29.1	28.4	27.6	26.9	26.2	25.4	24.6	23.8	22.9	22.0	21.0	20.0	19.1	18.2	17.2	16.3	15.3	14.4	13.2	12.0	10.8	9.4	8.2	6.8	4.9	3.3	1.7	0.4	0	0

WEEKS TO EXPIRATION

OPTION VALUES ARE IN CENTS – to nearest tenth.

WM GRANDMILL (1985) LTD.

OPTION VALUES on SOYBEAN FUTURES – Table No:76

OPTION VALUES ARE IN CENTS – to nearest tenth.

WEEKS TO EXPIRATION	30	29	28	27	26	25	24	23	22	21	20	19	18	17	16	15	14	13	12	11	10	9	8	7	6	5	4	3	2	1	0
IN THE MONEY $1.25	149.9	149.0	148.1	147.2	146.2	145.4	144.5	143.5	142.5	141.5	140.5	139.4	138.2	137.1	136.1	135.0	134.1	132.9	131.8	130.5	129.2	127.8	126.5	125.5	125.0	125.0	125.0	125.0	125.0	125.0	125.0
IN THE MONEY $1.00	126.7	125.7	124.7	123.8	122.9	121.9	121.0	120.0	119.0	118.0	116.9	115.8	114.6	113.6	112.5	111.4	110.3	109.1	108.0	106.8	105.7	104.3	103.0	102.0	101.4	100.7	100.2	100.2	100.0	100.0	100.0
IN THE MONEY 75¢	105.1	104.2	103.4	102.6	101.8	100.9	100.0	99.0	98.1	97.2	96.2	95.1	94.0	92.9	91.9	90.8	89.8	88.7	87.6	86.5	85.4	84.1	82.9	81.6	80.2	78.6	77.0	75.8	75.1	75.0	75.0
IN THE MONEY 50¢	92.8	92.0	91.2	90.4	89.6	88.7	87.8	86.8	85.8	84.8	83.7	82.6	81.4	80.2	79.1	77.8	76.5	75.1	73.7	72.2	70.6	68.9	67.0	65.0	62.8	60.0	57.2	54.3	51.4	50.1	50.0
IN THE MONEY 25¢	81.7	80.8	79.9	79.0	78.0	77.1	76.1	75.1	74.0	72.8	71.6	70.3	68.9	67.5	66.1	64.7	63.2	61.7	60.1	58.4	56.6	54.7	52.6	50.3	47.6	44.0	40.2	35.7	30.9	26.7	25.0
AT THE MONEY	70.0	69.2	68.4	67.6	66.8	65.9	65.0	64.0	63.0	62.0	60.9	59.7	58.4	57.1	55.8	54.4	53.0	51.4	49.8	47.9	46.0	43.8	41.5	38.9	35.9	31.9	27.6	22.5	16.5	10.0	0.0
OUT OF THE MONEY 25¢	60.4	59.6	58.8	58.0	57.2	56.3	55.4	54.4	53.4	52.4	51.3	50.1	48.8	47.5	46.2	44.8	43.4	41.9	40.3	38.5	36.6	34.5	32.2	29.7	26.7	22.8	18.7	13.9	8.4	2.5	0
OUT OF THE MONEY 50¢	51.4	50.6	49.8	49.0	48.1	47.4	46.6	45.6	44.6	43.5	42.5	41.3	40.1	38.8	37.6	36.3	34.9	33.4	31.9	30.2	28.4	26.5	24.4	22.1	19.5	16.2	12.7	8.8	4.6	0.6	0
OUT OF THE MONEY 75¢	47.4	46.6	45.9	45.1	44.2	43.4	42.6	41.6	40.6	39.6	38.5	37.4	36.2	34.9	33.6	32.3	30.9	29.4	27.8	26.1	24.2	22.2	20.1	17.8	15.2	11.9	8.5	5.1	1.8	0.1	0
OUT OF THE MONEY $1.00	40.3	39.5	38.8	38.0	37.2	36.4	35.5	34.6	33.7	32.7	31.6	30.5	29.3	28.0	26.8	25.5	24.3	22.8	21.3	19.8	18.2	16.5	14.6	12.9	10.9	8.5	6.1	3.6	1.4	0.4	0
OUT OF THE MONEY $1.25	32.2	31.4	30.6	29.9	29.1	28.4	27.6	26.7	25.8	24.9	23.9	22.8	21.7	20.7	19.7	18.6	17.7	16.5	15.4	14.3	13.1	11.7	10.3	8.9	7.4	5.4	3.7	1.9	0.4	0.0	0

WM GRANDMILL (1985) LTD.

OPTION VALUES on SOYBEAN FUTURES – Table No:75

OPTION VALUES ARE IN CENTS – to nearest tenth.

WEEKS TO EXPIRATION	30	29	28	27	26	25	24	23	22	21	20	19	18	17	16	15	14	13	12	11	10	9	8	7	6	5	4	3	2	1	0
OUT OF THE MONEY $1.25	31.4	30.6	29.9	29.2	28.4	27.6	26.8	26.0	25.1	24.2	23.3	22.3	21.2	20.2	19.1	18.1	17.1	16.1	15.1	13.9	12.8	11.4	10.1	8.7	7.2	5.2	3.6	1.8	0.4	0	0
OUT OF THE MONEY $1.00	39.5	38.8	38.0	37.3	36.4	35.6	34.8	33.9	33.0	32.0	31.1	29.9	28.6	27.5	26.1	24.9	23.6	22.3	20.8	19.2	17.7	16.0	14.4	12.5	10.6	8.2	5.9	3.5	1.3	0	0
OUT OF THE MONEY 75¢	46.6	45.9	45.1	44.3	43.4	42.6	41.8	40.9	39.9	38.9	38.0	36.8	35.5	34.3	32.9	31.6	30.2	28.9	27.3	25.5	23.7	21.7	19.7	17.3	14.7	11.5	8.3	5.0	1.8	0	0
OUT OF THE MONEY 50¢	50.6	49.8	49.0	48.2	47.4	46.6	45.8	44.9	43.9	42.9	41.9	40.7	39.4	38.2	36.9	35.6	34.2	32.9	31.3	29.6	27.9	26.0	24.0	21.6	19.0	15.8	12.4	8.7	4.5	0.6	0
OUT OF THE MONEY 25¢	59.6	58.8	58.0	57.2	56.3	55.5	54.6	53.7	52.7	51.7	50.6	49.4	48.1	46.9	45.5	44.1	42.8	41.3	39.7	37.9	36.0	34.0	31.7	29.2	26.2	22.4	18.4	13.6	8.2	2.4	0
AT THE MONEY	69.2	68.4	67.6	66.8	65.9	65.1	64.2	63.3	62.3	61.3	60.2	59.0	57.7	56.5	55.1	53.7	52.3	50.8	49.2	47.3	45.4	43.3	41.0	38.4	35.4	31.5	27.3	22.2	16.3	9.9	0.0
IN THE MONEY 25¢	80.8	80.0	79.0	78.1	77.1	76.3	75.3	74.3	73.2	72.1	70.9	69.6	68.1	66.8	65.4	64.0	62.6	61.1	59.5	57.8	56.1	54.2	52.1	49.8	47.1	43.6	39.9	35.5	30.8	26.6	25.5
IN THE MONEY 50¢	92.0	91.2	90.4	89.6	88.7	87.9	87.0	86.1	85.1	84.1	83.0	82.0	80.8	79.6	78.4	77.2	75.9	74.6	73.3	71.6	70.1	68.4	66.6	64.6	62.4	59.6	57.0	54.2	51.3	50.1	50.0
IN THE MONEY 75¢	104.2	103.4	102.6	101.8	100.9	100.0	99.2	98.3	97.4	96.5	95.5	94.5	93.4	92.4	91.3	90.3	89.3	88.3	87.3	86.1	85.0	83.8	82.7	81.4	80.0	78.4	77.0	75.7	75.1	75.0	75.0
IN THE MONEY $1.00	125.7	124.7	123.8	122.9	121.9	121.0	120.2	119.3	118.3	117.3	116.2	115.2	114.1	113.1	112.0	110.9	109.7	108.7	107.6	106.4	105.3	104.0	102.8	101.9	101.3	100.6	100.2	100.0	100.0	100.0	100.0
IN THE MONEY $1.25	149.0	148.1	147.2	146.3	145.4	144.6	143.7	142.8	141.8	140.8	139.8	138.7	137.6	136.6	135.5	134.5	133.5	132.5	131.3	130.0	128.7	127.5	126.3	125.4	125.0	125.0	125.0	125.0	125.0	125.0	125.0

WM GRANDMILL (1985) LTD.

OPTION VALUES on SOYBEAN FUTURES – Table No: 78

	30	29	28	27	26	25	24	23	22	21	20	19	18	17	16	15	14	13	12	11	10	9	8	7	6	5	4	3	2	1	0
IN THE MONEY $1.25	151.6	150.8	150.0	149.1	148.1	147.1	146.1	145.1	144.1	143.0	141.9	140.7	139.5	138.3	137.1	136.0	134.9	133.8	132.7	131.3	129.9	128.4	127.0	125.8	125.1	125.1	125.0	125.0	125.0	125.0	125.0
$1.00	128.4	127.6	126.7	125.8	124.7	123.8	122.7	121.6	120.6	119.5	118.4	117.1	115.9	114.7	113.6	112.5	111.3	110.1	108.8	107.5	106.3	105.0	103.5	102.3	101.6	100.8	100.3	100.0	100.0	100.0	100.0
75¢	106.8	106.0	105.2	104.3	103.4	102.5	101.6	100.6	99.6	98.5	97.5	96.3	95.2	94.0	92.9	91.8	90.7	89.6	88.4	87.2	86.0	84.7	83.4	82.1	80.5	78.9	77.3	75.9	75.1	75.0	75.0
50¢	94.5	93.7	92.9	92.1	91.2	90.3	89.4	88.4	87.4	86.3	85.1	83.9	82.7	81.5	80.2	79.0	77.7	76.3	74.8	73.2	71.5	69.8	67.7	65.7	63.4	60.4	57.6	54.6	51.5	50.1	50.0
25¢	83.4	82.6	81.8	80.9	80.0	78.9	77.9	76.8	75.7	74.5	73.2	71.9	70.4	69.0	67.5	66.0	64.6	63.0	61.3	59.4	57.6	55.7	53.4	51.1	48.3	44.6	40.7	36.2	31.3	26.8	25.0
AT THE MONEY	71.7	70.9	70.1	69.3	68.4	67.5	66.6	65.6	64.6	63.5	62.4	61.1	59.8	58.5	57.1	55.7	54.3	52.7	51.0	49.1	47.1	44.9	42.4	39.8	36.7	32.6	28.3	23.0	16.9	10.3	0.0
OUT OF THE MONEY 25¢	62.1	61.3	60.5	59.7	58.8	57.9	57.0	56.0	55.0	53.9	52.7	51.5	50.2	48.9	47.5	46.1	44.7	43.2	41.5	39.6	37.7	35.5	33.1	30.5	27.5	23.5	19.3	14.4	8.8	2.7	0.0
50¢	53.1	52.3	51.5	50.7	49.8	48.9	48.0	47.1	46.2	45.1	44.0	42.7	41.4	40.2	38.8	37.5	36.1	34.6	33.0	31.3	29.4	27.5	25.2	22.9	20.1	16.7	13.2	9.3	5.0	0.7	0.0
75¢	49.0	48.2	47.4	46.7	45.9	45.0	44.1	43.1	42.2	41.1	40.0	38.7	37.5	36.3	34.9	33.5	32.2	30.6	29.0	27.2	25.3	23.3	20.9	18.6	15.9	12.4	9.0	5.5	2.0	0.1	0.0
$1.00	41.8	41.2	40.4	39.6	38.8	38.0	37.1	36.1	35.2	34.1	33.0	31.8	30.6	29.4	28.0	26.7	25.4	24.0	22.4	20.7	19.1	17.3	15.3	13.5	11.3	8.9	6.4	3.8	1.5	0.0	0.0
$1.25	33.7	33.1	32.3	31.5	30.6	29.8	29.0	28.1	27.2	26.2	25.2	24.0	22.9	21.8	20.7	19.6	18.5	17.4	16.3	15.0	13.8	12.5	10.9	9.4	7.7	5.8	3.9	2.0	0.5	0.0	0.0

WEEKS TO EXPIRATION

OPTION VALUES ARE IN CENTS – to nearest tenth

WM GRANDMILL (1985) LTD.

OPTION VALUES on SOYBEAN FUTURES – Table No: 77

	30	29	28	27	26	25	24	23	22	21	20	19	18	17	16	15	14	13	12	11	10	9	8	7	6	5	4	3	2	1	0
IN THE MONEY $1.25	150.8	150.0	149.0	148.1	147.1	146.2	145.3	144.3	143.3	142.3	141.2	140.0	138.8	137.7	136.5	135.4	134.4	133.3	132.1	130.8	129.4	128.1	126.8	125.7	125.1	125.0	125.0	125.0	125.0	125.0	125.0
$1.00	127.6	126.7	125.7	124.7	123.8	122.8	121.8	120.8	119.8	118.8	117.6	116.4	115.2	114.2	113.0	112.0	110.8	109.6	108.4	107.1	105.9	104.7	103.3	102.2	101.5	100.7	100.3	100.0	100.0	100.0	100.0
75¢	106.0	105.2	104.2	103.4	102.5	101.7	100.8	99.8	98.8	97.9	96.9	95.7	94.5	93.5	92.3	91.3	90.2	89.2	88.0	86.8	85.6	84.4	83.2	81.9	80.4	78.6	77.3	75.8	75.1	75.0	75.0
50¢	93.7	92.9	92.0	91.2	90.3	89.5	88.6	87.6	86.5	85.6	84.5	83.2	82.0	80.8	79.6	78.4	77.1	75.7	74.3	72.7	71.0	69.3	67.3	65.3	63.0	60.2	57.5	54.4	51.5	50.1	50.0
25¢	82.6	81.7	80.8	80.0	78.9	78.0	77.0	75.9	74.8	73.7	72.4	71.1	69.7	68.2	66.7	65.3	63.9	62.4	60.7	58.9	57.1	55.2	53.1	50.7	47.9	44.3	40.6	35.9	31.1	26.7	25.0
AT THE MONEY	70.9	70.1	69.2	68.4	67.5	66.7	65.8	64.8	63.8	62.8	61.7	60.4	59.1	57.8	56.4	55.0	53.6	52.1	50.4	48.5	46.5	44.4	42.0	39.4	36.3	32.3	28.0	22.7	16.7	10.1	0.0
OUT OF THE MONEY 25¢	61.3	60.5	59.6	58.8	57.9	57.1	56.2	55.2	54.2	53.2	52.0	50.8	49.5	48.2	46.8	45.4	44.0	42.5	40.9	39.1	37.1	35.0	32.7	30.1	27.1	23.2	19.1	14.1	8.6	2.5	0.0
50¢	52.3	51.5	50.6	49.8	48.9	48.1	47.3	46.4	45.4	44.4	43.2	42.0	40.7	39.5	38.2	36.9	35.5	34.0	32.4	30.7	28.9	27.0	24.9	22.5	19.7	16.4	13.1	9.0	4.8	0.7	0.0
75¢	48.2	47.4	46.6	45.9	45.0	44.2	43.3	42.4	41.4	40.4	39.3	38.1	36.8	35.6	34.2	32.9	31.5	30.0	28.4	26.7	24.7	22.8	20.6	18.2	15.5	12.1	8.9	5.2	1.4	0.1	0.0
$1.00	41.2	40.4	39.5	38.8	37.9	37.2	36.3	35.4	34.4	33.5	32.4	31.2	29.9	28.7	27.4	26.1	24.8	23.4	21.9	20.2	18.6	16.9	15.1	13.2	11.1	8.7	6.3	3.7	1.4	0	0
$1.25	33.1	32.3	31.4	30.6	29.8	29.1	28.3	27.4	26.5	25.6	24.6	23.4	22.3	21.3	20.1	19.1	18.0	17.0	15.8	14.6	13.4	12.1	10.7	9.2	7.6	5.6	3.9	1.9	0.4	0	0

WEEKS TO EXPIRATION

OPTION VALUES ARE IN CENTS – to nearest tenth

WM GRANDMILL (1985) LTD.

OPTION VALUES on SOYBEAN FUTURES – Table No:80

Position	30	29	28	27	26	25	24	23	22	21	20	19	18	17	16	15	14	13	12	11	10	9	8	7	6	5	4	3	2	1	0
OUT $1.25	35.2	34.5	34.1	33.7	33.0	32.2	31.4	30.3	29.4	28.5	27.6	26.5	25.4	24.2	23.0	21.8	20.7	19.5	18.4	17.1	15.7	14.5	13.1	11.5	9.9	8.3	6.2	4.3	2.2	0.5	0.0
OUT $1.00	43.2	42.5	41.8	41.1	40.3	39.5	38.5	37.4	36.6	35.6	34.4	33.2	32.0	30.7	29.4	28.0	26.6	25.2	23.5	21.7	20.0	18.2	16.2	14.2	11.9	9.4	6.8	4.0	1.7	0.0	0
OUT 75¢	50.4	49.7	49.0	48.2	47.4	46.6	45.6	44.6	43.6	42.6	41.4	40.2	38.9	37.6	36.3	34.9	33.4	31.9	30.1	28.3	26.4	24.2	21.9	19.5	16.7	13.0	9.6	5.7	2.2	0.1	0
OUT 50¢	54.8	54.0	53.1	52.2	51.4	50.6	49.5	48.5	47.5	46.6	45.4	44.2	42.9	41.5	40.2	38.8	37.4	35.9	34.1	32.3	30.4	28.4	26.2	23.8	20.9	17.3	13.9	9.6	5.2	0.8	0
OUT 25¢	63.8	63.0	62.1	61.2	60.4	59.5	58.5	57.5	56.5	55.4	54.2	53.0	51.7	50.3	48.9	47.5	46.0	44.4	42.7	40.7	38.8	36.5	34.2	31.5	28.4	24.3	20.0	14.8	9.1	2.8	0
AT THE MONEY	73.4	72.6	71.7	70.8	70.0	69.1	68.1	67.1	66.1	65.0	63.8	62.6	61.3	59.9	58.5	57.1	55.6	54.0	52.2	50.2	48.2	45.9	43.5	40.8	37.6	33.4	29.0	23.5	17.3	10.5	0.0
IN 25¢	85.1	84.3	83.4	82.5	81.7	80.7	79.6	78.5	77.4	76.2	74.8	73.5	72.1	70.5	69.0	67.5	65.9	64.3	62.5	60.5	58.6	56.6	54.4	52.0	49.1	45.3	41.4	36.5	31.5	26.9	25.0
IN 50¢	96.2	95.4	94.5	93.7	92.8	91.9	90.9	89.9	88.9	87.8	86.6	85.4	84.1	82.8	81.5	80.2	78.9	77.5	75.8	74.2	72.4	70.6	68.6	66.8	64.0	61.0	58.1	54.8	51.7	50.2	50.0
IN 75¢	108.6	107.8	106.9	106.0	105.1	104.2	103.1	102.1	101.1	100.0	98.8	97.7	96.5	95.3	94.0	92.9	91.7	90.6	89.3	87.9	86.7	85.3	83.9	82.6	81.0	79.2	77.6	76.0	75.1	75.0	75.0
IN $1.00	130.2	129.4	128.4	127.5	126.7	125.7	124.4	123.3	122.2	121.0	119.8	118.6	117.3	116.0	114.7	113.6	112.4	111.2	109.7	108.3	107.0	105.6	104.5	102.7	101.8	100.9	100.4	100.0	100.0	100.0	100.0
IN $1.25	153.2	152.5	151.6	150.7	149.9	148.9	147.8	146.7	145.6	144.5	143.3	142.1	140.8	139.6	138.3	137.1	135.9	134.8	133.5	132.1	130.7	129.1	127.6	126.2	125.3	125.0	125.0	125.0	125.0	125.0	125.0

WEEKS TO EXPIRATION

OPTION VALUES ARE IN CENTS – to nearest tenth.

WM GRANDMILL (1985) LTD.

OPTION VALUES on SOYBEAN FUTURES – Table No:79

Position	30	29	28	27	26	25	24	23	22	21	20	19	18	17	16	15	14	13	12	11	10	9	8	7	6	5	4	3	2	1	0
OUT $1.25	34.5	33.7	33.1	32.2	31.4	30.5	29.6	28.7	27.8	26.8	25.8	24.7	23.5	22.4	21.3	20.1	19.0	17.8	16.6	15.4	14.1	12.8	11.3	9.6	8.0	6.0	4.1	2.1	0.5	0	0
OUT $1.00	42.5	41.8	41.2	40.3	39.5	38.7	37.7	36.8	35.8	34.8	33.7	32.5	31.3	30.0	28.7	27.4	26.0	24.5	22.9	21.2	19.5	17.7	15.9	13.8	11.6	9.2	6.6	3.9	1.6	0	0
OUT 75¢	49.7	49.0	48.2	47.4	46.6	45.8	44.8	43.8	42.8	41.8	40.6	39.4	38.2	36.9	35.6	34.2	32.8	31.2	29.5	27.7	25.8	23.7	21.5	19.0	16.2	12.8	9.2	5.6	2.1	0.1	0
OUT 50¢	54.0	53.1	52.3	51.4	50.6	49.7	48.7	47.7	46.8	45.7	44.6	43.4	42.1	40.8	39.5	38.1	36.7	35.2	33.6	31.8	29.9	27.9	25.8	23.3	20.4	17.1	13.5	9.4	5.1	0.8	0
OUT 25¢	63.0	62.1	61.3	60.4	59.6	58.7	57.7	56.7	55.7	54.6	53.4	52.2	50.9	49.6	48.2	46.8	45.3	43.7	42.0	40.1	38.2	36.0	33.7	31.0	27.9	23.9	19.6	14.6	8.9	2.7	0
AT THE MONEY	72.6	71.7	70.9	70.0	69.2	68.3	67.3	66.3	65.3	64.2	63.0	61.8	60.5	59.2	57.8	56.4	54.9	53.3	51.6	49.6	47.6	45.4	43.0	40.3	37.1	33.0	28.6	23.3	17.1	10.4	0.0
IN 25¢	84.3	83.4	82.6	81.7	80.8	79.8	78.7	77.6	76.5	75.3	74.0	72.6	71.2	69.8	68.2	66.7	65.2	63.6	61.9	60.0	58.1	56.1	54.0	51.5	48.6	45.0	41.0	36.3	31.4	26.9	25.0
IN 50¢	95.4	94.5	93.7	92.8	92.0	91.0	89.9	88.9	88.1	87.0	85.8	84.6	83.3	82.1	80.9	79.6	78.3	76.8	75.3	73.7	71.9	70.1	68.3	66.0	63.7	60.8	57.8	54.7	51.6	50.2	50.0
IN 75¢	107.8	106.9	106.0	105.9	105.1	104.2	103.3	102.3	101.3	100.3	99.2	98.1	97.0	95.8	94.6	93.5	92.3	91.2	90.0	88.8	87.5	86.3	85.0	83.7	82.3	80.7	79.1	77.4	75.9	75.1	75.0
IN $1.00	129.4	128.4	127.6	126.7	125.7	124.6	123.5	122.4	121.3	120.2	119.0	117.8	116.6	115.3	114.2	113.0	111.8	110.5	109.2	107.8	106.6	105.3	103.9	102.5	101.7	100.9	100.3	100.0	100.0	100.0	100.0
IN $1.25	152.5	151.6	150.8	149.9	149.0	148.0	146.9	145.8	144.8	143.7	142.5	141.3	140.1	138.8	137.6	136.5	135.3	134.2	133.0	131.6	130.2	128.7	127.4	126.0	125.2	125.0	125.0	125.0	125.0	125.0	125.0

WEEKS TO EXPIRATION

OPTION VALUES ARE IN CENTS – to nearest tenth.

WM GRANDMILL (1985) LTD.

OPTION VALUES on SOYBEAN FUTURES – Table No:82

	30	29	28	27	26	25	24	23	22	21	20	19	18	17	16	15	14	13	12	11	10	9	8	7	6	5	4	3	2	1	0
IN THE MONEY $1.25	154.8	154.0	153.2	152.4	151.5	150.7	149.5	148.4	147.2	146.0	144.8	143.5	142.2	140.8	139.6	138.2	137.0	135.6	134.3	132.9	131.4	129.9	128.1	126.6	125.4	125.5	125.5	125.5	125.5	125.5	125.5
IN $1.00	131.8	131.0	130.2	129.3	128.4	127.5	126.5	125.3	124.1	122.9	121.7	120.6	119.3	117.9	116.6	115.3	114.1	112.9	111.6	110.2	108.7	107.2	105.9	104.4	103.1	101.9	101.0	100.4	100.0	100.0	100.0
IN 75¢	110.3	109.5	108.6	107.7	106.7	105.8	104.7	103.7	102.6	101.5	100.3	99.0	97.8	96.5	95.3	93.9	92.8	91.4	90.1	88.7	87.3	86.0	84.4	83.0	81.4	79.5	77.7	76.1	75.2	75.0	75.0
IN 50¢	97.8	97.0	96.2	95.3	94.4	93.5	92.5	91.5	90.4	89.3	88.1	86.8	85.5	84.1	82.8	81.4	80.1	78.5	76.9	75.1	73.4	71.5	69.4	67.2	64.9	61.6	58.4	55.1	51.9	50.2	50.0
IN 25¢	86.6	85.9	85.1	84.2	83.3	82.4	81.4	80.3	79.0	77.8	76.5	75.1	73.6	72.1	70.5	68.9	67.2	65.5	63.7	61.7	59.6	57.6	55.3	52.8	49.8	46.0	41.9	37.0	31.9	27.0	25.0
AT THE MONEY	75.0	74.2	73.4	72.5	71.6	70.7	69.7	68.7	67.6	66.5	65.3	64.0	62.7	61.3	59.9	58.4	56.9	55.2	53.4	51.4	49.3	47.0	44.5	41.7	38.4	34.2	29.6	24.1	17.7	10.7	0.0
OUT 25¢	65.4	64.6	63.8	62.9	62.0	61.1	60.1	59.1	58.0	56.9	55.7	54.4	53.1	51.7	50.3	48.8	47.3	45.6	43.8	41.9	39.8	37.6	35.1	32.4	29.2	25.0	20.5	15.4	9.5	3.0	0
OUT 50¢	56.4	55.6	54.7	53.9	53.0	52.1	51.1	50.1	49.0	47.9	46.8	45.6	44.3	42.9	41.5	40.1	38.6	37.0	35.3	33.4	31.5	29.4	27.1	24.6	21.6	18.0	14.3	10.1	5.5	0.9	0
OUT 75¢	51.8	51.1	50.3	49.6	48.9	48.0	47.1	46.2	45.1	44.0	42.8	41.6	40.3	38.9	37.6	36.2	34.7	33.0	31.3	29.4	27.4	25.2	22.9	20.3	17.3	13.7	10.0	6.1	2.4	0.2	0
OUT $1.00	44.6	43.9	43.1	42.5	41.7	40.9	40.0	39.0	38.0	37.0	35.8	34.6	33.3	32.0	30.7	29.3	27.9	26.2	24.6	22.8	20.9	19.1	17.0	14.8	12.5	9.9	7.1	4.3	1.8	0	0
OUT OF THE MONEY $1.25	36.7	35.9	35.1	34.5	33.6	32.9	31.9	30.9	29.9	28.9	27.8	26.7	25.5	24.2	23.0	21.7	20.6	19.2	17.6	16.5	15.1	13.8	12.1	10.4	8.7	6.6	4.5	2.4	0.6	0	0

WEEKS TO EXPIRATION

OPTION VALUES ARE IN CENTS – to nearest tenth.

WM GRANDMILL (1985) LTD.

OPTION VALUES on SOYBEAN FUTURES – Table No:81

	30	29	28	27	26	25	24	23	22	21	20	19	18	17	16	15	14	13	12	11	10	9	8	7	6	5	4	3	2	1	0
IN THE MONEY $1.25	153.9	153.1	152.4	151.6	150.7	149.7	148.6	147.5	146.3	145.2	144.1	142.8	141.4	140.2	138.8	137.6	136.4	135.1	133.9	132.5	131.0	129.4	127.8	126.4	125.4	125.0	125.0	125.0	125.0	125.0	125.0
IN $1.00	130.9	130.1	129.3	128.4	127.5	126.5	125.5	124.3	123.1	121.9	120.7	119.6	118.3	116.9	115.6	114.3	113.1	111.9	110.6	109.2	107.7	106.2	104.9	103.4	102.1	100.9	100.4	100.0	100.0	100.0	100.0
IN 75¢	109.4	108.5	107.7	106.8	105.9	104.9	103.9	102.9	101.8	100.7	99.6	98.3	97.1	95.9	94.6	93.4	92.2	90.9	89.7	88.3	86.9	85.6	84.2	82.8	81.2	79.4	77.6	76.0	75.2	75.0	75.0
IN 50¢	96.9	96.1	95.3	94.5	93.9	92.7	91.7	90.7	89.6	88.5	87.4	86.1	84.7	83.4	82.1	80.8	79.4	78.0	76.4	74.7	72.9	70.9	69.1	66.8	64.4	61.3	58.3	55.0	51.8	50.2	50.0
IN 25¢	85.8	85.0	84.2	83.4	82.5	81.6	80.5	79.3	78.1	76.9	75.7	74.3	72.7	71.3	69.8	68.1	66.5	64.9	63.1	61.1	59.1	57.0	54.9	52.3	49.5	45.7	41.6	36.8	31.7	27.0	25.0
AT THE MONEY	74.1	73.3	72.5	71.7	70.8	69.9	68.9	67.9	66.8	65.7	64.6	63.3	61.9	60.6	59.2	57.7	56.2	54.6	52.8	50.8	48.7	46.4	44.0	41.2	38.0	33.8	29.3	23.8	17.5	10.6	0.0
OUT 25¢	64.5	63.7	62.9	62.1	61.2	60.3	59.3	58.3	57.2	56.1	54.9	53.7	52.3	51.0	49.6	48.1	46.6	45.0	43.3	41.3	39.3	37.0	34.7	31.9	28.8	24.7	20.2	15.1	9.3	2.9	0
OUT 50¢	55.5	54.7	53.9	53.1	52.2	51.3	50.3	49.3	48.2	47.2	46.1	44.9	43.5	42.2	40.8	39.4	37.9	36.5	34.7	32.9	30.9	28.8	26.7	24.1	21.3	17.7	14.0	9.9	5.3	0.8	0
OUT 75¢	51.0	50.3	49.7	49.0	48.1	47.3	46.4	45.4	44.3	43.2	42.2	40.9	39.5	38.3	36.9	35.5	34.0	32.5	30.7	28.8	26.9	24.6	22.4	19.8	17.1	13.4	9.7	5.9	2.3	0.1	0
OUT $1.00	43.8	43.1	42.5	41.8	41.1	40.2	39.3	38.3	37.3	36.2	35.2	33.9	32.6	31.4	30.0	28.6	27.2	25.7	24.1	22.3	20.4	18.5	16.7	14.5	12.3	9.6	6.9	4.2	1.7	0	0
OUT OF THE MONEY $1.25	35.8	35.0	34.5	33.7	32.9	32.1	31.2	30.2	29.2	28.2	27.2	26.0	24.8	23.6	22.4	21.2	20.0	18.7	17.5	16.1	14.7	13.4	11.9	10.2	8.5	6.4	4.4	2.3	0.6	0	0

WEEKS TO EXPIRATION

OPTION VALUES ARE IN CENTS – to nearest tenth.

WM GRANDMILL (1985) LTD.

OPTION VALUES on SOYBEAN FUTURES – Table No: 84

OPTION VALUES ARE IN CENTS – to nearest tenth.

	30	29	28	27	26	25	24	23	22	21	20	19	18	17	16	15	14	13	12	11	10	9	8	7	6	5	4	3	2	1	0
OUT OF THE MONEY $1.25	38.5	37.6	36.7	35.8	35.0	34.2	33.3	32.4	31.3	30.3	29.2	28.0	26.7	25.5	24.1	22.8	21.6	20.2	18.7	17.2	15.8	14.4	12.8	11.0	9.1	6.9	4.8	2.6	0.7	0	0
$1.00	46.4	45.5	44.6	43.8	43.1	42.2	41.4	40.5	39.4	38.4	37.3	36.0	34.7	33.4	31.9	30.5	29.1	27.5	25.8	23.8	21.9	19.9	17.8	15.5	13.1	10.3	7.5	4.6	1.9	0.1	0
75¢	53.6	52.7	51.8	51.0	50.2	49.4	48.6	47.5	46.5	45.5	44.3	43.0	41.7	40.3	38.8	37.4	36.0	34.3	32.5	30.4	28.0	26.2	23.8	21.1	18.1	14.8	10.5	6.4	2.6	0.2	0
50¢	58.2	57.3	56.4	55.5	54.1	53.6	52.6	51.6	50.5	49.4	48.2	47.0	45.7	44.3	42.8	41.3	39.9	38.2	36.5	34.4	32.5	30.3	28.0	25.4	22.4	18.7	14.8	10.5	5.8	1.0	0
25¢	67.2	66.3	65.4	64.5	63.6	62.6	61.6	60.6	59.5	58.4	57.2	55.9	54.5	53.1	51.6	50.1	48.6	46.9	45.0	43.0	40.9	38.6	36.1	33.3	30.0	25.7	21.2	15.9	9.8	3.3	0
AT THE MONEY	76.8	75.9	75.0	74.1	73.2	72.2	71.2	70.2	69.1	68.0	66.8	65.5	64.1	62.7	61.2	59.7	58.2	56.5	54.6	52.5	50.4	48.0	45.5	42.6	39.3	34.9	30.3	24.6	18.1	11.0	0.0
IN THE MONEY 25¢	88.4	87.5	86.6	85.8	84.9	83.9	82.9	81.9	80.7	79.5	78.1	76.7	75.2	73.6	72.0	70.3	68.7	66.8	64.9	62.8	60.7	58.5	56.2	53.6	50.6	46.7	42.3	37.5	32.2	27.2	25.0
50¢	99.6	98.7	97.8	96.9	96.0	95.0	94.0	93.0	91.9	90.8	89.6	88.3	86.9	85.5	84.0	82.6	81.2	79.7	78.0	76.1	74.3	72.3	70.2	67.9	65.2	62.1	58.8	55.4	52.0	50.2	50.0
75¢	112.1	111.2	110.3	109.4	108.4	107.4	106.6	105.6	104.1	103.0	101.8	100.5	99.1	97.8	96.4	95.1	93.8	92.4	90.9	89.4	88.0	86.6	85.0	83.5	81.8	79.8	78.1	76.3	75.2	75	75.0
$1.00	133.6	132.7	131.8	131.0	130.1	129.0	128.2	127.2	126.0	124.7	124.3	122.9	121.5	120.1	118.7	117.2	115.8	114.5	113.1	111.6	109.9	108.4	106.9	105.3	103.6	102.1	101.2	100.5	100.0	100.0	100.0
$1.25	156.6	155.7	154.8	153.9	153.0	152.1	151.1	150.1	148.9	147.7	146.3	145.0	143.6	142.2	140.7	139.4	138.0	136.6	135.1	133.6	132.2	130.6	128.7	127.1	125.6	125.0	125.0	125.0	125.0	125.0	125.0

WEEKS TO EXPIRATION

WM GRANDMILL (1985) LTD.

OPTION VALUES on SOYBEAN FUTURES – Table No: 83

OPTION VALUES ARE IN CENTS – to nearest tenth.

	30	29	28	27	26	25	24	23	22	21	20	19	18	17	16	15	14	13	12	11	10	9	8	7	6	5	4	3	2	1	0
OUT OF THE MONEY $1.25	37.7	36.8	35.9	35.1	34.4	33.5	32.7	31.7	30.6	29.6	28.5	27.4	26.1	24.9	23.5	22.3	21.0	19.7	18.4	16.9	15.5	14.0	12.6	10.8	8.9	6.8	4.7	2.5	0.6	0	0
$1.00	45.6	44.7	43.8	43.1	42.4	41.6	40.8	39.8	38.8	37.7	36.6	35.4	34.1	32.7	31.3	29.9	28.4	26.8	25.2	23.3	21.4	19.4	17.5	15.2	12.9	10.1	7.4	4.5	1.9	0	0
75¢	52.8	51.9	51.1	50.3	49.6	48.8	47.8	46.9	45.9	44.8	43.6	42.4	41.0	39.6	38.2	36.8	35.3	33.6	31.9	29.9	27.9	25.7	23.4	20.7	17.8	14.1	10.3	6.3	2.5	0.2	0
50¢	57.4	56.5	55.6	54.7	53.8	52.9	51.9	50.9	49.8	48.7	47.5	46.3	45.0	43.6	42.2	40.7	39.2	37.6	35.9	33.9	32.0	29.8	27.6	25.0	22.1	18.4	14.7	10.3	5.7	1.0	0
25¢	66.4	65.5	64.6	63.7	62.8	61.9	60.9	59.9	58.8	57.7	56.5	55.2	53.8	52.4	50.9	49.4	47.9	46.2	44.4	42.4	40.3	38.1	35.6	32.9	29.7	25.4	20.9	15.7	9.7	3.2	0
AT THE MONEY	76.0	75.1	74.2	73.3	72.4	71.5	70.5	69.5	68.4	67.3	66.1	64.8	63.4	62.0	60.5	59.0	57.5	55.8	54.0	51.9	49.8	47.5	45.0	42.2	38.9	34.6	30.0	24.4	17.9	10.9	0.0
IN THE MONEY 25¢	87.6	86.7	85.8	85.0	84.1	83.2	82.2	81.2	80.0	78.7	77.3	75.9	74.4	72.9	71.2	69.6	67.9	66.1	64.3	62.2	60.1	58.0	55.8	53.2	50.3	46.4	42.3	37.3	32.1	27.1	25.0
50¢	98.8	97.6	96.9	96.1	95.2	94.3	93.3	92.3	91.2	90.1	88.9	87.6	86.2	84.8	83.3	82.0	80.6	79.1	77.5	75.6	73.9	71.8	69.9	67.6	65.0	61.8	58.7	55.3	52.0	50.2	50.0
75¢	111.3	110.4	109.5	108.5	107.6	106.6	105.6	104.5	103.4	102.3	101.1	99.8	98.4	97.2	95.8	94.5	93.2	91.9	90.6	89.1	87.6	86.2	84.8	83.3	81.6	79.7	77.9	76.2	75.2	75.0	75.0
$1.00	132.8	131.9	131.0	130.1	129.2	128.2	127.2	126.0	124.7	123.5	122.2	120.8	119.4	118.0	116.5	115.2	113.9	112.6	111.2	109.5	108.0	106.5	105.1	103.4	102.0	100.5	100.5	100.2	100.0	100.0	100.0
$1.25	155.8	154.9	154.0	153.1	152.3	151.4	150.4	149.3	148.1	146.9	145.6	144.3	142.9	141.5	140.1	138.8	137.4	136.1	134.8	133.3	131.8	130.1	128.5	126.9	125.5	125.0	125.0	125.0	125.0	125.0	125.0

WEEKS TO EXPIRATION

WM GRANDMILL (1985) LTD.

OPTION VALUES on SOYBEAN FUTURES – Table No:86

Column headings = WEEKS TO EXPIRATION. OPTION VALUES ARE IN CENTS – to nearest tenth.

	30	29	28	27	26	25	24	23	22	21	20	19	18	17	16	15	14	13	12	11	10	9	8	7	6	5	4	3	2	1	0
IN THE MONEY $1.25	161.2	160.3	159.5	158.5	157.5	156.5	155.5	154.4	153.2	152.1	150.8	149.3	147.7	146.0	144.5	143.0	141.3	139.7	137.9	136.1	134.3	132.7	130.7	128.6	126.7	125.2	125.0	125.0	125.0	125.0	125.0
$1.00	138.4	137.5	136.5	135.5	134.5	133.5	132.5	131.4	130.2	129.0	127.6	126.0	124.3	122.6	121.0	119.5	117.8	116.1	114.5	112.6	110.7	108.9	107.0	105.2	103.2	101.7	100.7	100.1	100.0	100.0	100.0
75¢	117.1	116.1	115.2	114.1	113.1	112.0	111.0	109.9	108.6	107.4	106.0	104.5	103.0	101.5	100.0	98.5	97.0	95.4	93.7	91.9	90.1	88.5	86.7	84.9	83.1	80.7	78.7	76.7	75.3	75.0	75.0
50¢	104.3	103.4	102.5	101.5	100.5	99.4	98.4	97.4	96.4	95.0	93.7	92.3	90.8	89.3	87.8	86.3	84.6	82.9	81.1	79.1	77.0	74.9	72.5	70.0	67.3	63.7	60.2	56.4	52.7	50.3	50.0
25¢	93.0	92.1	91.3	90.3	89.3	88.4	87.3	86.2	85.1	83.9	82.6	81.2	79.5	77.8	76.2	74.5	72.6	70.7	68.5	66.1	63.8	61.3	58.7	56.0	52.9	48.6	44.2	38.9	33.1	27.6	25.0
AT THE MONEY	81.5	80.6	79.7	78.8	77.7	76.7	75.7	74.6	73.4	72.2	70.9	69.5	68.0	66.5	65.0	63.5	61.8	60.0	58.0	55.8	53.5	51.0	48.3	45.3	41.8	37.1	32.2	26.2	19.3	11.7	0.0
OUT OF THE MONEY 25¢	72.0	71.1	70.1	69.1	68.1	67.1	66.1	65.0	63.8	62.6	61.3	59.9	58.4	56.9	55.4	53.9	52.2	50.4	48.4	46.2	43.9	41.5	38.9	35.9	32.5	27.9	23.1	17.4	11.0	4.0	0
50¢	62.9	62.0	61.1	60.1	59.1	58.1	57.1	56.0	54.8	53.6	52.3	50.9	49.4	47.9	46.6	45.1	43.4	41.6	39.7	37.6	35.6	33.1	30.5	27.8	24.7	20.4	16.4	11.7	6.6	1.4	0
75¢	58.0	57.2	56.3	55.4	54.4	53.5	52.5	51.4	50.4	49.4	48.2	46.9	45.5	44.0	42.6	41.1	39.4	37.7	35.8	33.8	31.4	29.1	26.5	23.6	20.4	16.2	12.1	7.6	3.3	0.3	0
$1.00	50.8	50.0	49.1	48.2	47.2	46.3	45.3	44.2	43.2	42.2	41.1	39.8	38.4	37.0	35.6	34.1	32.5	30.8	28.9	26.8	24.7	22.5	20.0	17.6	14.9	11.6	8.7	5.4	2.3	0.1	0
$1.25	43.0	42.2	41.3	40.4	39.4	38.4	37.4	36.4	35.2	34.2	33.1	31.7	30.3	28.9	27.6	26.2	24.7	23.1	21.5	19.7	17.9	16.3	14.5	12.7	10.5	8.0	5.6	3.1	1.0	0.0	0

WM GRANDMILL (1985) LTD.

OPTION VALUES on SOYBEAN FUTURES – Table No:85

Column headings = WEEKS TO EXPIRATION. OPTION VALUES ARE IN CENTS – to nearest tenth.

	30	29	28	27	26	25	24	23	22	21	20	19	18	17	16	15	14	13	12	11	10	9	8	7	6	5	4	3	2	1	0
IN THE MONEY $1.25	159.1	158.2	157.3	156.4	155.4	154.4	153.4	152.4	151.3	150.1	148.8	147.2	145.7	144.2	142.7	141.2	139.7	138.1	136.5	134.9	133.4	131.6	129.9	127.9	126.1	125.1	125.0	125.0	125.0	125.0	125.0
$1.00	136.1	135.2	134.3	133.4	132.4	131.4	130.4	129.3	128.1	126.9	125.5	123.8	122.3	120.7	119.2	117.7	116.1	114.5	113.0	111.3	109.6	107.8	106.3	104.5	102.6	101.5	100.6	100.1	100.0	100.0	100.0
75¢	114.8	113.8	112.9	111.9	110.9	109.9	108.8	107.4	106.5	105.3	104.0	102.6	101.2	99.7	98.2	96.9	95.4	93.8	92.3	90.7	89.2	87.5	86.0	84.2	82.5	80.3	78.3	76.5	75.2	75.0	75.0
50¢	102.1	101.2	100.3	99.4	98.4	97.4	96.4	95.3	94.2	93.0	91.7	90.4	89.0	87.5	86.0	84.5	82.9	81.3	79.6	77.7	75.7	73.7	71.5	69.1	66.3	62.9	59.9	55.9	52.9	50.3	50.0
25¢	90.9	90.0	89.1	88.2	87.2	86.2	85.3	84.2	83.1	81.9	80.6	79.0	77.5	75.8	74.2	72.5	70.8	68.8	66.7	64.6	62.4	59.9	57.6	54.9	51.8	47.7	43.3	38.2	32.7	27.3	25.0
AT THE MONEY	79.3	78.4	77.5	76.6	75.6	74.6	73.6	72.6	71.4	70.2	69.0	67.6	66.2	64.7	63.2	61.7	60.1	58.3	56.4	54.3	52.1	49.6	47.0	44.0	40.6	36.1	31.3	25.4	18.7	11.3	0.0
OUT OF THE MONEY 25¢	69.7	68.8	67.9	67.0	66.0	65.0	64.0	62.9	61.8	60.6	59.4	58.0	56.6	55.1	53.6	52.1	50.5	48.7	46.8	44.7	42.6	40.1	37.6	34.7	31.3	26.9	22.1	16.7	10.4	3.6	0
50¢	60.7	59.8	58.9	58.0	57.0	56.0	55.0	53.9	52.8	51.6	50.4	49.0	47.5	46.0	44.8	43.3	41.7	40.0	38.1	36.2	34.0	31.8	29.4	26.7	23.6	19.6	15.6	11.1	6.2	1.2	0
75¢	55.9	55.1	54.2	53.4	52.4	51.4	50.5	49.6	48.8	47.5	46.5	45.1	43.7	42.3	40.8	39.3	37.8	36.1	34.2	32.2	30.0	27.7	25.2	22.4	19.3	15.3	11.3	7.0	2.9	0.3	0
$1.00	48.7	47.9	47.0	46.2	45.2	44.2	43.4	42.5	41.6	40.5	39.4	38.0	36.7	35.3	33.8	32.4	30.9	29.2	27.4	25.4	23.4	21.2	19.1	16.7	14.0	11.0	8.1	5.0	2.1	0.1	0
$1.25	40.9	40.1	39.2	38.3	37.3	36.3	35.4	34.5	33.5	32.4	31.2	29.9	28.6	27.3	25.9	24.6	23.1	21.6	20.1	18.5	17.0	15.7	13.8	11.9	9.8	7.5	5.1	2.9	0.9	0	0

WM GRANDMILL (1985) LTD.

OPTION VALUES on SOYBEAN FUTURES – Table No: 88

	30	29	28	27	26	25	24	23	22	21	20	19	18	17	16	15	14	13	12	11	10	9	8	7	6	5	4	3	2	1	0
IN THE MONEY																															
$1.25	166.7	165.7	164.6	163.6	162.7	161.6	160.6	159.5	158.3	157.0	155.6	154.1	152.6	151.0	149.3	147.4	145.5	143.6	141.5	139.3	137.2	135.1	133.0	130.8	128.2	125.8	125.0	125.0	125.0	125.0	125.0
$1.00	144.2	143.2	142.1	141.0	140.0	138.9	137.8	136.6	135.3	134.0	132.6	131.1	129.5	127.8	126.0	124.0	122.1	120.1	118.0	115.7	113.7	111.6	109.2	107.1	104.8	102.3	101.1	100.2	100.0	100.0	100.0
75¢	123.1	122.0	120.9	119.8	118.8	117.6	116.4	115.2	113.9	112.6	111.3	109.6	107.9	106.2	104.5	102.8	101.0	99.1	97.2	95.0	93.0	90.9	88.8	86.8	84.5	82.0	79.6	77.3	75.4	75.0	75.0
50¢	110.1	109.1	108.0	106.9	105.9	104.8	103.7	102.5	101.3	100.0	98.6	97.1	95.5	93.9	92.3	90.6	88.8	86.9	84.8	82.5	80.3	78.0	75.3	72.6	69.5	65.6	61.7	57.5	53.4	50.4	50.0
25¢	98.7	97.7	96.6	95.6	94.6	93.5	92.4	91.3	90.1	88.8	87.4	86.0	84.4	82.8	81.2	79.2	77.3	75.2	72.9	70.2	67.6	64.9	61.9	58.8	55.4	51.0	46.2	40.6	34.2	28.1	25.0
AT THE MONEY																															
25¢	87.2	86.2	85.1	84.1	83.1	82.0	80.9	79.7	78.5	77.2	75.8	74.3	72.7	71.1	69.5	67.8	66.0	64.1	62.0	59.6	57.2	54.6	51.6	48.4	44.6	39.7	34.4	28.0	20.6	12.5	0.0
OUT OF THE MONEY																															
25¢	77.6	76.6	75.5	74.6	73.6	72.5	71.3	70.1	68.9	67.6	66.2	64.7	63.1	61.5	59.9	58.2	56.4	54.5	52.4	50.0	47.6	45.0	42.1	39.0	35.2	30.4	25.2	19.1	12.2	4.8	0
50¢	68.5	67.5	66.4	65.5	64.5	63.4	62.3	61.1	59.9	58.6	57.2	55.7	54.1	52.5	50.9	49.2	47.5	45.7	43.6	41.2	38.9	36.5	33.6	30.6	27.2	22.8	18.2	13.1	7.5	2.0	0
75¢	63.4	62.5	61.4	60.5	59.5	58.5	57.5	56.3	55.2	53.9	52.6	51.2	49.8	48.5	46.9	45.3	43.5	41.7	39.6	37.3	35.0	32.5	29.6	26.6	23.0	18.5	13.9	8.9	4.0	0.6	0
$1.00	56.1	55.1	54.1	53.1	52.2	51.2	50.2	49.1	48.0	46.7	45.4	44.0	42.6	41.3	39.8	38.2	36.5	34.7	32.7	30.4	28.1	25.7	23.0	20.1	17.1	13.4	10.0	6.3	2.8	0.3	0
$1.25	48.4	47.5	46.4	45.5	44.5	43.5	42.5	41.3	40.2	38.9	37.5	36.0	34.6	33.2	31.7	30.1	28.5	26.7	24.9	22.7	20.8	18.7	16.6	14.6	12.3	9.3	6.7	3.9	1.5	0.0	0

WEEKS TO EXPIRATION

OPTION VALUES ARE IN CENTS – to nearest tenth.

WM GRANDMILL (1985) LTD.

OPTION VALUES on SOYBEAN FUTURES – Table No: 87

	30	29	28	27	26	25	24	23	22	21	20	19	18	17	16	15	14	13	12	11	10	9	8	7	6	5	4	3	2	1	0
IN THE MONEY																															
$1.25	163.9	163.0	162.0	161.1	160.1	159.2	158.1	157.0	155.8	154.5	153.2	151.8	150.3	148.5	146.8	145.1	143.4	141.5	139.7	137.6	135.7	133.9	132.0	129.8	127.5	125.4	125.0	125.0	125.0	125.0	125.0
$1.00	141.3	140.3	139.3	138.3	137.3	136.2	135.1	134.0	132.8	131.5	130.2	128.6	127.1	125.1	123.4	121.6	119.9	118.0	116.1	114.1	112.2	110.2	108.2	106.2	104.0	101.9	100.9	100.2	100.0	100.0	100.0
75¢	120.1	119.1	118.0	117.0	115.9	114.9	113.7	112.6	111.3	110.0	108.6	107.0	105.5	103.8	102.2	100.6	98.9	97.2	95.4	93.4	91.5	89.7	87.8	85.9	83.8	81.4	79.2	77.0	75.4	75.0	75.0
50¢	107.2	106.2	105.2	104.2	103.2	102.2	101.1	100.0	98.8	97.5	96.2	94.7	93.2	91.6	90.0	88.4	86.7	84.8	82.9	80.8	78.7	76.4	74.1	71.4	68.4	64.6	60.9	56.9	53.0	50.4	50.0
25¢	95.9	94.9	93.9	92.9	91.9	91.0	89.9	88.8	87.6	86.3	85.1	83.6	82.1	80.4	78.6	76.8	74.9	72.9	70.7	68.1	65.7	63.1	60.3	57.5	54.1	49.8	45.2	39.7	33.7	27.8	25.0
AT THE MONEY																															
25¢	84.4	83.4	82.4	81.4	80.4	79.4	78.3	77.2	76.0	74.7	73.4	71.9	70.4	68.8	67.2	65.6	63.9	62.0	60.0	57.7	55.4	52.8	50.0	46.9	43.2	38.4	33.3	27.1	19.9	12.1	0.0
OUT OF THE MONEY																															
25¢	74.9	73.9	72.9	71.9	70.9	69.8	68.7	67.6	66.4	65.1	63.8	62.3	60.8	59.2	57.6	56.0	54.3	52.4	50.4	48.1	45.8	43.3	40.5	37.5	33.9	29.2	24.2	18.2	11.6	4.4	0
50¢	65.8	64.8	63.8	62.8	61.8	60.8	59.7	58.6	57.4	56.1	54.8	53.3	51.8	50.2	48.6	47.1	45.3	43.6	41.6	39.4	37.2	34.7	32.2	29.3	25.9	21.6	17.3	12.4	7.1	1.7	0
75¢	60.8	59.8	58.9	58.0	57.0	56.0	55.0	53.9	52.8	51.5	50.4	48.9	47.4	46.3	44.7	43.1	41.5	39.6	37.7	35.5	33.2	30.7	28.1	25.1	21.6	17.3	12.9	8.3	3.6	0.5	0
$1.00	53.4	52.5	51.6	50.7	49.8	48.8	47.8	46.7	45.6	44.3	43.2	42.0	40.7	39.2	37.6	36.1	34.5	32.7	30.8	28.6	26.4	24.1	21.6	19.0	16.0	12.5	9.3	5.8	2.5	0.2	0
$1.25	45.8	44.8	43.9	42.9	42.0	41.0	40.0	38.9	37.7	36.4	35.2	33.9	32.6	31.0	29.5	28.1	26.6	24.9	23.1	21.1	19.3	17.5	15.6	13.7	11.4	8.7	6.1	3.6	1.2	0	0

WEEKS TO EXPIRATION

OPTION VALUES ARE IN CENTS – to nearest tenth.

WM GRANDMILL (1985) LTD.

OPTION VALUES on SOYBEAN FUTURES – Table No: 90

OPTION VALUES ARE IN CENTS – to nearest tenth.

WEEKS TO EXPIRATION	IN $1.25	IN $1.00	IN 75¢	IN 50¢	IN 25¢	AT 25¢	OUT 25¢	OUT 50¢	OUT 75¢	OUT $1.00	OUT $1.25
30	172.1	149.9	128.9	115.7	104.2	92.8	83.2	74.0	68.5	61.2	53.6
29	171.1	148.8	127.7	114.6	103.1	91.7	82.1	72.9	67.6	60.2	52.6
28	170.0	147.7	126.6	113.5	102.0	90.6	81.0	71.9	66.6	59.2	51.6
27	168.9	146.5	125.4	112.4	101.0	89.5	79.9	70.8	65.6	58.3	50.6
26	167.8	145.4	124.3	111.3	99.9	88.4	78.8	69.7	64.5	57.2	49.6
25	165.6	144.3	123.2	110.2	98.8	87.3	77.7	68.6	63.5	56.2	48.5
24	164.4	143.1	121.9	109.0	97.6	86.1	76.5	67.4	62.4	55.0	47.4
23	163.2	141.8	120.6	107.8	96.4	84.9	75.4	66.3	61.3	53.9	46.3
22	161.8	140.5	119.3	106.4	95.1	83.6	74.1	65.0	60.0	52.7	45.0
21	160.4	139.1	117.8	105.0	93.7	82.2	72.7	63.6	58.7	51.4	43.7
20	158.9	137.6	116.2	103.5	92.2	80.7	71.2	62.1	57.3	50.1	42.3
19	157.2	135.9	114.6	101.9	90.7	79.1	69.5	60.5	55.7	48.5	40.7
18	155.5	134.2	112.8	100.2	89.0	77.4	67.8	58.8	54.1	46.9	39.1
17	153.8	132.5	111.0	98.5	87.3	75.7	66.1	57.2	52.6	45.4	37.5
16	152.1	130.8	109.3	96.8	85.7	74.0	64.4	55.4	50.9	43.7	35.8
15	150.2	129.1	107.4	95.0	83.9	72.2	62.6	53.6	49.4	42.2	34.2
14	147.9	127.0	105.4	93.1	82.0	70.3	60.7	51.7	47.6	40.6	32.5
13	145.7	124.5	103.2	91.0	79.7	68.2	58.6	49.6	45.7	38.6	30.4
12	143.5	122.1	101.0	88.8	77.3	66.0	56.4	47.5	43.5	36.5	28.5
11	141.1	119.5	98.5	86.3	74.5	63.5	53.9	45.1	41.1	34.1	26.2
10	138.8	116.9	96.2	83.7	71.6	60.9	51.3	42.5	38.6	31.7	24.0
9	136.4	114.4	93.7	81.1	68.6	58.1	48.5	39.8	35.9	29.0	21.5
8	134.2	112.0	91.3	78.4	65.3	55.0	45.4	36.9	32.9	26.1	19.1
7	132.0	109.1	88.7	75.2	61.8	51.5	42.0	33.5	29.5	22.9	16.5
6	129.2	106.5	86.2	71.8	58.0	47.5	38.1	29.8	25.7	19.4	14.0
5	126.3	103.4	83.3	67.6	53.2	42.2	32.9	25.0	20.7	15.2	10.8
4	125.0	101.4	80.5	63.3	48.2	36.6	27.4	20.0	15.8	11.3	7.8
3	125.0	100.3	77.8	58.5	42.1	29.8	20.7	14.5	10.2	7.2	4.6
2	125.0	100.0	75.7	54.0	35.3	21.9	13.4	8.5	4.8	3.4	1.7
1	125.0	100.0	75.0	50.5	28.6	13.3	5.5	2.5	0.8	0.4	0.1
0	125.0	100.0	75.0	50.0	25.0	0.0	0	0	0	0	0.0

WM GRANDMILL (1985) LTD.

OPTION VALUES on SOYBEAN FUTURES – Table No: 89

OPTION VALUES ARE IN CENTS – to nearest tenth.

WEEKS TO EXPIRATION	IN $1.25	IN $1.00	IN 75¢	IN 50¢	IN 25¢	AT 25¢	OUT 25¢	OUT 50¢	OUT 75¢	OUT $1.00	OUT $1.25
30	169.3	146.9	125.8	112.8	101.4	89.9	80.3	71.2	66.0	58.7	51.0
29	168.3	145.9	124.8	111.8	100.4	88.9	79.3	70.2	65.0	57.7	50.1
28	167.4	144.9	123.8	110.8	99.4	87.9	78.3	69.2	64.1	56.8	49.2
27	166.4	143.9	122.7	109.8	98.4	86.9	77.3	68.2	63.2	55.8	48.2
26	165.3	142.8	121.6	108.7	97.3	85.8	76.2	67.1	62.2	54.8	47.2
25	164.2	141.6	120.4	107.5	96.2	84.7	75.2	66.1	61.1	53.7	46.1
24	163.1	140.4	119.2	106.3	95.0	83.5	74.0	64.9	59.9	52.6	44.9
23	161.9	139.2	117.9	105.1	93.8	82.3	72.8	63.7	58.8	51.5	43.8
22	160.7	137.9	116.6	103.8	92.5	81.0	71.5	62.4	57.5	50.3	42.5
21	159.4	136.4	115.1	102.4	91.2	79.6	70.0	61.0	56.2	49.0	41.2
20	158.0	135.0	113.6	101.0	89.8	78.2	68.6	59.6	54.9	47.7	39.9
19	156.5	133.5	112.0	99.5	88.3	76.7	67.1	58.1	53.5	46.3	38.4
18	154.9	131.9	110.4	97.9	86.7	75.1	65.5	56.5	51.9	44.7	36.8
17	153.2	130.2	108.6	96.2	85.1	73.4	63.8	54.8	50.4	43.2	35.2
16	151.6	128.4	106.8	94.5	83.4	71.7	62.1	53.1	49.0	41.8	33.7
15	149.9	126.7	105.1	92.8	81.7	70.0	60.4	51.4	47.4	40.3	32.2
14	147.9	124.5	103.2	91.0	80.0	68.2	58.6	49.6	45.7	38.6	30.1
13	145.7	122.3	101.2	89.0	77.5	66.2	56.6	47.6	43.7	36.7	28.6
12	143.5	120.0	99.0	86.8	75.1	64.0	54.4	45.6	41.6	34.6	26.7
11	141.1	117.6	96.8	84.4	72.4	61.6	52.0	43.2	39.2	32.3	24.5
10	138.8	115.2	94.5	82.0	69.7	59.1	49.5	40.7	36.8	29.9	22.3
9	136.4	112.9	92.2	79.5	66.6	56.3	46.7	38.0	34.1	27.3	20.0
8	134.2	110.5	90.0	76.8	63.6	53.3	43.7	35.2	31.2	24.5	17.8
7	132.0	108.2	87.8	74.1	60.3	50.0	40.5	32.2	28.1	21.6	15.6
6	129.2	105.7	85.4	70.7	56.7	46.1	36.7	28.5	24.3	18.3	13.2
5	126.3	102.8	82.7	66.7	52.2	41.0	31.7	24.0	19.7	14.4	10.1
4	125.0	101.4	80.0	62.4	47.2	35.5	26.3	19.1	14.8	10.6	7.2
3	125.0	100.3	77.5	58.0	41.3	28.9	19.9	13.8	9.5	6.7	4.2
2	125.0	100.0	75.5	53.7	34.7	21.2	12.7	8.0	4.4	3.1	1.6
1	125.0	100.0	75.0	50.5	28.4	12.9	5.2	2.3	0.7	0.4	0
0	125.0	100.0	75.0	50.0	25.0	0.0	0	0	0	0	0

WM GRANDMILL (1985) LTD.

OPTION VALUES on SOYBEAN FUTURES – Table No: 92

OPTION VALUES ARE IN CENTS – to nearest tenth.

	30	29	28	27	26	25	24	23	22	21	20	19	18	17	16	15	14	13	12	11	10	9	8	7	6	5	4	3	2	1	0
IN THE MONEY $1.25	177.5	176.4	175.3	174.1	173.1	171.9	170.7	169.4	168.0	166.6	165.1	163.5	161.7	159.9	158.2	156.4	154.4	152.3	149.9	146.9	144.1	141.1	138.1	135.1	132.2	128.3	125.5	125.3	125.0	125.0	125.0
IN THE MONEY $1.00	155.6	154.5	153.4	152.1	150.9	149.7	148.4	147.1	145.6	144.1	142.6	140.8	139.0	137.1	135.2	133.4	131.4	129.2	126.7	123.5	120.6	117.6	114.5	110.4	108.4	104.9	102.0	100.5	100.0	100.0	100.0
IN THE MONEY 75¢	134.8	133.6	132.5	131.2	129.8	128.4	127.3	126.0	124.5	123.0	121.4	119.6	117.7	115.7	113.8	111.9	109.9	107.6	105.1	102.3	99.6	96.8	93.8	91.0	88.0	84.6	81.6	78.5	75.9	75.0	75.0
IN THE MONEY 50¢	121.3	120.2	119.1	117.9	116.6	115.5	114.2	112.9	111.5	110.0	108.5	106.7	104.9	103.0	101.2	99.4	97.4	95.2	92.8	90.1	87.4	84.4	81.3	78.1	74.3	69.7	65.0	59.7	54.7	50.5	50.0
IN THE MONEY 25¢	109.7	108.6	107.5	106.3	105.2	104.0	102.7	101.4	100.1	98.6	97.1	95.4	93.6	91.7	90.0	88.2	86.2	84.1	81.7	78.7	75.7	72.4	68.8	65.0	60.7	55.6	50.3	43.7	36.3	28.5	25.0
AT THE MONEY	98.4	97.3	96.2	95.0	93.8	92.6	91.3	90.0	88.6	87.1	85.6	83.9	82.1	80.2	78.4	76.6	74.6	72.4	70.0	67.3	64.6	61.6	58.3	54.7	50.4	44.8	38.9	31.6	23.2	14.1	0.0
OUT OF THE MONEY 25¢	88.7	87.6	86.5	85.3	84.2	83.0	81.7	80.4	79.0	77.5	76.0	74.4	72.6	70.7	68.8	67.0	65.0	62.8	60.4	57.7	55.0	52.0	48.7	45.1	40.9	35.4	29.7	22.5	14.5	5.3	0
OUT OF THE MONEY 50¢	79.5	78.4	77.3	76.1	75.0	73.8	72.5	71.3	69.9	68.4	66.9	65.3	63.5	61.6	59.8	58.0	56.0	53.8	51.4	48.7	46.2	43.2	40.0	36.6	32.5	27.4	22.1	15.9	9.4	2.4	0
OUT OF THE MONEY 75¢	73.5	72.5	71.5	70.4	69.4	68.3	67.2	66.0	64.7	63.3	61.9	60.3	58.6	56.8	55.1	53.4	51.4	49.6	47.4	44.8	42.2	39.2	36.1	32.6	28.5	23.2	17.8	11.6	5.6	0.7	0
OUT OF THE MONEY $1.00	66.1	65.1	64.1	63.0	62.0	61.0	59.8	58.7	57.4	56.0	54.6	53.0	51.3	49.6	47.9	46.2	44.2	42.4	40.3	37.7	35.2	32.3	29.2	25.8	21.9	17.3	12.9	8.3	3.9	0.4	0
OUT OF THE MONEY $1.25	66.1	65.1	64.1	63.0	62.0	61.0	59.8	58.7	57.4	56.0	54.6	53.0	51.3	49.6	47.9	46.2	44.2	42.4	40.3	37.7	35.2	32.3	29.2	25.8	21.6	18.8	15.8	12.4	8.9	5.3	0.0

WEEKS TO EXPIRATION

WM GRANDMILL (1985) LTD.

OPTION VALUES on SOYBEAN FUTURES – Table No: 91

OPTION VALUES ARE IN CENTS – to nearest tenth.

	30	29	28	27	26	25	24	23	22	21	20	19	18	17	16	15	14	13	12	11	10	9	8	7	6	5	4	3	2	1	0
IN THE MONEY $1.25	174.5	173.6	172.7	171.6	170.7	169.4	168.1	166.9	165.6	164.2	162.8	161.2	159.5	157.7	155.9	154.1	152.3	150.2	147.7	144.9	142.3	139.5	136.7	134.1	131.3	127.6	125.3	125.0	125.0	125.0	125.0
IN THE MONEY $1.00	152.5	151.5	150.5	149.4	148.4	147.1	145.7	144.4	143.1	141.6	140.1	138.4	136.5	134.7	132.9	131.1	129.2	127.0	124.3	121.4	118.8	115.9	113.2	110.4	107.5	104.1	100.8	100.5	100.0	100.0	100.0
IN THE MONEY 75¢	131.6	130.6	129.5	128.4	127.2	126.0	124.6	123.3	121.9	120.4	118.9	117.1	115.2	113.3	111.4	109.6	107.6	105.4	103.0	100.4	97.9	95.2	92.5	89.9	87.2	83.9	81.0	78.1	75.8	75.0	75.0
IN THE MONEY 50¢	118.3	117.2	116.3	115.2	114.1	112.9	111.6	110.3	109.0	107.5	106.0	104.3	102.5	100.7	98.7	97.1	95.2	93.1	90.8	88.2	85.6	82.7	79.8	76.6	73.2	68.6	64.1	59.1	54.4	50.6	50.0
IN THE MONEY 25¢	106.7	105.8	104.8	103.7	102.6	101.4	100.2	98.9	97.6	96.2	94.7	93.0	91.3	89.5	87.7	86.0	84.1	82.0	79.5	76.7	73.7	70.4	66.9	63.4	59.4	54.4	49.2	43.0	35.8	28.9	25.0
AT THE MONEY	95.4	94.4	93.4	92.3	91.2	90.0	88.7	87.4	86.1	84.7	83.2	81.5	79.7	77.9	76.1	74.3	72.4	70.3	68.0	65.4	62.8	59.8	56.6	53.1	49.0	43.5	37.7	30.7	22.6	13.7	0.0
OUT OF THE MONEY 25¢	85.7	84.8	83.8	82.7	81.6	80.4	79.1	77.8	76.5	75.2	73.7	72.0	70.1	68.3	66.5	64.7	62.8	60.7	58.4	55.8	53.2	50.2	47.0	43.5	39.6	34.2	28.5	21.6	14.0	5.9	0
OUT OF THE MONEY 50¢	76.5	75.6	74.6	73.5	72.4	71.3	70.0	68.7	67.4	66.1	64.6	62.9	61.1	59.3	57.5	55.7	53.8	51.7	49.4	46.9	44.4	41.4	38.3	35.0	31.2	26.2	21.0	15.2	8.9	2.8	0
OUT OF THE MONEY 75¢	70.8	69.9	69.0	68.1	67.1	66.0	64.8	63.6	62.4	61.1	59.6	58.0	56.3	54.6	52.9	51.2	49.6	47.6	45.5	42.9	40.4	37.5	34.4	31.0	27.0	21.9	16.8	10.9	5.2	1.0	0
OUT OF THE MONEY $1.00	63.4	62.5	61.6	60.7	59.7	58.7	57.5	56.3	55.0	53.7	52.3	50.8	49.1	47.4	45.7	44.0	42.4	40.6	38.4	35.9	33.5	30.6	27.6	24.3	20.5	16.2	12.0	7.7	3.7	0.5	0
OUT OF THE MONEY $1.25	55.9	55.0	54.1	53.1	52.1	51.1	49.9	48.6	47.4	46.1	44.6	43.0	41.3	39.6	37.8	36.0	34.4	32.5	30.3	27.9	25.6	22.9	20.3	17.7	15.0	11.5	8.3	4.9	1.9	0.1	0

WEEKS TO EXPIRATION

WM GRANDMILL (1985) LTD.

OPTION VALUES on SOYBEAN FUTURES – Table No:94

	30	29	28	27	26	25	24	23	22	21	20	19	18	17	16	15	14	13	12	11	10	9	8	7	6	5	4	3	2	1	0
IN THE MONEY $1.25	191.5	190.3	189.0	187.5	186.2	184.8	183.3	181.9	180.3	178.7	177.0	175.0	173.1	171.1	169.0	166.9	164.7	162.3	159.7	156.8	153.6	150.3	146.1	142.0	137.5	132.8	128.1	125.1	125.0	125.0	125.0
$1.00	170.0	168.6	167.3	166.0	164.5	163.1	161.8	160.3	158.6	156.9	155.1	153.0	150.9	148.8	146.6	144.4	142.2	139.6	136.9	133.8	130.6	127.1	122.7	118.5	114.0	109.0	104.7	101.5	100.1	100.0	100.0
75¢	150.2	148.8	147.5	145.2	143.7	142.3	141.0	139.3	137.8	136.0	134.2	132.0	129.9	127.7	125.5	123.3	121.0	118.3	115.5	112.4	109.0	105.5	101.6	97.6	93.3	88.6	84.4	80.3	76.8	75.1	75.0
50¢	135.6	134.4	133.0	131.6	130.3	128.9	127.3	125.9	124.3	122.5	120.8	118.8	116.6	114.6	112.5	110.3	108.1	105.5	102.8	99.8	96.6	93.2	89.4	85.3	80.7	75.0	69.3	62.9	56.6	51.3	50.0
25¢	123.5	122.3	121.1	119.7	118.4	117.0	115.6	114.0	112.5	110.9	109.2	107.2	105.2	103.1	101.1	98.9	96.7	94.2	91.5	88.6	85.5	82.1	77.9	73.4	68.0	61.5	55.2	47.7	39.3	30.6	25.0
AT THE MONEY	112.5	111.2	109.9	108.6	107.2	105.8	104.4	102.9	101.3	99.6	97.9	95.9	93.8	91.7	89.6	87.4	85.2	82.7	80.0	77.0	73.8	70.4	66.6	62.5	57.6	51.2	44.4	36.1	26.6	16.1	0.0
OUT OF THE MONEY 25¢	102.6	101.2	100.0	98.8	97.5	96.1	94.7	93.2	91.6	89.9	88.2	86.2	84.2	82.1	80.0	77.8	75.6	73.2	70.5	67.4	64.2	60.8	57.0	52.9	48.0	41.7	35.0	26.9	17.8	8.0	0
50¢	93.8	92.4	91.1	89.8	88.3	86.9	85.4	84.0	82.4	80.7	79.0	77.0	75.0	72.9	70.9	68.7	66.5	64.1	61.4	58.4	55.2	51.8	48.0	44.1	39.3	33.2	27.0	19.6	11.9	4.4	0
75¢	87.3	86.0	84.7	83.5	82.0	80.6	79.3	77.7	76.2	74.6	73.1	71.3	69.4	67.6	65.7	63.6	61.5	59.2	56.6	53.7	50.7	47.7	44.1	40.1	35.4	29.2	22.8	15.3	7.8	1.7	0
$1.00	79.8	78.7	77.4	76.0	74.7	73.3	72.0	70.4	68.8	67.2	65.7	63.9	62.0	60.2	58.4	56.3	54.2	51.9	49.4	46.5	43.5	40.7	37.1	33.2	28.5	22.6	16.9	11.0	5.6	1.2	0
$1.25	71.5	70.2	68.9	67.7	66.3	65.0	63.5	62.8	61.4	59.9	58.3	56.4	54.5	52.6	50.7	48.6	46.5	44.2	41.6	38.7	35.6	32.6	29.0	25.3	21.1	16.4	12.1	7.5	3.3	0.4	0

WEEKS TO EXPIRATION

WM GRANDMILL (1985) LTD.

OPTION VALUES ARE IN CENTS – to nearest tenth.

OPTION VALUES on SOYBEAN FUTURES – Table No:93

	30	29	28	27	26	25	24	23	22	21	20	19	18	17	16	15	14	13	12	11	10	9	8	7	6	5	4	3	2	1	0
IN THE MONEY $1.25	184.8	183.2	182.0	180.8	179.6	178.3	177.0	175.6	174.1	172.7	171.2	169.3	167.4	165.5	163.5	161.6	159.7	157.4	154.8	152.1	149.0	145.5	142.0	138.4	134.8	130.6	126.6	125.0	125.0	125.0	125.0
$1.00	162.8	161.6	160.4	159.1	157.8	156.5	155.1	153.7	152.1	150.5	148.9	146.9	145.0	143.0	140.9	138.9	136.7	134.4	131.8	129.0	125.7	122.1	118.5	114.8	111.2	106.9	103.1	101.0	100.0	100.0	100.0
75¢	141.8	140.7	139.5	138.3	137.0	135.6	134.2	132.8	131.2	129.5	127.8	125.8	123.9	121.8	119.7	117.6	115.4	113.0	110.3	107.4	104.2	101.0	97.6	94.1	90.6	86.6	83.0	79.4	76.4	75.0	75.0
50¢	128.5	127.2	126.0	124.8	123.5	122.1	120.8	119.4	117.9	116.3	114.7	112.8	110.9	108.0	106.8	104.8	102.7	100.4	97.8	95.0	92.0	88.8	85.3	81.6	77.5	72.3	67.1	61.3	55.6	51.0	50.0
25¢	116.5	115.4	114.2	113.0	111.8	110.5	109.2	107.8	106.3	104.8	103.2	101.4	99.5	97.5	95.5	93.5	91.5	89.2	86.6	83.9	80.8	77.3	73.4	69.1	64.3	58.5	52.7	45.7	37.8	29.9	25.0
AT THE MONEY	105.4	104.2	103.0	101.8	100.5	99.2	97.9	96.5	95.0	93.4	91.8	89.9	88.0	86.0	84.0	82.0	79.9	77.6	75.0	72.2	69.2	66.0	62.5	58.6	54.0	48.0	41.6	33.8	24.9	15.1	0.0
OUT OF THE MONEY 25¢	95.7	94.4	93.2	92.1	90.8	89.5	88.2	86.8	85.3	83.8	82.2	80.3	78.4	76.4	74.5	72.5	70.3	68.0	65.4	62.6	59.6	56.4	52.9	49.0	44.4	38.6	32.3	24.7	16.2	7.1	0
50¢	86.4	85.3	84.1	82.9	81.6	80.3	79.0	77.6	76.1	74.6	73.0	71.2	69.3	67.3	65.4	63.4	61.3	59.0	56.4	53.6	50.6	47.5	44.1	40.3	35.9	30.3	24.5	17.7	10.8	3.7	0
75¢	80.2	78.9	77.9	76.7	75.5	74.2	73.1	71.8	70.4	69.0	67.7	66.0	64.1	62.3	60.4	58.5	56.5	54.3	51.8	49.4	46.6	43.5	40.1	36.4	31.9	26.2	20.2	13.4	6.7	1.4	0
$1.00	72.8	71.7	70.5	69.4	68.1	66.8	65.7	64.4	63.0	61.6	60.3	58.7	56.8	54.9	53.0	51.2	49.3	47.1	44.6	42.2	39.5	36.5	33.2	29.5	25.2	19.9	14.7	9.6	4.7	0.9	0
$1.25	64.2	63.1	62.1	61.9	60.7	59.5	58.3	56.9	55.5	54.1	52.7	51.0	49.2	47.3	45.4	43.5	41.5	39.3	36.7	34.2	31.4	28.5	25.3	21.9	18.4	14.4	10.4	6.4	2.8	0.3	0

WEEKS TO EXPIRATION

WM GRANDMILL (1985) LTD.

OPTION VALUES ARE IN CENTS – to nearest tenth.

OPTION VALUES on SOYBEAN FUTURES – Table No:96

	30	29	28	27	26	25	24	23	22	21	20	19	18	17	16	15	14	13	12	11	10	9	8	7	6	5	4	3	2	1	0
IN THE MONEY $1.25	219.2	217.6	216.1	214.5	213.0	211.4	209.4	207.5	205.6	203.7	201.6	199.0	196.4	193.7	191.1	188.3	186.0	182.4	179.1	175.3	171.6	167.4	162.9	157.9	151.9	143.5	135.8	128.5	125.0	125.0	125.0
$1.00	197.9	196.2	194.6	192.9	191.3	189.6	187.6	185.7	183.8	181.9	179.8	177.3	174.7	172.0	169.5	166.6	163.8	160.3	157.3	153.4	149.4	145.0	140.2	134.9	128.8	120.0	112.3	105.1	102.9	100.0	100.0
75¢	177.2	175.7	174.2	172.8	171.3	169.8	167.9	166.0	164.0	162.1	160.0	157.5	154.9	152.2	149.6	146.8	143.0	139.9	136.5	132.5	128.4	123.9	119.0	113.5	107.2	99.0	91.6	84.8	79.1	75.4	75.0
50¢	163.5	161.8	160.2	158.5	156.9	155.2	153.2	151.2	149.6	147.7	145.6	143.1	140.5	137.8	135.1	132.4	129.6	126.5	123.0	119.1	115.2	110.9	106.1	100.9	94.8	86.8	78.8	69.9	60.9	53.1	50.0
25¢	152.0	150.4	148.7	147.0	145.3	143.5	141.5	139.5	137.5	135.5	133.5	130.5	128.4	125.7	123.1	120.5	117.7	114.6	111.3	107.5	103.7	99.5	94.8	89.7	83.7	75.1	65.8	55.8	45.1	33.8	25.0
AT THE MONEY	140.7	139.0	137.3	135.7	134.0	132.3	130.5	128.6	126.6	124.5	122.4	119.9	117.3	114.6	112.0	109.3	106.5	103.4	100.0	96.2	92.3	88.0	83.3	78.1	72.0	64.0	55.5	45.1	33.2	20.1	0.0
OUT OF THE MONEY 25¢	131.0	129.3	127.7	126.0	124.4	122.7	120.7	118.7	116.6	114.5	112.4	110.0	107.3	104.6	102.1	99.4	96.6	93.5	90.3	86.5	82.7	78.4	73.8	68.5	62.4	54.4	45.9	35.7	24.1	11.7	0.0
50¢	121.6	120.1	118.2	116.6	115.0	113.4	111.4	109.5	107.6	105.7	103.6	101.0	98.5	95.8	93.2	90.4	87.6	84.5	81.1	77.3	73.5	69.3	64.7	59.5	53.4	45.6	37.3	27.6	17.2	7.2	0
75¢	116.0	114.2	112.5	110.7	109.0	107.2	105.2	103.2	101.3	99.4	97.3	94.7	92.2	89.5	86.8	84.3	81.5	78.4	75.0	71.5	68.1	64.1	59.7	54.8	49.2	41.6	33.3	23.4	12.9	3.7	0
$1.00	108.2	107.0	105.3	103.5	101.8	100.0	98.0	96.0	94.0	92.0	89.9	87.5	84.7	82.0	79.4	76.8	74.0	70.9	67.6	64.1	60.7	56.8	52.4	47.6	42.0	34.6	26.5	17.5	9.3	2.6	0
$1.25	100.8	98.3	96.8	95.1	93.5	91.9	89.8	87.6	85.5	83.4	81.4	78.9	76.2	73.5	71.0	68.3	65.5	62.4	60.2	57.0	53.2	49.2	44.7	39.8	34.1	26.7	19.4	12.6	6.1	1.3	0

WEEKS TO EXPIRATION

OPTION VALUES ARE IN CENTS – to nearest tenth.

WM GRANDMILL (1985) LTD.

OPTION VALUES on SOYBEAN FUTURES – Table No:95

	30	29	28	27	26	25	24	23	22	21	20	19	18	17	16	15	14	13	12	11	10	9	8	7	6	5	4	3	2	1	0
IN THE MONEY $1.25	205.9	204.3	202.8	201.3	199.7	198.2	196.6	194.8	193.1	191.3	189.3	187.0	184.6	182.1	179.7	177.5	174.9	172.2	169.4	166.1	162.7	159.0	154.8	150.2	144.3	137.5	132.5	126.5	125.0	125.0	125.0
$1.00	184.0	182.5	181.0	179.5	178.0	176.5	175.0	173.3	171.4	169.6	167.7	165.3	163.1	160.5	158.1	155.6	152.9	150.2	147.1	143.6	140.0	136.0	131.8	127.0	120.8	114.0	108.2	102.6	100.4	100.0	100.0
75¢	164.1	162.7	161.2	159.7	158.2	156.7	155.2	153.3	151.4	149.6	147.8	144.3	142.1	139.5	137.3	134.8	132.0	129.2	126.0	122.4	118.8	114.7	110.3	105.4	99.8	93.3	87.8	82.5	75.2	75.2	75.0
50¢	149.8	148.3	146.8	145.3	143.8	142.3	140.5	138.7	137.0	135.2	133.2	130.9	128.5	126.1	123.8	121.3	118.7	116.0	112.9	109.5	105.9	102.0	97.8	92.3	87.6	80.7	74.1	66.3	58.6	52.2	50.0
25¢	137.7	136.2	134.7	133.2	131.7	130.2	128.7	126.8	125.1	123.3	121.4	119.2	116.8	114.4	112.1	109.7	107.1	104.5	101.4	98.1	94.6	90.8	86.6	82.0	75.9	68.0	60.3	51.8	42.2	32.3	25.0
AT THE MONEY	126.6	125.1	123.6	122.1	120.6	119.1	117.5	115.7	113.9	112.1	110.2	107.9	105.6	103.1	100.8	98.4	95.8	93.1	90.0	86.6	83.1	79.2	75.0	70.3	64.8	57.6	50.0	40.6	29.9	18.1	0.0
OUT OF THE MONEY 25¢	116.7	115.1	113.6	112.1	110.6	109.1	107.6	105.9	104.0	102.2	100.4	98.1	95.9	93.3	91.1	88.7	86.1	83.5	80.4	77.0	73.6	69.6	65.4	60.7	55.2	48.0	40.5	31.3	20.8	9.9	0
50¢	107.8	106.3	104.8	103.3	101.8	100.3	98.6	96.9	95.2	93.2	91.4	89.0	86.7	84.1	81.9	79.5	76.9	74.3	71.3	67.9	64.5	60.6	56.4	51.7	46.4	39.3	32.2	23.6	14.6	5.9	0
75¢	101.4	100.0	98.5	97.0	95.5	93.9	92.3	90.4	88.7	86.8	84.9	82.7	80.4	78.0	75.8	73.5	71.2	68.7	66.0	62.9	59.5	55.8	51.8	47.6	42.4	35.4	28.1	19.3	10.3	2.7	0
$1.00	94.1	92.6	91.1	89.6	88.1	86.5	85.0	83.1	81.2	79.5	77.7	75.4	73.1	70.7	68.4	66.1	63.8	61.4	58.7	55.5	52.2	48.6	44.6	40.6	35.4	28.5	21.6	14.0	7.3	2.0	0
$1.25	85.5	84.0	82.5	81.0	79.6	78.1	76.5	74.6	72.9	71.1	69.3	67.1	64.8	62.2	61.0	58.7	56.3	53.8	51.1	47.9	44.5	40.8	36.7	32.5	27.4	21.1	15.6	9.8	4.6	0.7	0

WEEKS TO EXPIRATION

OPTION VALUES ARE IN CENTS – to nearest tenth.

WM GRANDMILL (1985) LTD.

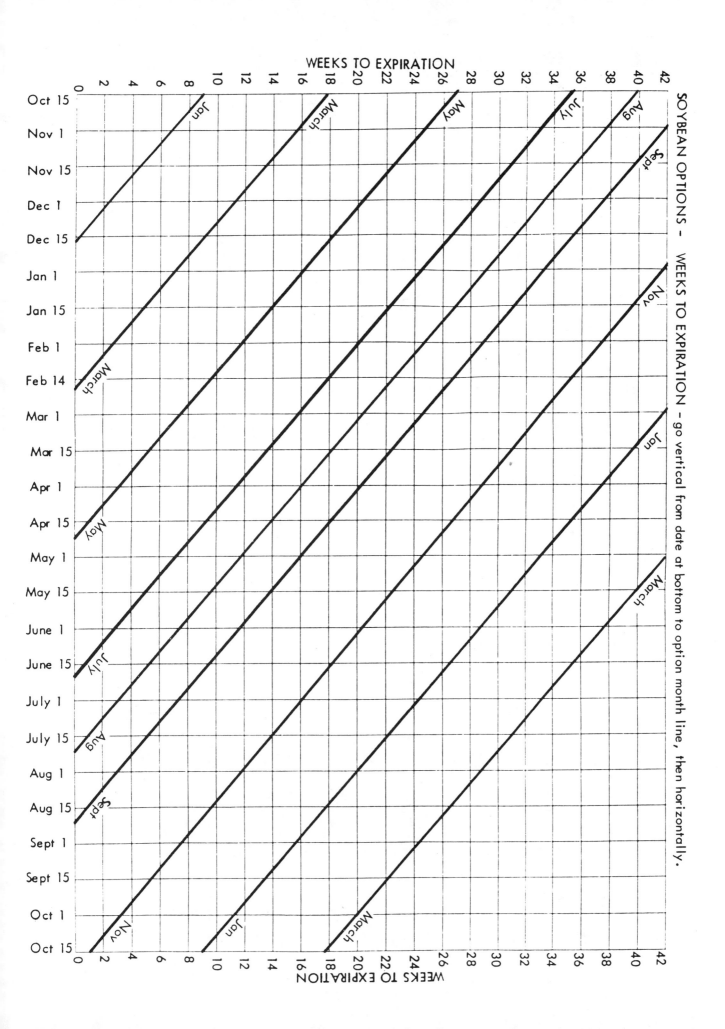

THE DAY FINDER – FIRST YEAR

Day of month	Jan	Feb	Mar	Apr	May	Jun	Jul	Aug	Sep	Oct	Nov	Dec	Day of month
1	1	32	60	91	121	152	182	213	244	274	305	335	1
2	2	33	61	92	122	153	183	214	245	275	306	336	2
3	3	34	62	93	123	154	184	215	246	276	307	337	3
4	4	35	63	94	124	155	185	216	247	277	308	338	4
5	5	36	64	95	125	156	186	217	248	278	309	339	5
6	6	37	65	96	126	157	187	218	249	279	310	340	6
7	7	38	66	97	127	158	188	219	250	280	311	341	7
8	8	39	67	98	128	159	189	220	251	281	312	342	8
9	9	40	68	99	129	160	190	221	252	282	313	343	9
10	10	41	69	100	130	161	191	222	253	283	314	344	10
11	11	42	70	101	131	162	192	223	254	284	315	345	11
12	12	43	71	102	132	163	193	224	255	285	316	346	12
13	13	44	72	103	133	164	194	225	256	286	317	347	13
14	14	45	73	104	134	165	195	226	257	287	318	348	14
15	15	46	74	105	135	166	196	227	258	288	319	349	15
16	16	47	75	106	136	167	197	228	259	289	320	350	16
17	17	48	76	107	137	168	198	229	260	290	321	351	17
18	18	49	77	108	138	169	199	230	261	291	322	352	18
19	19	50	78	109	139	170	200	231	262	292	323	353	19
20	20	51	79	110	140	171	201	232	263	293	324	354	20
21	21	52	80	111	141	172	202	233	264	294	325	355	21
22	22	53	81	112	142	173	203	234	265	295	326	356	22
23	23	54	82	113	143	174	204	235	266	296	327	357	23
24	24	55	83	114	144	175	205	236	267	297	328	358	24
25	25	56	84	115	145	176	206	237	268	298	329	359	25
26	26	57	85	116	146	177	207	238	269	299	330	360	26
27	27	58	86	117	147	178	208	239	270	300	331	361	27
28	28	59	87	118	148	179	209	240	271	301	332	362	28
29	29		88	119	149	180	210	241	272	302	333	363	29
30	30		89	120	150	181	211	242	273	303	334	364	30
31	31		90		151		212	243		304		365	31

TO FIND THE NUMBER OF DAYS BETWEEN TWO DATES: 1. Locate the nearest date in the "first year" table. 2. Locate the other date (you may need the "second year" table). 3. Subtract the two amounts.

THE DAY FINDER – SECOND YEAR

Day of month	Jan	Feb	Mar	Apr	May	Jun	Jul	Aug	Sep	Oct	Nov	Dec	Day of month
1	366	397	425	456	486	517	547	578	609	639	670	700	1
2	367	398	426	457	487	518	548	579	610	640	671	701	2
3	368	399	427	458	488	519	549	580	611	641	672	702	3
4	369	400	428	459	489	520	550	581	612	642	673	703	4
5	370	401	429	460	490	521	551	582	613	643	674	704	5
6	371	402	430	461	491	522	552	583	614	644	675	705	6
7	372	403	431	462	492	523	553	584	615	645	676	706	7
8	373	404	432	463	493	524	554	585	616	646	677	707	8
9	374	405	433	464	494	525	555	586	617	647	678	708	9
10	375	406	434	465	495	526	556	587	618	648	679	709	10
11	376	407	435	466	496	527	557	588	619	649	680	710	11
12	377	408	436	467	497	528	558	589	620	650	681	711	12
13	378	409	437	468	498	529	559	590	621	651	682	712	13
14	379	410	438	469	499	530	560	591	622	652	683	713	14
15	380	411	439	470	500	531	561	592	623	653	684	714	15
16	381	412	440	471	501	532	562	593	624	654	685	715	16
17	382	413	441	472	502	533	563	594	625	655	686	716	17
18	383	414	442	473	503	534	564	595	626	656	687	717	18
19	384	415	443	474	504	535	565	596	627	657	688	718	19
20	385	416	444	475	505	536	566	597	628	658	689	719	20
21	386	417	445	476	506	537	567	598	629	659	690	720	21
22	387	418	446	477	507	538	568	599	630	660	691	721	22
23	388	419	447	478	508	539	569	600	631	661	692	722	23
24	389	420	448	479	509	540	570	601	632	662	693	723	24
25	390	421	449	480	510	541	571	602	633	663	694	724	25
26	391	422	450	481	511	542	572	603	634	664	695	725	26
27	392	423	451	482	512	543	573	604	635	665	696	726	27
28	393	424	452	483	513	544	574	605	636	666	697	727	28
29	394		453	484	514	545	575	606	637	667	698	728	29
30	395		454	485	515	546	576	607	638	668	699	729	30
31	396		455		516		577	608		669		730	31

Wm. Grandmill (1985) Ltd.

INTERPOLATOR FOR USE WITH THE SOYBEAN OPTION TABLES

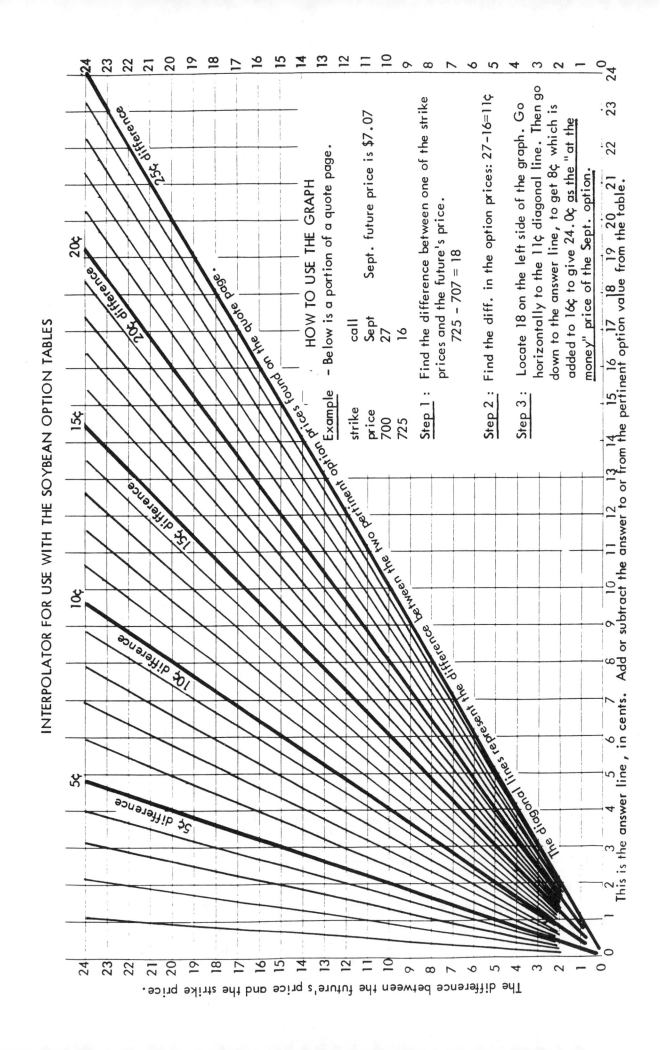

HOW TO USE THE GRAPH
- Below is a portion of a quote page.

Example

strike price	call Sept	Sept. future price is $7.07
700	27	
725	16	

Step 1 : Find the difference between one of the strike prices and the future's price.
725 - 707 = 18

Step 2 : Find the diff. in the option prices: 27-16=11¢

Step 3 : Locate 18 on the left side of the graph. Go horizontally to the 11¢ diagonal line. Then go down to the answer line, to get 8¢ which is added to 16¢ to give 24.0¢ as the "at the money" price of the Sept. option.

The diagonal lines represent the difference between the two pertinent option prices found on the quote page.

This is the answer line, in cents. Add or subtract the answer to or from the pertinent option value from the table.

The difference between the future's price and the strike price.

5¢ difference
10¢ difference
15¢ difference
20¢ difference
25¢ difference

5¢
10¢
15¢
20¢

WORLD SOYBEANS - showing the relationship between the U.S. Chicago price and the world soybean carryover as % of world total use.

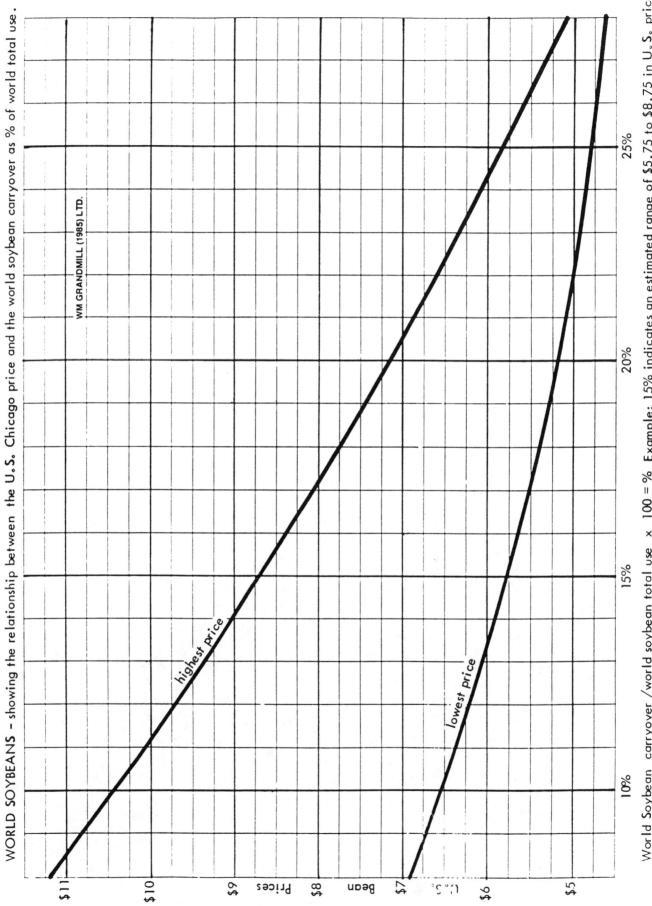

World Soybean carryover /world soybean total use × 100 = % Example: 15% indicates an estimated range of $5.75 to $8.75 in U.S. prices.

SOYBEANS - showing the relationship between the soybean price and the soybean carryover expressed as % of the total use.

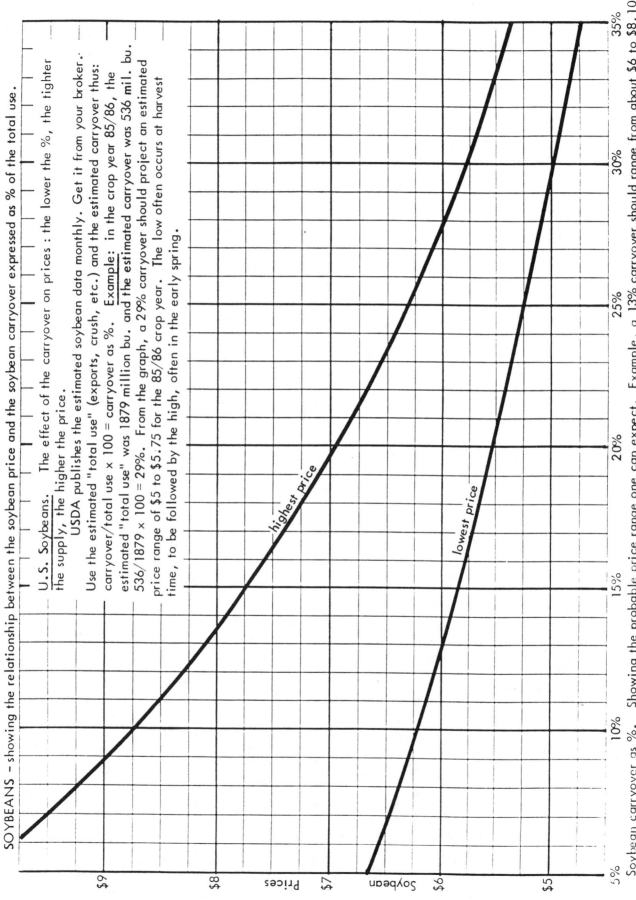

U.S. Soybeans.   The effect of the carryover on prices : the lower the %, the tighter the supply, the higher the price.

USDA publishes the estimated soybean data monthly. Get it from your broker.

Use the estimated "total use" (exports, crush, etc.) and the estimated carryover thus: carryover/total use x 100 = carryover as %.   Example: in the crop year 85/86, the estimated "total use" was 1879 million bu. and the estimated carryover was 536 mil. bu. 536/1879 x 100 = 29%. From the graph, a 29% carryover should project an estimated price range of $5 to $5.75 for the 85/86 crop year. The low often occurs at harvest time, to be followed by the high, often in the early spring.

highest price

lowest price

Soybean Prices

$9

$8

$7

$6

$5

5%   10%   15%   20%   25%   30%   35%

Soybean carryover as %.   Showing the probable price range one can expect. Example, a 13% carryover should range from about $6 to $8.10.

WHEN DO THE BEST TRADES HAPPEN? This chart indicates the interaction between the time to expiration for Soybean Options, and the price and volatility. The closer the option price is to the expiration date, the faster is its erosion of value. On the other hand is the price and volatility – the higher the price and the rate of volatility, the greater the risk and usually a larger profit.

The "weeks to expiration" are indicated on the side of the chart. The price and volatility is indicated by the Option Table Number which would be used in that option trade.

BUY FOR THE LONG TERM

Options are cheap in this area. At worst you could lose about 7¢ ($350) because prices are very unlikely to fall below 5¢ at the 12th week, while the profit potential is unlimited. Because there is little downside risk, buying a call is an ideal trade, and there is lots of time for the profit to materialize.

Buy a May call in October or November to take advantage of the seasonal price uptrend. This trade is rated as Very Good. Do not sell a call or a put in this area because the premium gained is too small.

BUY FOR THE LONG TERM

This is the mid price range. Therefore, there is plenty of scope for a large price move up or down. This means that you should trade only when your price indicators point the direction i.e. your charts and moving average crossover lines and also the seasonal trends.

If you buy a call or a put only when your indicators show the way, then your chances of success are Good. You have plenty of time for the profit to materialize. Do not sell a call or a put because of very little price erosion from the passing of time here.

STAY OUT OF THE MARKET

Option prices are very expensive in this area. This means that you should not buy a call or buy a put in this area because the future's price would have to make a large move just so you could break even. The cost is too high.

Also, you should not sell a call or sell a put here because there is very little price deterioration so far away from the expiration date. For best results you should sell close to the expiration date.

BUY FOR THE MEDIUM TERM

Prices are cheap so you couldn't lose much money even under the worst conditions, while the profit potential is unlimited for buying a call.

Buy a call when your charts indicate an uptrend in the future's price. This trade is rated as Good.

Do not buy a put because there is little downside room to make a profit. Do not sell a call or a put in this area because there is too much risk for the small amount of premium that you would gain.

BUY OR SELL FOR THE MEDIUM TERM

This is the mid price range so one can buy or sell options in this area. Know the price trend from your charts and seasonal trends, before you take your position.

Buying a call or a put and selling a call or a put are all rated as Average – that means an average risk and an average profit potential. This is the area where most of your trades will be done.

Remember, the comments on this page are based on average weather during the growing season.

SELL FOR THE MEDIUM TERM

Option premiums are high in this area. So, when you sell a call or a put, you will receive a large premium into your account, which gets you off to a good start. Be sure that you have noted the price trend from your charts before you make the sale.

Do not buy a call or a put in this area. The cost will be excessive and you would need a good price move just to break even. Buying is risky when prices are high.

Selling an option is rated as Good.

STAY OUT OF THE MARKET

Do not buy a call or a put because the time is short – too close to the expiration date, and the price erosion is greatest when you have a short time span.

Do not sell a call or a put because the premiums are too low, as compared to the risk.

SELL A CALL OR A PUT

Because of the short time span, there is good price erosion here as the expiration date draws near – which is to your advantage when selling but to your disadvantage when buying.

Sell a put when your charts indicate a neutral or bullish price trend. Sell a call when your charts show a neutral or bearish trend.

Both of the trades above are rated as Good. Do not buy a call or buy a put here because price erosion is working against you when buying.

SELL! SELL! SELL!

This is a seller's dream area. Here we have high premiums and just a few weeks from the expiration date. This means that you would receive a large premium and it would deteriorate at a very rapid rate, which is to your advantage. It couldn't be better for you.

Sell a call "at the money" when the price trend is neutral or falling. Rated as Very Good.
Sell a put "at the money" when the price trend is neutral or rising. Rated as Very Good.

40+ to 22 wks.

22 to 6 wks.

6 to 0 wks.

Weeks to expiration

If Tables 1 to 15 are used

If Tables 15 to 55 are used

If tables 55 and up are used

PROFIT PROFILE AT EXPIRATION

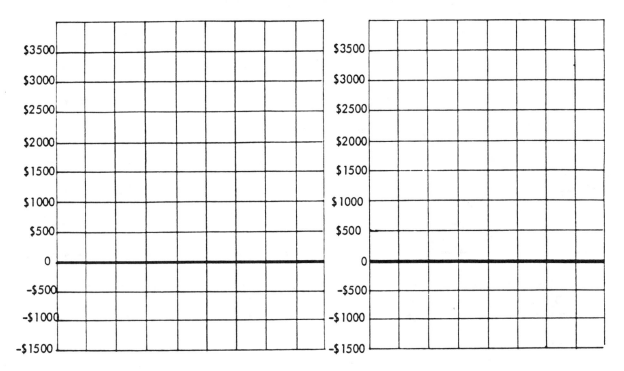

Strike Prices

Strike Prices

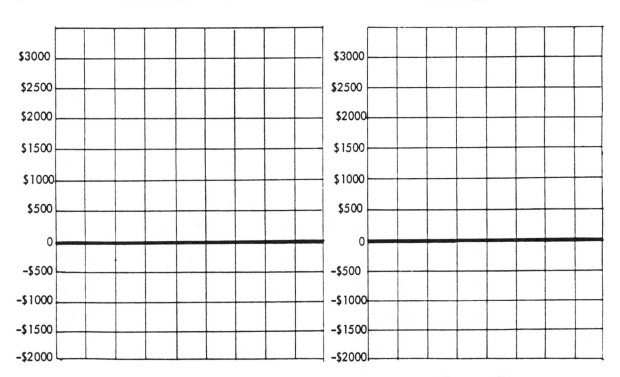

Strike Prices

Strike Prices

	weeks to expiration				weeks to expiration			
+$1								
+.75								
+.50								
+.25								
0								
-.25								
-.50								
-.75								
-$1								

changes in the soybean future's price

	weeks to expiration				weeks to expiration			
+$1								
+.75								
+.50								
+.25								
0								
-.25								
-.50								
-.75								
-$1								

changes in the soybean future's price